Dara Birnbaum

NOTE(S): WORK (ING) PROCESS (ES)
RE: CONCERNS (THAT TAKE ON / DEAL WITH)

Primary Information

Notes to Self **Alex Kitnick**

This book offers a collection of drawings, notes, contact sheets, and proposals that the artist Dara Birnbaum created at the start of her career while making her first works with slide projection, Super 8 film, and video. These works include *Back Piece* (March 1975), *Attack Piece* (August 1975), *Mirroring* (1975), *Pivot: Turning Around Suppositions* (March 1976), *Liberty: A Dozen or So Views* (May 1976), and *Lesson Plans to Keep the Revolution Alive* (1977). Birnbaum organized these papers into a manuscript in 1977 for the exhibition *Notebooks, Workbooks, Scripts, Scores* at the downtown art space Franklin Furnace, titling it *Note(s): Work(ing) Process(es) Re: Concerns (That Take On/Deal With)*.[1] In a way, Birnbaum's contribution was a "book dummy" for a book never meant to be printed, which is perhaps to the point: the material gathered here stresses process over product, as does the book's title (which also privileges prepositions). "End statements have their origins in non-rational processes and are therefore not subject to rational scrutiny," the book's epigraph reads, paraphrasing Marx. "*Means*, however, can be scrutinized from the perspective of their ends and are consequently subject to rational evaluation."[2] Like Birnbaum's own artwork at the time, this book analyzes the media's material processes (its means of production) while also offering the reader a view of an artist in formation, attempting to process a new technology. As such, it represents an early, and largely unknown, document of video art.

Born in New York City in 1946, Dara Birnbaum discovered video art in 1974, in Florence, Italy, where she moved after studying architecture at Carnegie Mellon University in Pittsburgh (B.Arch 1969), and painting at the San Francisco Art Institute (BFA 1973). In addition to witnessing the first wave of videomaking at Maria Gloria Bicocchi's gallery Centro Diffusione Grafica (later called Art/Tapes/22), Birnbaum met a number of key video artists, including Vito Acconci. Upon returning to New York, where she soon met Dan Graham, Birnbaum began making work that built on the concerns established by such artists, including Lacan's theory of the mirror stage, and topology.[3] Alternating between single-channel tapes and installation, Birnbaum's work sought to confront the self (often the artist's own self) and do "work" (in an almost therapeutic sense) on the viewer. Notes for *Back Piece*, for example, an installation from 1975, allude to the viewer's "inner conflicts" and "emotional tensions." Peppered with references ranging from psychoanalyst Carl Jung to the guru Ram Dass and "California culture," Birnbaum's work contextualizes her "depressed patient" in a contemporary world. An American high school cheer, though not included in the final work, provided the piece with its title: "Go back (back into the woods) / You haven't got (3) / Go back / If you give me your back."

FRANKLIN FURNACE

112 Franklin Street, New York, N.Y. 10013 — (212) 925-4671

NOTEBOOKS WORKBOOKS SCRIPTS SCORES

Kathy Acker / Laurie Anderson / David Appel / Jill Bellos /
Dara Birnbaum / Jon Deak / Mary Beth Edelson / Simone Forti /
Tina Girouard / Michael Harvey / Julia Heyward / Jacqui Holmes /
Scott Johnson / Paula Longendyke / Larry Miller / Meredith Monk /
Alec Nicolescu / Carolee Schneeman / Stuart Sherman /
Michael Smith / Herbert Wentscher

OPENING: SATURDAY, FEBRUARY 12, 1977

4-7 P.M.

This exhibition will be on view through May. It is the first group in an ongoing series sponsored by the Archive.

Announcement for *Notebooks, Workbooks, Scripts, Scores.*
Courtesy of Franklin Furnace Archive, Inc.

Note(s) is a collection of working papers, but Birnbaum was also fascinated by the form of the book in its own right, and how it might abet an understanding of new media. This was not uncommon to media study — the journal *Radical Software*, first published in 1970, created a clearinghouse for media theory and video how-to skills — but Birnbaum looked to earlier precedents as well: "I was in architecture at the time when McLuhan was coming out," Birnbaum said in a 2005 interview, "and I think just the whole way of presentation, of changing the form of the book as an extension of our senses.... Yeah, he was one of my big heroes."[4] Even as Birnbaum pushed art into contact with new media and novel encounters with the body, she also used historical forms to process her thought. Indeed, text recurs throughout Birnbaum's work. A year after *Note(s)*, also at Franklin Furnace, Birnbaum presented *(Reading) Versus (Reading Into)*, a reworking of a billboard for the *Daily Telegraph* picturing three men perusing the newspaper. ("The voice of the quiet majority," the original states matter-of-factly.) Broken into a tripartite structure and installed across the gallery's street-facing windows, the work includes an institutional statement of intent from Franklin Furnace director Martha Wilson on its backside (apparently at certain times of day the text could be seen from the outside of the gallery, as well). In examining reading habits alongside watching patterns, Birnbaum was able to focus on the changing status of spectatorship in late twentieth-century life.

If ways of looking are key to these works, Birnbaum paid attention to subject matter, too. *Pivot: Turning Around Suppositions*, an "investigative exercise," presents the artist through a variety of performative movements and differing camera angles, making facial expressions and delivering canned lines (e.g., "You must really be the devil").[5] In *Note(s)*, Birnbaum discusses the work in relation to film clichés, especially the gender codes of film noir. *Screen*, a leading British film journal steeped in psychoanalytic theory, often ran articles on this topic in the 1970s (see, for example, Laura Mulvey's canonical "Visual Pleasure and Narrative Cinema" from the Autumn 1975 issue), and in doing so established a discourse around questions of ideology and popular culture that certain video artists found energizing.[6] Birnbaum's notes for *Pivot* mark one of the first instances that the stuff of mass media breaks into the artist's work; they are also an early instance in which the artist's feminism is made explicit. Under the section heading "AMERICAN FILM ROLES (ROLE-PLAYING)," Birnbaum homes in on three films in particular: *Gilda*, starring Rita Hayworth ("the promiscuity was only to make him jealous," Birnbaum writes); *The Big Sleep*, featuring Lauren Bacall ("protecting the innocent sister"); and *The Strange Love of Martha Ivers* with Barbara Stanwyck ("better than she seemed"). The artist creates a shorthand for conventions of female behavior and character-types, what Birnbaum later called "the iconic depiction of women in typecast roles," but other factors may have inspired Birnbaum's focus on these films, too.[7] All three films premiered in 1946, the year of the artist's birth, marking a connection — albeit implicitly — between popular culture and the artist's

FRANKLIN FURNACE

112 Franklin Street, New York, N.Y. 10013 — (212) 925-4671

FOR IMMEDIATE RELEASE

April 11 - 27, Franklin Furnace Archive will present an installation by DARA BIRNBAUM entitled (READING) VERSUS (READING INTO) / an ad and an extraction.

Opening: April 11, 1978, 5-7 p.m.

This installation uses both the "store-front" window of the Franklin Furnace as well as the walled interior (exhibition) space of the gallery. A double sided 'banner' (as billboard) wraps the window area higher than normal viewing height - visible up and down the street (much in the way that commercial advertising normally 'reads'). The 'banner' spans both the storefront of the Furnace as well as the window area of the 'residential building' 112 Franklin Street. Directed outwards towards the street is a photo blow-up from an outdoor London billboard (1977) now relocated in time and space. The ad itself deals with 'reading' and the 'selling of' written statements (ie: a commercial for The Daily Telegraph). On the opposite side of this statement of visual 'language' is an extraction of 'literal' text regarding the inner political and organizational workings of the Furnace itself. This 'inner banner' (written word) once again spans the three separated windowed areas of '112 Franklin Street' - yet from the gallery area alone only two of the sections of this text can be 'read'. The third section becomes separated out through the actual usages of the 'interiorized space' - so that the first section must be seen from the 'private space' of the residentially designated area next door.

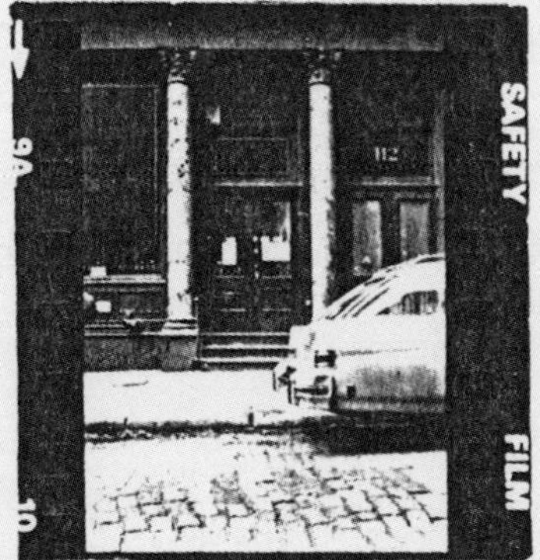

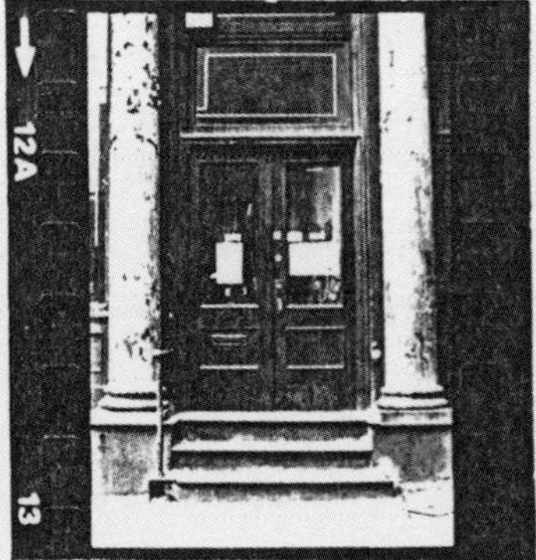

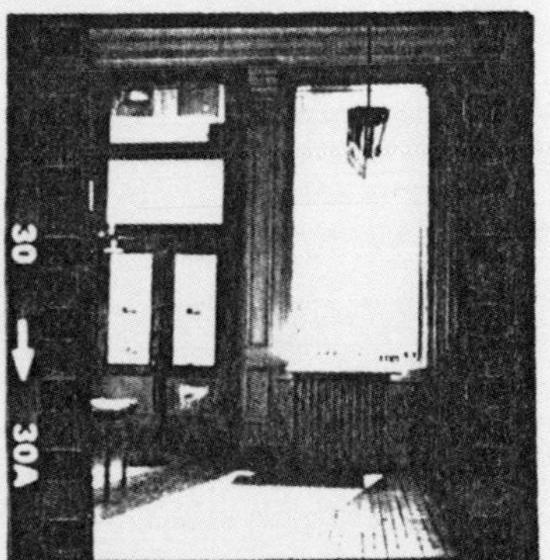

A display wall at right angles to the windowed areas contains a second 'banner' that juxtaposes further extractions from both the original photographic and literary material. Both representations are joined by the common structural unity of the 'selling' (as of: ideas) through visual language(s).

Dara Birnbaum has recently exhibited her work at Artists Space and The Kitchen, N.Y.C. Her films and tapes have been presented at Global Village, Anthology Film Archives and on Manhattan Cable, Channel D, N.Y.C.

Franklin Furnace Archive, Inc. is a non-profit corporation dedicated to the cataloging, exhibition and preservation of book-like works by artists

Press release for *Notebooks, Workbooks, Scripts, Scores.*
Courtesy of Franklin Furnace Archive, Inc.

own subject formation. What roles do media offer? the artist seems to ask. What effects do different media have on persons, and how might persons use media to challenge them in turn? Enlisting video to probe the ideology of film, the notes to *Pivot* appear to be part of the artist's attempt to sort this out.

In *Liberty: A Dozen or So Views*, made two months after *Pivot*, Birnbaum turns to iconography and symbolism, as well as documentary modes.[8] Made in 1976, the United States Bicentennial year, the work reflects on America's history in elliptical fashion.[9] The Statue of Liberty in New York Harbor stands at the center of the work, but equally important are the people Birnbaum interviews on the Staten Island Ferry, who also played a part in making the work. The subjects she interviews represent ethnic types, or at least Birnbaum recorded them as such in her notes: Black, Chinese, Italian American, Jewish, etc. A societal cross-section. The video consists of each person stating "objective" facts about themselves, including age, race, eye color, weight, and so forth, as if they were delivering information to a census, or registering as immigrants (Ellis Island is nearby).[10] According to Birnbaum's notes, the framing of these video portraits is based on a Swedish advertisement for eyeglasses ("Look good – and look good in autumn glasses," the ad reads[11]). Capitalist conventions are key here – Birnbaum wanted to present her subjects in a "cool," clear, almost ethnographic light – but unlike mainstream film, the artist resisted images that would encourage the viewer to form an intimate bond with the recorded subject. In a 1975 interview published in the *SoHo Weekly News* (and pasted in her notebook), Birnbaum notes, "Video is very seductive. It has a warm side, personal, familiar. It has a cool side, manipulative. In *Liberty* I explored this problem. I let tourists on the boat to the Statue of Liberty handle the camera. Their vision was expanded and they could see the object in a new way."[12] The video, in other words, documents a social encounter. The process of making is just as significant as what the viewer finally sees.

Note(s) marks an important early chapter in Birnbaum's practice. The final work included, *Lesson Plans to Keep the Revolution Alive*, offers a starting point for the artist's first exhibition at Artists Space, in 1977. Importantly, it is also a transitional work. While Birnbaum embraced TV (she examines the one-season wonder *Westside Medical*, as one example), she resisted video: the installation consisted of twenty-five photographs shot from a television monitor, paired with exactly timed transcripts of dialogue. Soon after, Birnbaum would finally combine TV and video to create pop culture-inflected single-channel videos, including *Technology/Transformation: Wonder Woman* (1978) and *Kiss the Girls: Make Them Cry* (1979), which form the basis for Birnbaum's first monograph, *Rough Edits: Popular Image Video, Works 1977–1980*, edited by Benjamin Buchloh for the Press of the Nova Scotia College of Art and Design. (*Lesson Plans*, a crossover work, is the first work covered in that volume.) While these later artworks differ in texture and feeling from what we see in *Note(s)* (particularly striking is their near-pedagogical emphasis on convention and technique – as well as the introduction of color), similarities remain.

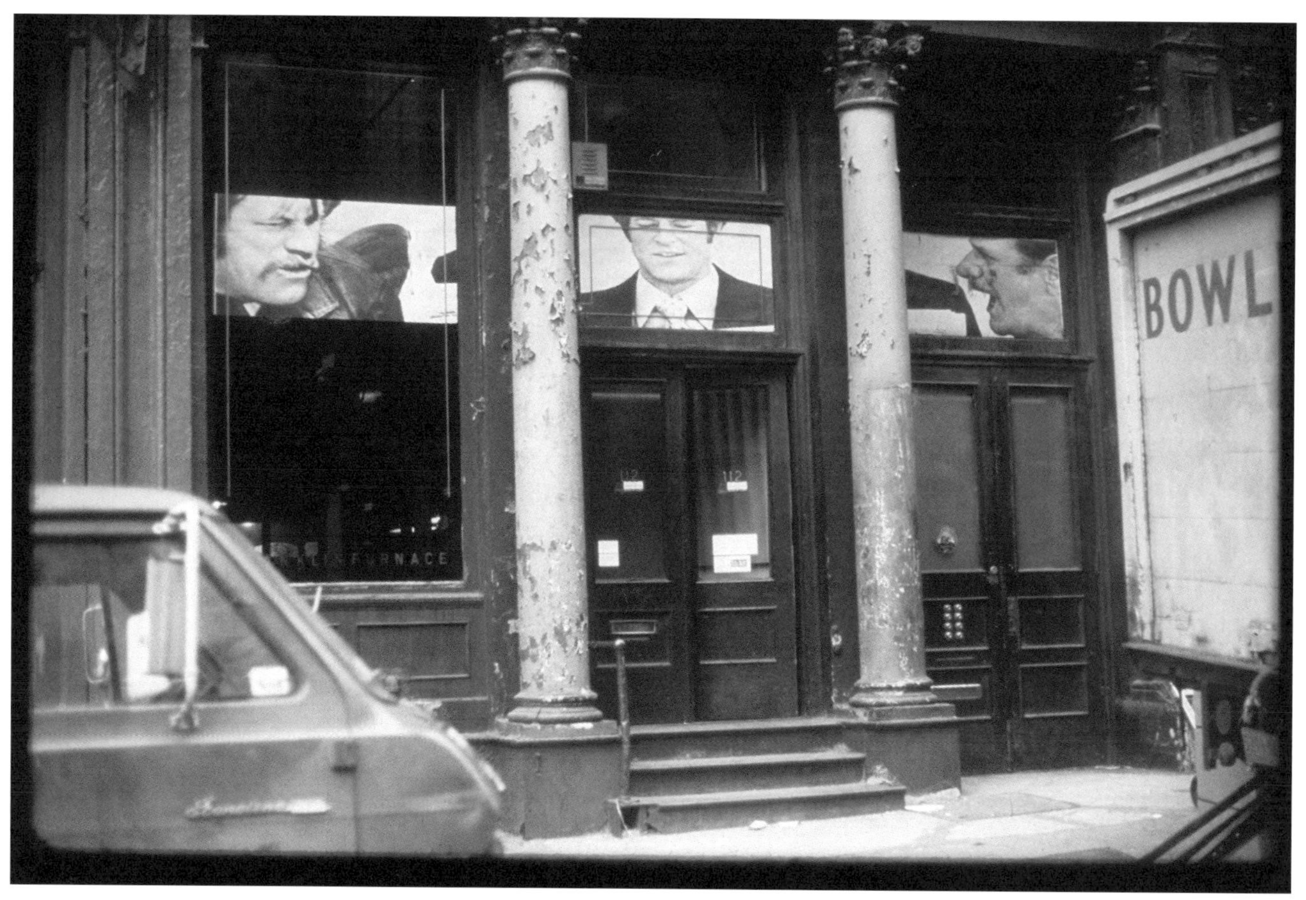

Installation view of Dara Birnbaum's *(Reading) Versus (Reading Into)* at Franklin Furnace Archive, Inc., 112 Franklin Street, Tribeca, NY (April 11-April 27, 1978). Courtesy of Franklin Furnace Archive, Inc.

I can't help but see, for example, a connection between Lady Liberty and Wonder Woman. Strong, patriotic, idealized — and armored in attire — both represent a version of mass art. But the shift in medium (from patinated bronze to network television) is significant, as is the move in Birnbaum's technique (from documentary to appropriation). Birnbaum wanted to meet the present head on, to "talk back to the media," and investigating TV, she believed, using the "medium on itself," was the most powerful way of doing so. While much of Birnbaum's subsequent work critiques the image of woman as captured by media, it draws on lessons learned from looking at sculpture and film, which, intriguingly, she processed in the old-fashioned form of the book. Indeed, there are manifesto-like moments here. (Remember, we began with Marx.) In one of the manuscript's final methodological sections, "New Structures, New Approaches," Birnbaum declares, "We force the ACTION. (We push/We fight)."

[1] The exhibition, which opened on February 12, 1977, was organized by the artist Jacki Apple, and included work by Kathy Acker, Laurie Anderson, Mary Beth Edelson, Simone Forti, Meredith Monk, Carolee Schneemann, Stuart Sherman, and Michael Smith, among others. It was supposed to be the first show in an ongoing series of "one-of-a-kind informal books, containing in-progress documentation (scores) of performance works, workbooks of writings, drawings for installations and performances, video and film storyboards, scripts, worknotes *[sic]*, and concepts, composers' notebooks, choreographers' scores, and personal journal notebooks." [Franklin Furnace Archive, "Notebooks, Workbooks, Scripts, Scores," press release, February 12, 1977.]

[2] Bill Harrell, "Marx and Critical Thought," *Paunch*, no. 44-45 (May 1976), 13.

[3] "I did works that related to the videowork of the post-minimal artists," Birnbaum said in a 1983 interview. "Artists like Dan Graham and Acconci dealt with the nature of the video image in relation to subjective/objective perceptions." Dara Birnbaum, *Rough Edits: Popular Image Video, Works 1977-1980*, ed. Benjamin H. D. Buchloh (Halifax: The Press of the Nova Scotia College of Art and Design, 1987), 66.

[4] *The Early Show: Video from 1969-1979* (New York: Hunter College, 2006), 21.

[5] "This early single-channel video is an investigation of the physical and psychological roles played by director, camera, and performer in the film or video shoot," Rebecca Cleman writes. "These roles have gendered significance; Birnbaum herself is cameraman Michael Lanley's object, a loaded dynamic demonstrating a woman's subjection to the male gaze." Karen Kelly, Barbara Schröder, and Giel Vandecaveye, eds., *Dara Birnbaum: The Dark Matter of Media Light* (New York: DelMonico Books, 2011), 178.

[6] "At the time I was meeting people like Dan Graham, who introduced me to the writings in *Screen* Magazine which primarily dealt with film theory and psychoanalytic approaches to film. I didn't understand why these magazines analyzed 40s American Film. It seemed so important to look at what was happening now, what a contemporary vocabulary would be...meaning television, not film." Birnbaum, *Rough Edits*, 67.

[7] Dara Birnbaum, "Author's introduction," *Rough Edits*, 14. In an interview with Norman Klein, Birnbaum stated, "Television for me meant the use of stereotypical roles, it was about the delivery of certain forms of gesture and message." *Rough Edits*, 90. Pamela Lee's description of Birnbaum's video *Kiss the Girls: Make Them Cry* (1979) makes clear how these issues continued to be of primary importance in the artist's work: "Each actor plays her own role in assuming the guise of knowing brunette, flirty blonde, sassy child. Together they display the imagined spectrum of 'feminine' behavior." Pamela Lee, *New Games: Postmodernism after Contemporary Art* (New York: Routledge, 2013), 178.

[8] Birnbaum was enrolled in editing classes at New York's Global Village Experimental Television Center at the time, which might have encouraged her to turn to documentary.

[9] Chantal Akerman's film *News from Home*, released the same year, also features a long final shot depicting the Statue of Liberty as seen from the Staten Island Ferry.

[10] There are similarities in this regard between Birnbaum's video and Martha Rosler's much more sardonic *Vital Statistics of a Citizen, Simply Obtained*, made in 1977.

[11] The Swedish reads, "Se bra — och se bra ut i hastens glasögon."

[12] The interview excerpted in *Liberty: A Dozen or So Views* was conducted by Stephanie Woodard and first appeared in "Views and Interviews: Dara Birnbaum" in *SoHo Weekly News*, January 6, 1977.

NOTE(S): WORK (ING) PROCESS (ES)

RE: CONCERNS (THAT TAKE ON / DEAL WITH)

IE: STILL PROJECTION FORMAT
SLIDE USAGE(S) / INSTALLATION THEORY

STILL VS CONTINUOUS PROJECTION FORMAT
SLIDE / FILM USAGE

VIDEO FORMAT

INTER•PROCESS(ES)
INTER•PLAY(S) FORMAT

NOTE(S): FOR DISTRIBUTION
AS INSIGHT INTO THE MEANS OF PAST /
PRESENT / AND PROJECTED WORK -
AS IN: WORK(ING) PROCESS(ES)-

"END STATEMENTS HAVE THEIR ORIGIN
IN NON-RATIONAL PROCESSES AND ARE
THEREFORE NOT SUBJECT TO RATIONAL
SCRUTINY. MEANS, HOWEVER, CAN BE
SCRUTINIZED FROM THE PERSPECTIVES
OF THEIR ENDS AND ARE CONSEQUENT-
LY SUBJECT TO RATIONAL EVALUATION."
(MARX AND CRITICAL THOUGHT)

RE: CONCERNS (THAT TAKE ON / DEAL WITH)
STILL PROJECTION FORMAT / SLIDE USAGE(S)
INSTALLATION THEORY

IE: BACK PIECE
NYC 1975

BACK PIECE
(SIMULTANEOUS PROJECTIONS: INSTALLATION)
NEW YORK CITY, NEW YORK

BACK PIECE '75 IS AN INSTALLATION; AN ENVIRONMENT. IT IS TO PLACE THE VIEWER (PARTICPANT) INTO A PHYSICAL SPACE WHICH INDUCES MOVEMENT THAT IS THE PHYSICAL MANIFESTATION OF THE INNER CONFLICTS AND EMOTIONAL TENSIONS INHERENT TO THE PIECE. THE CONFLICT STRESSED IS THE DIVISION BETWEEN PHYSICAL AND TEMPORAL PRESENCE. (IN 1971, WE HAVE A CALIFORNIA CULTURE EXPRESSING THIS PRINCIPLE THROUGH BABA RAM DASS, IN TERMS OF "BE HERE NOW".) BACK PIECE CONCERNS ITSELF WITH STRESS PATTERNS DEVELOPED IN WHAT JUNG CATEGORIZES AS "TOPOLOGICAL FEELING TYPES": A SET OF INDIVIDUALS WHO CAN ONLY RELATE TO THE PRESENT IN TERMS OF A PAST SET OF EXPERIENCES. THIS LOGICALLY INHIBITS MANY GROWTH FACTORS WITHIN THE GIVEN INDIVIDUAL, WHO CANNOT SEE NEW CONDITIONS FROM A NON-BIASED POINT OF VIEW. THE EXCITEMENT OF WHAT IS NEW IS GONE AND EVENTUALLY BECOMES THREATENING. THIS LATER PROGRESSES TO A STATE OF "PARALYSIS OF WILL". THE INDIVIDUAL REALIZES THAT SHE/HE MUST MOVE FORWARD INTO A STATE OF AFFAIRS CONSTANTLY IN FLUX (WHERE THE PAST USUALLY CAN NO LONGER PLAY A DOMINANT ROLE). THIS VERY REALIZATION PRESENTS SUCH FEAR AND ANXIETY THAT SHE/HE CAN NOW GO NEITHER FORWARD NOR BACKWARD. THUS, WE COME TO A SORT OF CIRCULAR MOTION (A SPINNING / TURNING / CONFUSION) WITH NO LOGICAL PROGRESSION. EVENTUALLY THIS SET PATTERN TURNS IN ON ITSELF AND YIELDS TO A STATE OF "PARALYSIS".

INSTALLATION SET-UP: IN THE INSTALLATION, THE "VIEWER" IS PRESENTED WITH A CONTAINED SPACE. SHE/HE IS ENCLOSED BETWEEN A WALL (THAT MOUNTS TWO SLIDE PROJECTORS ON A DISSOLVE UNIT) AND A HANGING SCREEN OF CANVAS (SIMILAR TO A FLOATING PAINTING). A PLATFORM 1' HIGH IS ON THE GROUND BEHIND THE VIEWER; BETWEEN THE WALL AND HANGING SCREEN. IT TOO IS CANVAS AND FORMS THE SECOND PROJECTION SURFACE. ON THE HANGING SCREEN IS PROJECTED A SERIES OF SLIDES THAT ARE A LOGICAL PROGRESSION THROUGH THE VERY SPACE (IN ENTIRETY) THAT THE INSTALLATION OCCUPIES (STRESSING THE "BE HERE NOW" THEORY). THE PICTURES HAVE BEEN SHOT THROUGH AN EXTREME WIDE ANGLE LENS (STRESSING THE DISTORTED WAYS IN WHICH ONE ALWAYS VIEWS A REALITY). EACH SLIDE DISSOLVES IMMEDIATELY UPON VIEWING INTO A SLIDE THAT IS THROWN THROUGH OVERHEAD PROJECTION ONTO THE SCREENED PLATFORM BEHIND THE VIEWER. THE THROWN IMAGE IS WHAT MAY BE CALLED A "BLOCK CARD". IT IS THE SAME SPACE/ OR NON-SPACE AS THAT WHICH HAS JUST BEEN VIEWED BEFORE HER/HIM. BUT NOW A SECONDARY IMAGE IS BLOCKING OUR CLEAR VISION OF THIS SPACE. THESE IMAGES ARE A SERIES OF PHOTOS TAKEN IN EUROPE (FROM WHERE THE ARTIST HAD JUST RETURNED). THE PHOTOS ARE ALL AMBIGUOUS SPACES (IE: DOORWAYS; ENTRIES TO PLACES UNKNOWN; RIVERS/ WITH BRIDGES THAT CONNECT TO LAND BANKS; ETC.). EACH IMAGE SUCCESSFULLY BLOCKS THE PRESENT FORM AND IS REPRESENTATIVE OF A MORE "ROMANTIC" PAST. FOR THE VIEWER TO VIEW BOTH SERIES (PRESENT AND PAST) SHE/HE MUST PLACE ONESELF IN CONSTANT MOTION: TURNING TO EACH SCREEN RESPECTIVELY. IF HE/SHE CONTINUES TURNING (TRYING TO RELATE TO BOTH IMAGES), HE/SHE WILL SEE NEXT TO NOTHING (FOR THE DISSOLVE UNIT IS ON TOO FAST AND AT BEST

CAN BE SEEN ONLY DISSOLVING IMAGES). IF THE "VIEWER" SHOULD CHOOSE ONE SERIES OVER THE OTHER THE CONSEQUENCE IS OBVIOUS. IF SHE/HE CHOSES TO MOVE ONLY A PORTION OF HER/HIS BODY, SHE/HE MAY VIEW BOTH SERIES IN ENTIRETY (BY A SIMPLE TWISTING OF THE NECK) BUT ONLY AT THE EXPENSE OF REMOVING ONESELF PHYSICALLY FROM THE SPACIAL LIMITS OF THE PIECE. THE TURNING MOVEMENT THAT MUST OCCUR FOR VIEWING WHEN WITHIN THE DESIGNATED PHYSICAL BOUNDARIES OF THE PIECE BECOMES CIRCULAR. (IN OTHER WORDS, IT BECOMES THE PHYSICAL MANIFESTATION OF "PARALYSIS OF WILL": TURNING IN ON ITSELF / LEADING NOWHERE BUT TO UTTER FRUSTRATION.)

AUDIO REQUIREMENTS: THERE ARE TWO AUDIO TRACKS PRESENT (2 TAPES IN SMALL CASSETTE CATRIDGES); EACH CAN BE HEARD ONLY IF WALKED OVER TO .... AGAIN A PARALYZING FACTOR THAT INHIBITS RELATING TO THE REST OF THE INSTALLATION. ONE TAPE IS ENTIRELY EMOTIONAL (AMBIGUOUS / A ONE-WAY PHONE CONVERSATION IN MANY RESPECTS). IT RANGES AMONGST : A SET OF DEMANDS; DEFINITIVE STATEMENTS; IMPLORING COMMENTS; AND COMMANDS (EVENTUALLY DIRECTED TOWARD THE VIEWER). ALTHOUGH IT IS OBVIOUS THAT THESE STATEMENTS START OFF RELATING TO SOMEONE IN THE PERSON'S PAST (IE: "LOVER"), THEY BECOME PATTERNED ENOUGH AND ARE AMBIGUOUS ENOUGH THAT THE "VIEWER" WILL EVENTUALLY FIT HER/HIMSELF INTO THE CREATED PATTERN OF EXCHANGE.

THE SECOND TAPE IS DIALECTICAL: STRAIGHT READINGS FROM JUNG ON "TOPOLOGICAL FEELING TYPES" (WITH AN ADDENDUM OF A FAIRY TALE STORY OF HOW TOLSTOY MAKES THIS CASE AND POINT IN WAR AND PEACE).

A THIRD TAPE MAY BE SUBSTITUTED FOR THE OTHER TWO / OR IS TO BE USED ON A THIRD CHANNEL (FADING IN AND OUT OF THE EXISTING TAPES). THIS IS A 45 MINUTE REPETITIVE CHORUS:

(DIRECTIVES: WHISPERED / PACE INCREASING IN TYPICAL CHEERLEADING FASHION)

BACK PIECE: GO BACK, GO BACK, GO BACK INTO THE WOODS
CAUSE YOU HAVEN'T, YOU HAVEN'T, YOU HAVEN'T
GOT THE GOODS
AND YOU HAVEN'T
GOT THE RHYTHM
YOU HAVEN'T GOT THE JAZZ
AND YOU HAVEN'T GOT THE TEAM
TEAM THAT OUR TEAM HAS.

REPEATED AD INFINITUM

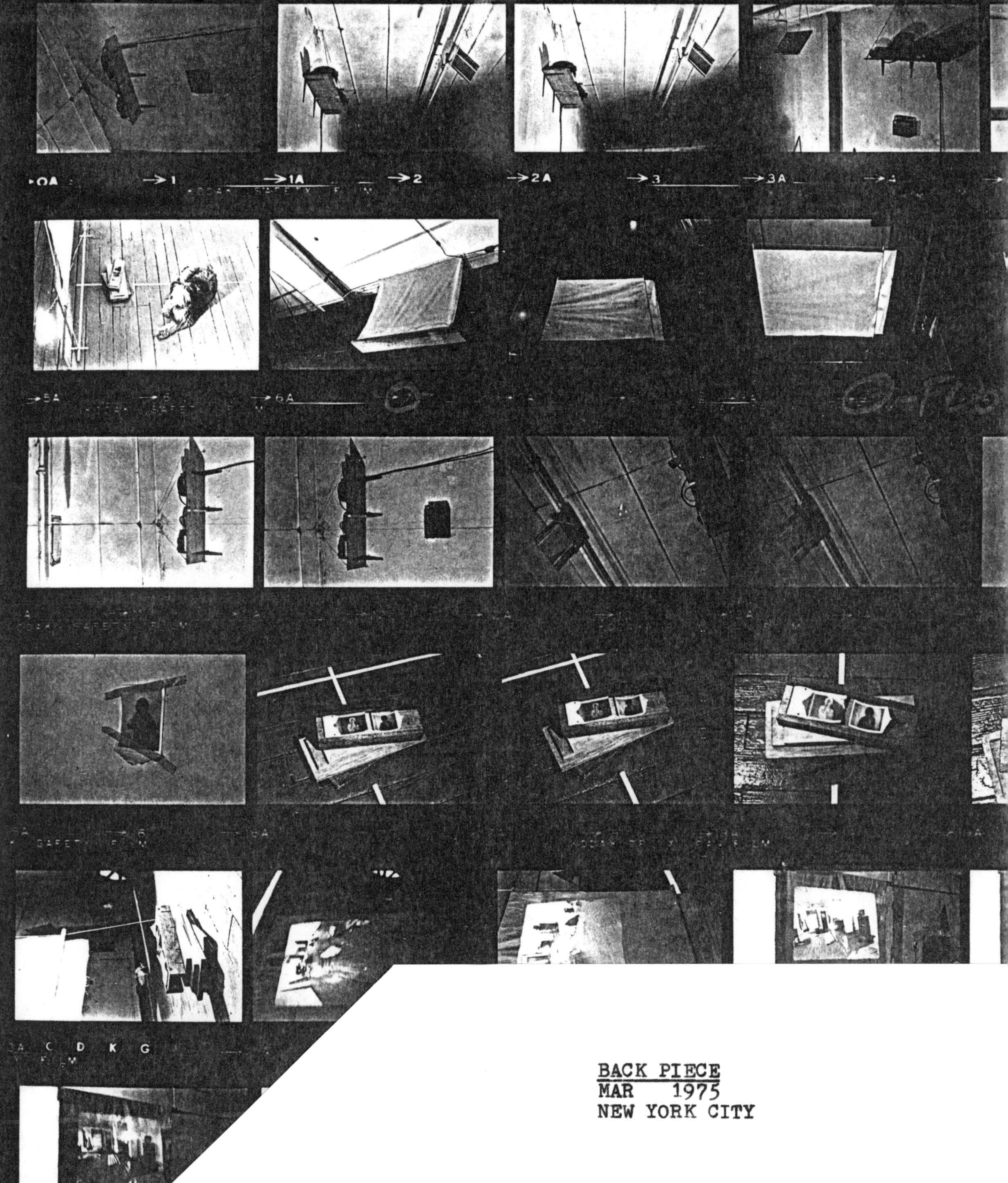

BACK PIECE
MAR 1975
NEW YORK CITY

BACK PIECE:

TAPE STARTS:
WHAT DO YOU WANT ME TO SAY ABOUT GOING BACK?

ISN'T IT ENOUGH TO SAY THAT I DON'T WANT TO GO BACK ANYMORE???

(all sorts of commands eventually thrown in - that seem to be directed toward viewer as well as the "other" of this internal dialogue -)

IE: DON'T TURN YOUR BACK !
DON'T
LOOK AROUND !

see - Freud's "regression" in "dreams" .

ambiguious references made
to ideas that (have) (do) fixate (me) into the past -
ie: affair / Amsterdam will become referential to slides shown (as postcards / pictures) of past -
postcards = the cliche(s) of that (type of) place(ment)

I DIDN'T WANT TO TALK ABOUT THAT TIME (ALWAYS TRYING TO DENY IT)

the tapes trying to act as reparation?
a solution to(ward) getting out of the situation of paralysis by denying going back to this past again .

(perhaps also look for personal pictures in relation to / juxtaposed to / the postcard series)

depression is a "pathetic immobility a suspension of existence"
As a result the patient experiences a sense of incompleteness, of impotence (and of unreality

---

TEMPORAL REGRESSION / IN SO FAR AS WHAT IS IN QUESTION IS A HARKING BACK TO OLDER PSYCHICAL STRUCTURES - / FREUD

BACK PIECE:
RELATION(SHIP(S)) TO TIME AND SPACE:

THE QUESTION OF THE DEPRESSED PATIENT'S ATTITUDE TOWARD TIME HAS OCCUPIED THE ATTENTION OF MANY EXISTENTIAL WRITERS. THEY HAVE SHOWED (EMPHASIZED) THAT TIME SEEMS TO HAVE SLOWED DOWN FOR THE DEPRESSED PATIENT. IN HIS SUBJECTIVE EXPERIENCE ONLY THE PAST MATTERS. PAINFUL MEMORIES DOMINATE HIS THINKING AND REMIND HIM OF HIS UNWORTHINESS AND INABILITY TO ACCOMPLISH.

THERE ARE FOUR (4) BASIC TEMPORAL ORIENTATIONS:
FEELING TYPES RELATE PRIMARILY TO THE PAST /
SEIZURES OF DEPRESSIVE ANXIETY ARE FREQUENT OCCURENCES IN FEELING TYPES / FEELING TYPES RELATE PRIMARILY TO THE PAST ...

BACK PIECE

THE AUDIO: BECOMES A SONG
(CHEERLEADER PACING)

CALLED BACK PIECE - YEA
+ ITS ABOUT GOING BACK / OR NOT GOING BACK
GO BACK GO BACK
______________________________ CHEER SONG
____
_______________ ______________________________

BACK PIECE / BACK PIECE
GO BACK (BACK BACK INTO THE WOODS)
YOU HAVEN'T GOT (3)
GO BACK
IF YOU GIVE ME YOUR BACK
I MEAN IF YOU'RE ALWAYS BACK THERE
YOU CAN'T FACE WHAT'S UP HERE MAN
UP HERE IS FRONT LINE
FRONT BUSINESS ALL THE TIME
LET'S GO
GO BACK GO BACK BACK TO THE WOODS
YOU HAVEN'T
______________________________ OUR TEAM
BACK PIECE
IT KEEPS GETTING STUCK
LIKE STUCK IN THE ____________________.
BACK PIECE
GO BACK / BACK PIECE / GO BACK / BACK PIECE / GO BACK / BACK PIECE
GO BACK / BACK PIECE / GO BACK / BACK PIECE / GO BACK / BACK PIECE/GB
GIVE ME A PIECE OF WHERE IT'S AT
YEA
BACK PIECE / GO BACK / BACK PIECE / GO BACK / BACK PIECE / GO BACK
BUT MAKE SURE / MAKE SURE YOU GIVE
ME A PIECE OF WHERE IT'S AT
BACK PIECE / GO BACK
HAVEN'T / HAVEN'T / GO BACK

I CAN FACE IT ANYTIME
MAYBE NOT DIRECTLY
BUT I CAN FACE IT
YEA
MAYBE BY BACKING UP ALITTLE
I CAN FACE ALL YOU GUYS
I'M SURE I CAN
THAT'S WHY THIS IS CALLED BACK PIECE - YEA (3X)
GO BACK - MOAN /GB /BP /GB /BP -
GO BACK TO WHERE IT'S AT
GB / GB / GB / GB / GB / GB / GB / GB / GB / GB / GB -
FADE

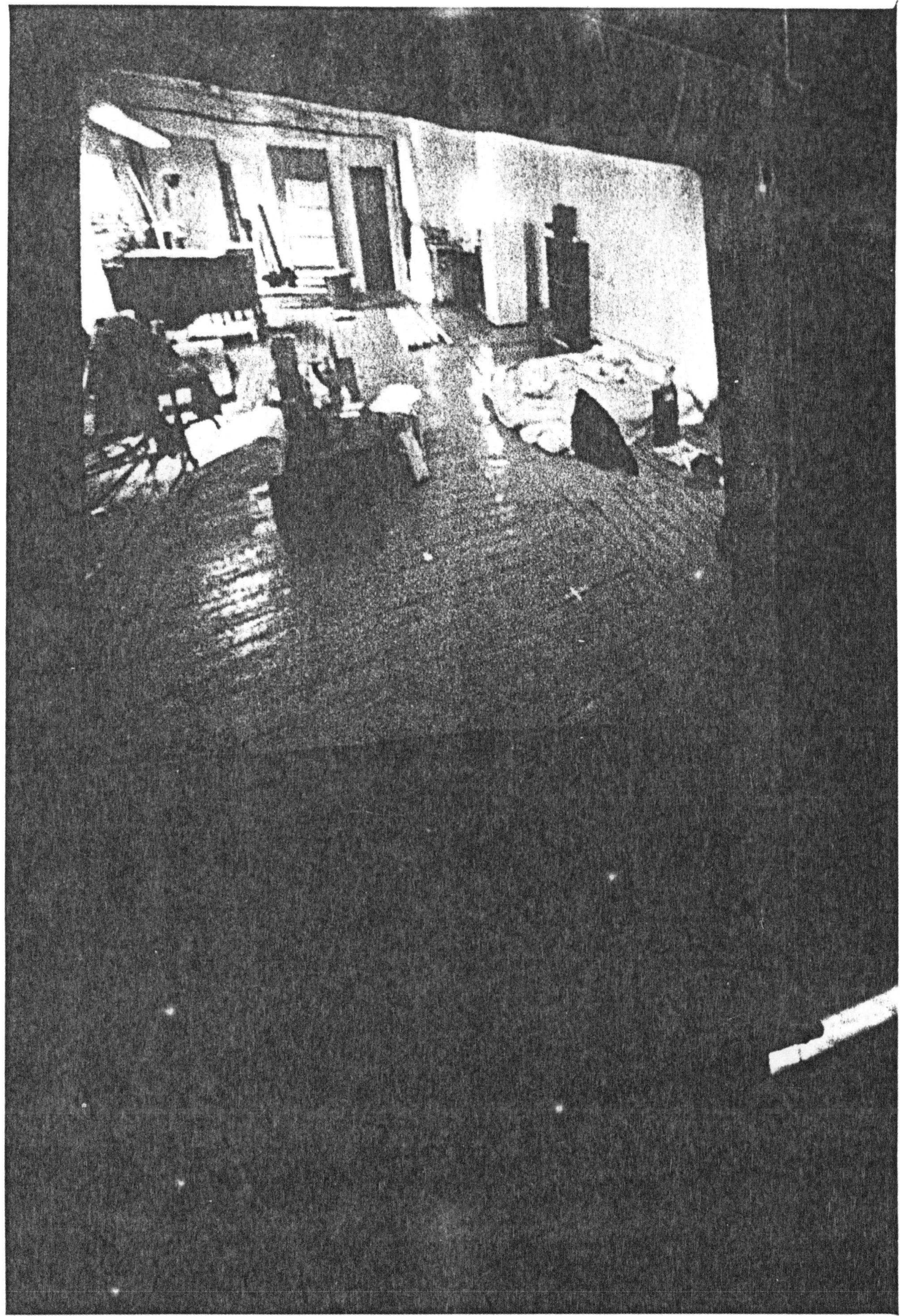

BACK PIECE
MAR 1975
NEW YORK CITY

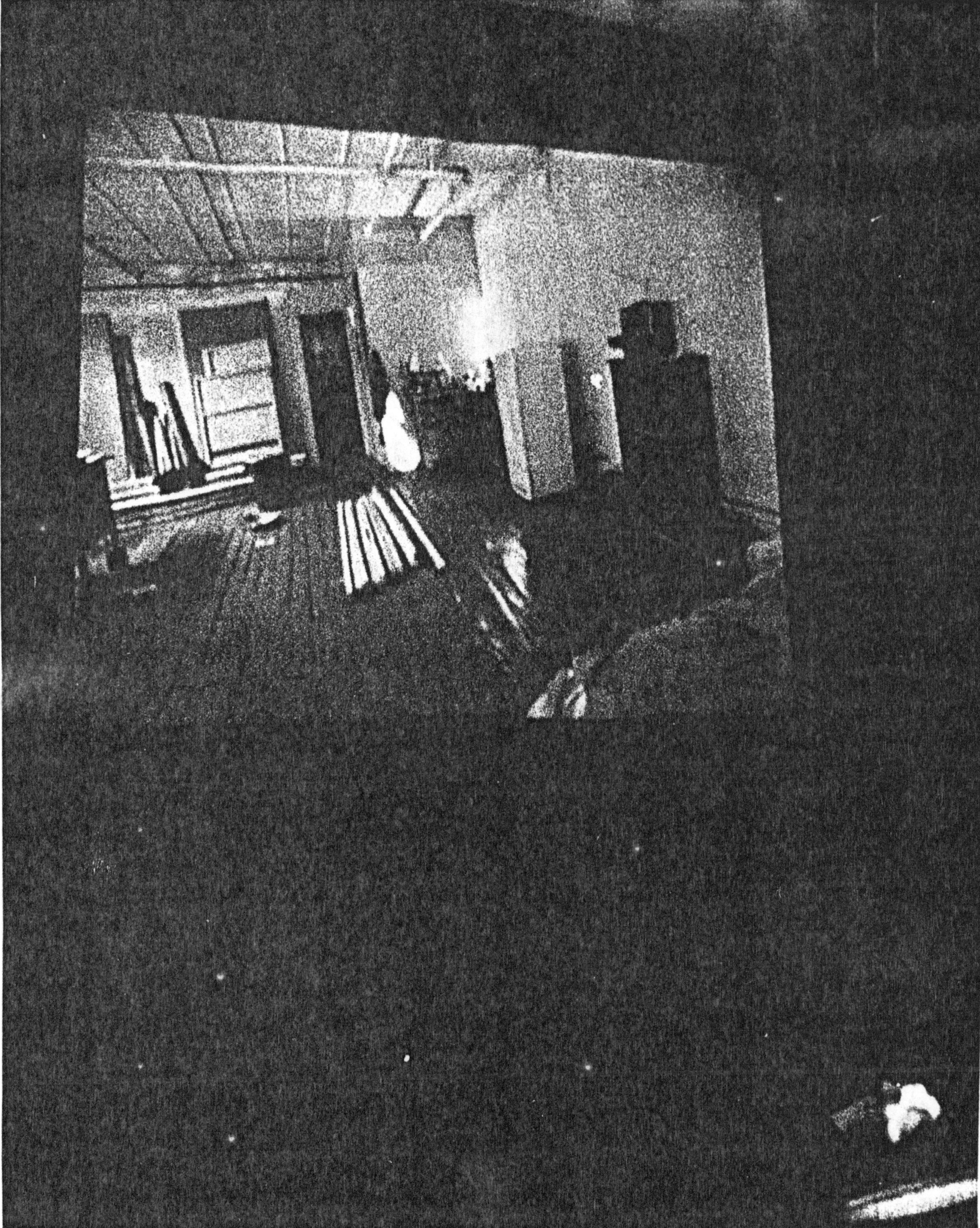

BACK PIECE
MAR 1975
NEW YORK CITY

GOING BACK

I can't go back
I won't go back
I don't want to go back

<u>can't</u>
implies it is ~~[illegible]~~ physically not possible.

<u>won't</u>
implies will

<u>don't want to</u>
inner feeling not having complete control over the outcome (manifest destiny)

to a physical reality (environment) outer
physical state of being (body condition) inner
i.e. being fat. sick. etc.).

<u>mental</u> state (inner self)
mental environment (relationships to other –
- those that are close as lovers
- those that are by necessity – as a business
- those that are general – everyday acquaintances

won't
implies will

as a business
◦ those that are general – everyday acquaintances

don't want to
inner feeling not having complete control over the outcome (manifest destiny).

---

involving another (co-ercion).
you can't make me
you won't make me
(I don't think) you want to make me.
you want to
you don't want to (you don't want me to)
can act positively or negatively depending upon stand of original person.

i.e. / I don't want to
you don't want me to } affirmation.

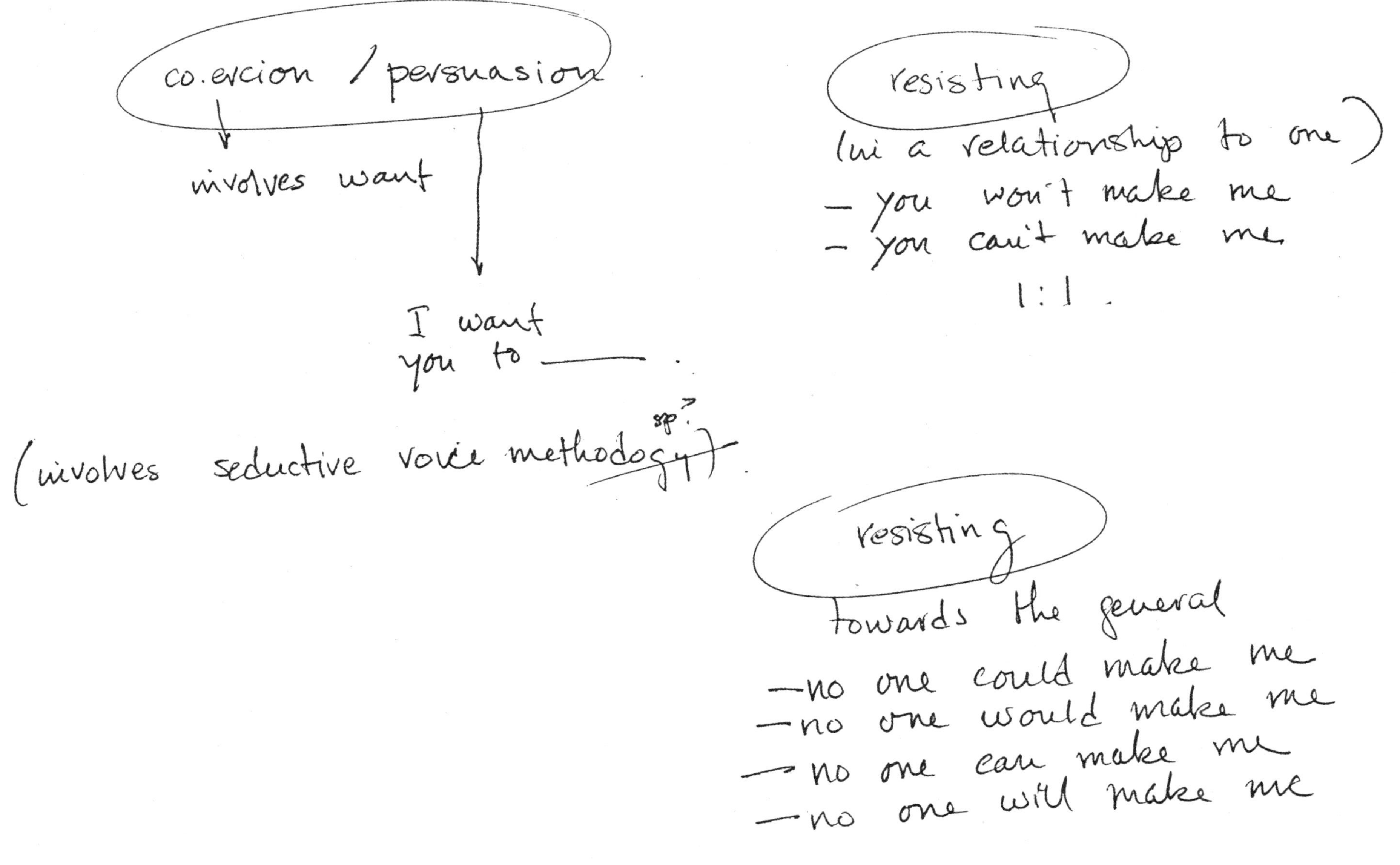
co.ercion / persuasion
involves want
I want
you to ____.
(involves seductive voice methodogy sp?).
resisting
(in a relationship to one)
– you won't make me
– you can't make me
1:1.
resisting
towards the general
–no one could make me
–no one would make me
–no one can make me
–no one will make me

BACK PIECE

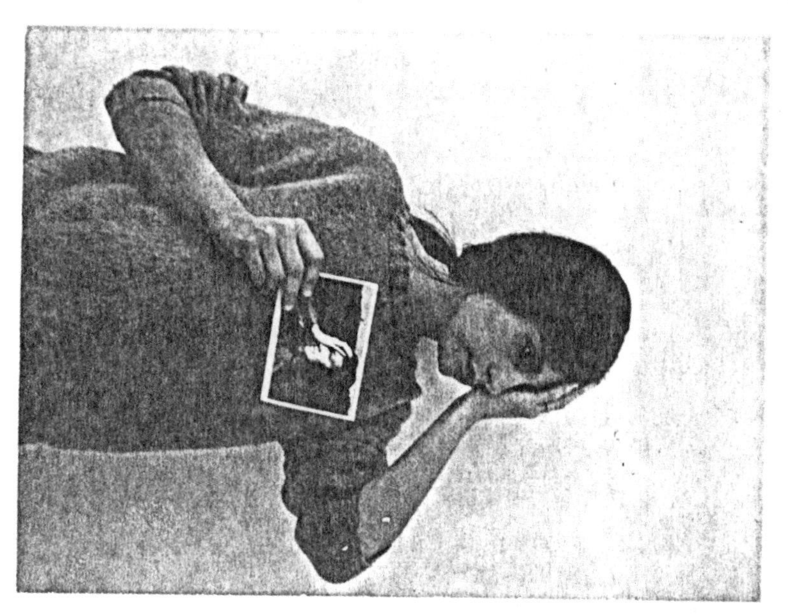

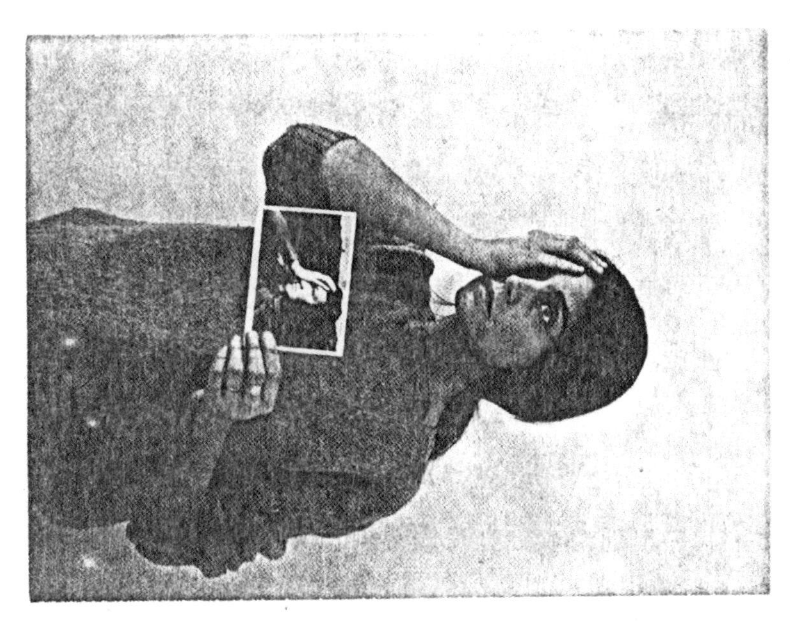

Tape Starts:
what do you want me to say – about going back? (that) I can't face it?

BACK PIECE

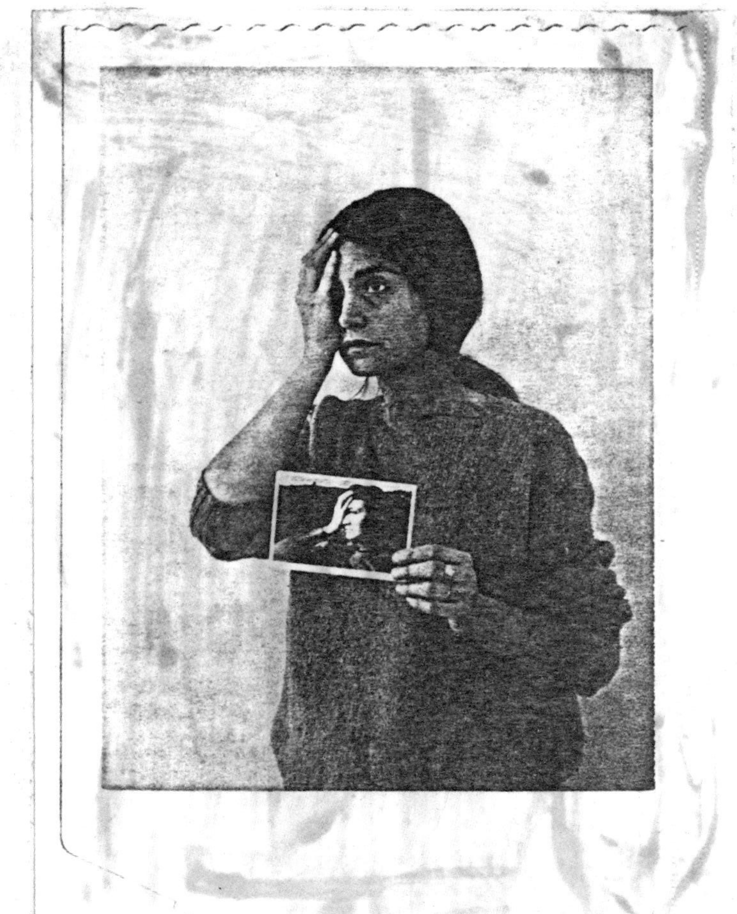

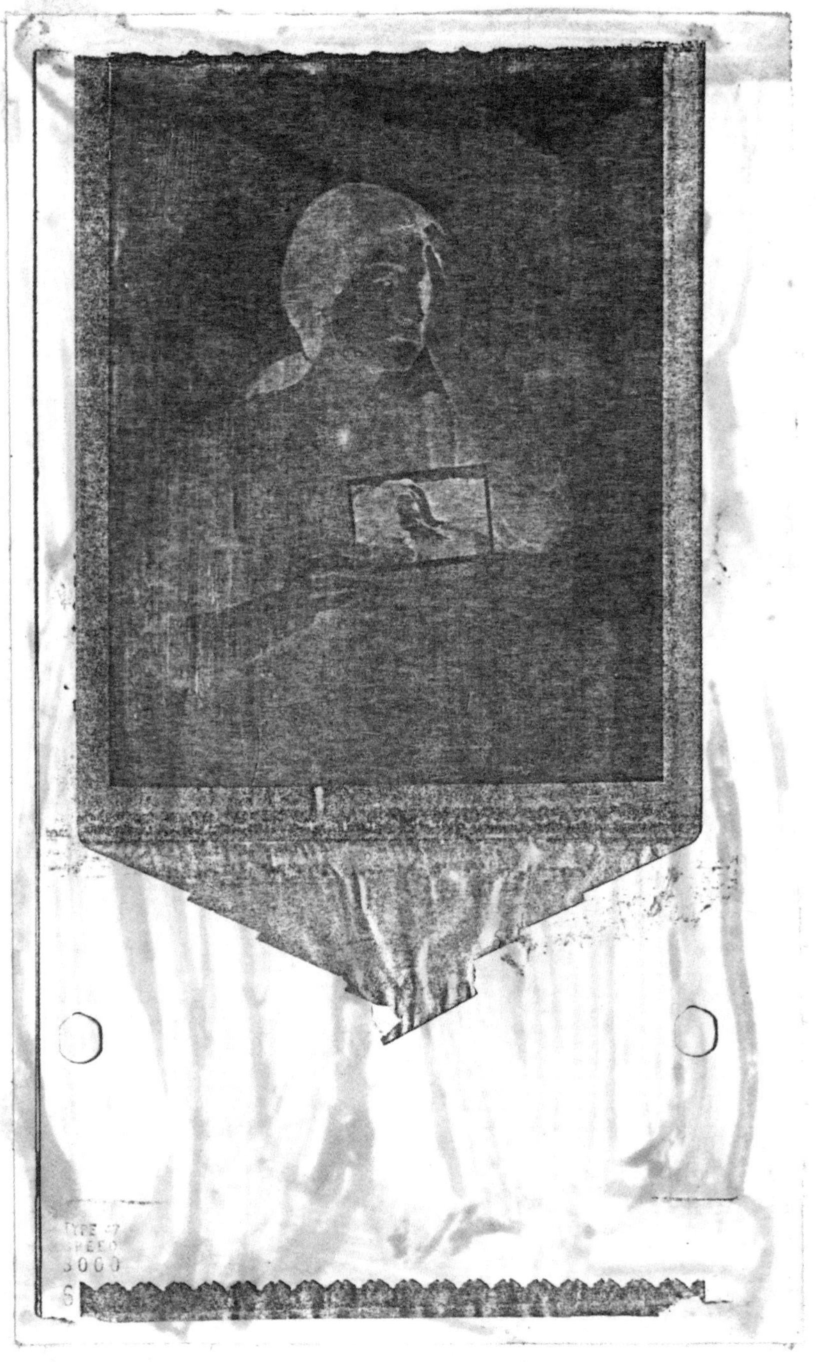

Tape starts

what do you want me to say—
about going back?
(that) I must turn my back
on it? / ~~or~~ (to command)
Don't turn back! Don't turn
your back on it ——

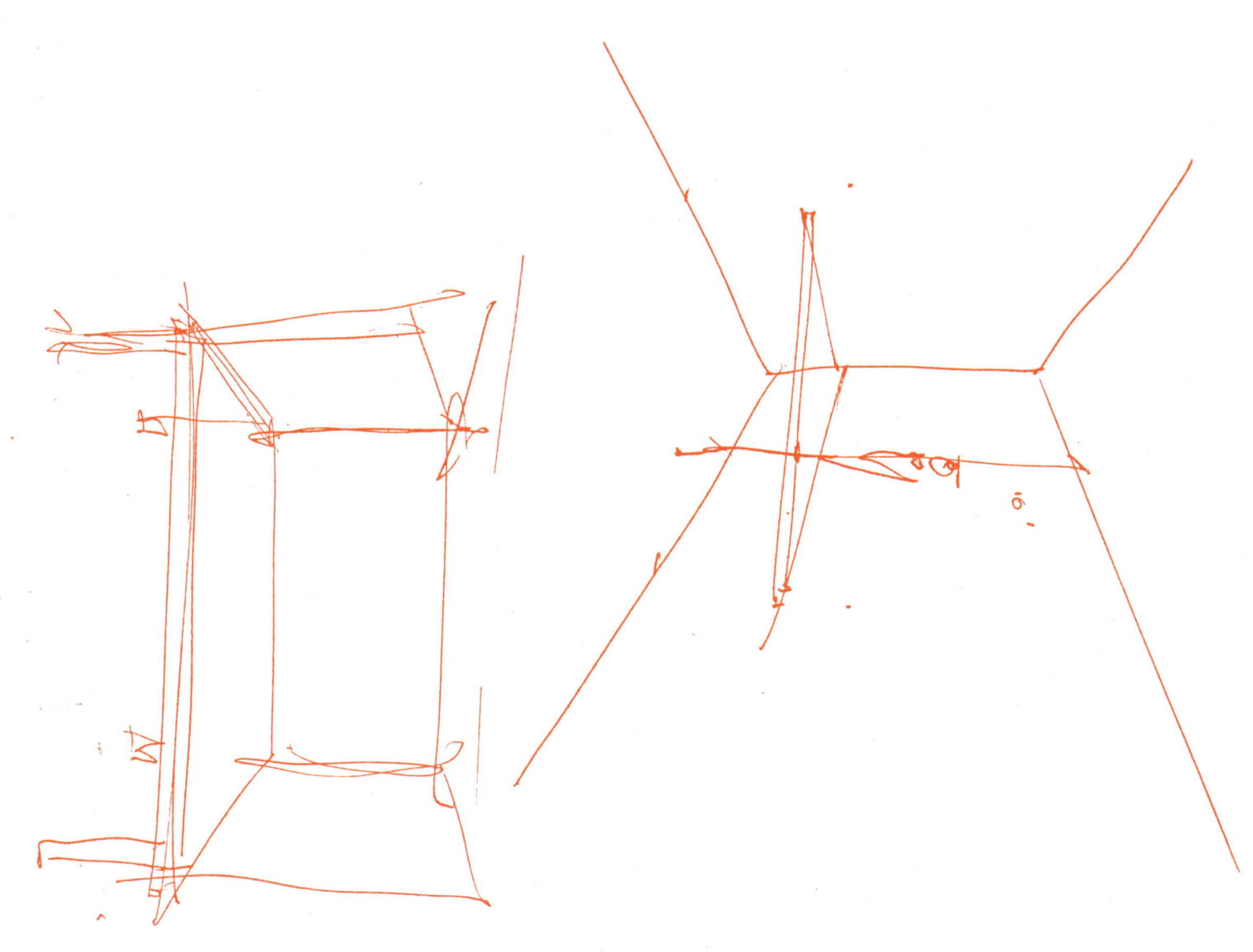

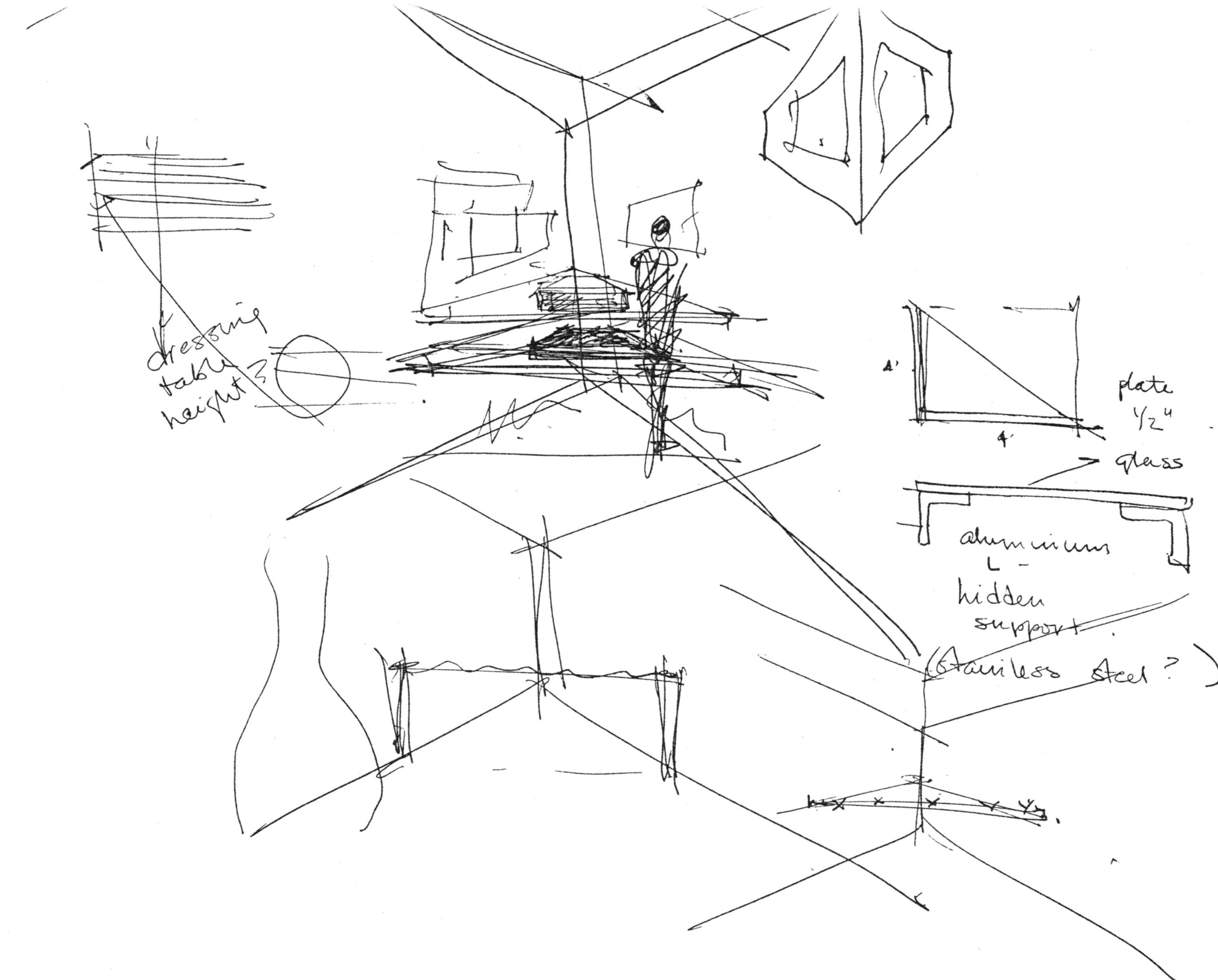
dressing table height?
4'
4'
plate 1/2"
glass
aluminium L - hidden support
(stainless steel ?)

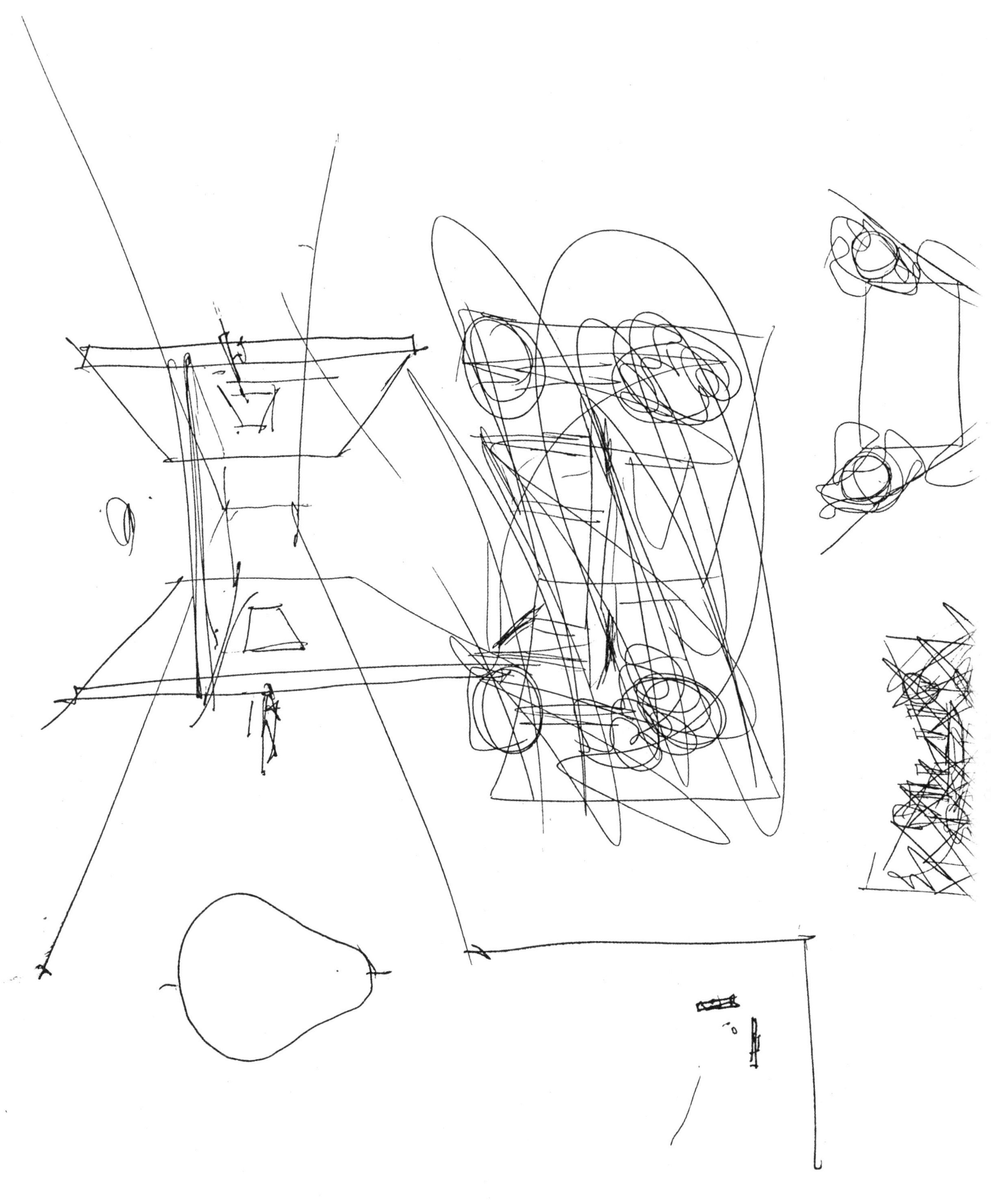

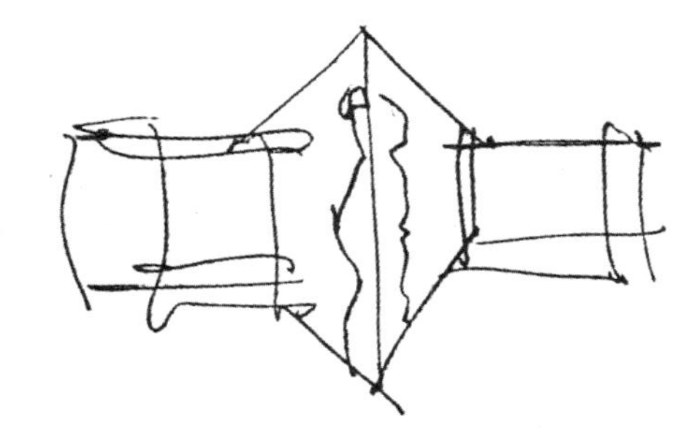

black + white slide film

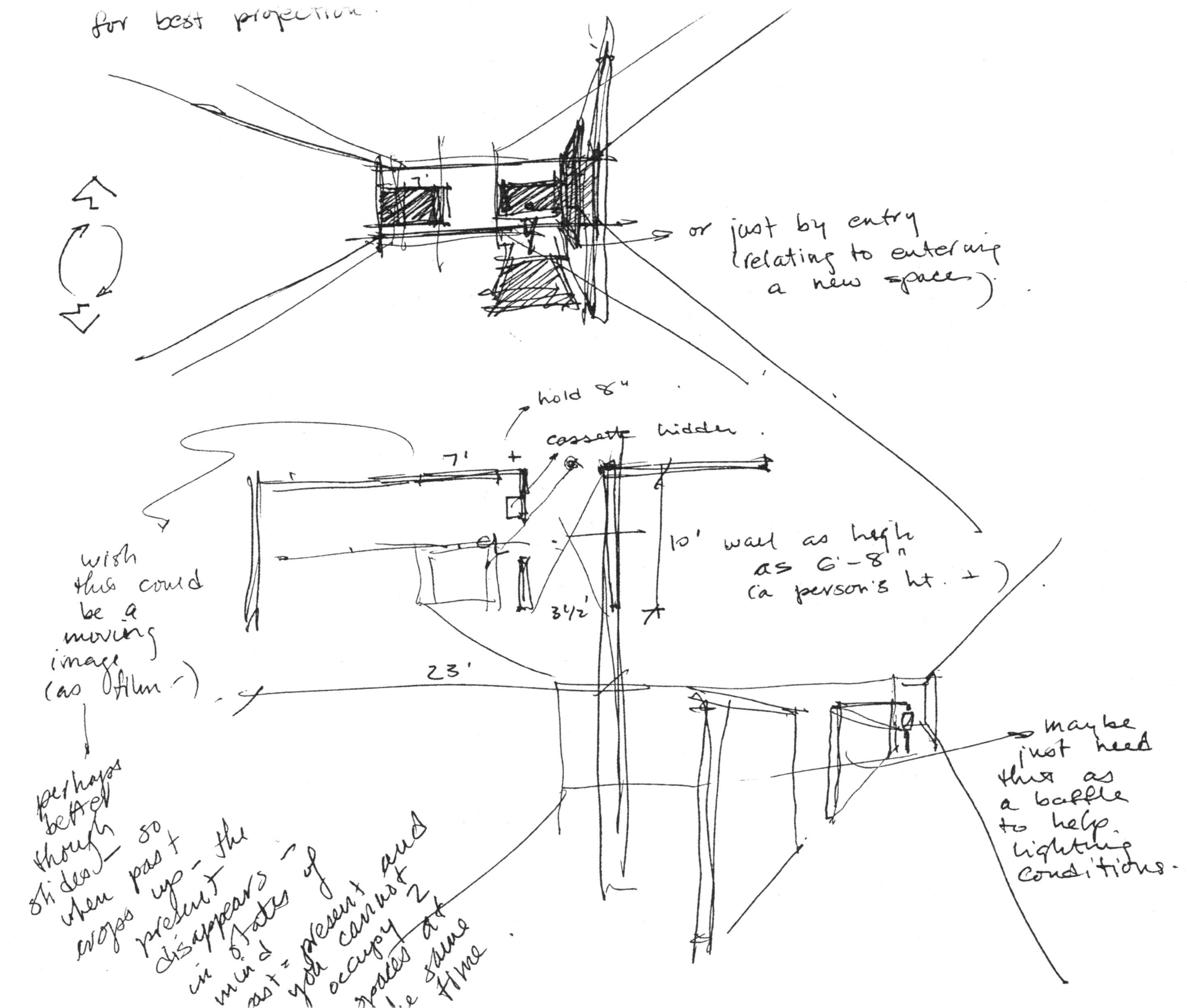
for best projection.
or just by entry (relating to entering a new space).
hold 8"
cassette hidden.
7'
10' wall as high as 6'-8" (a person's ht. +)
3½'
wish this could be a moving image (as film -)
23'
perhaps better though slides - so when past crops up - the present disappears - of states of mind past = present and you cannot occupy 2 spaces at the same time.
maybe just need this as a baffle to help lighting conditions.

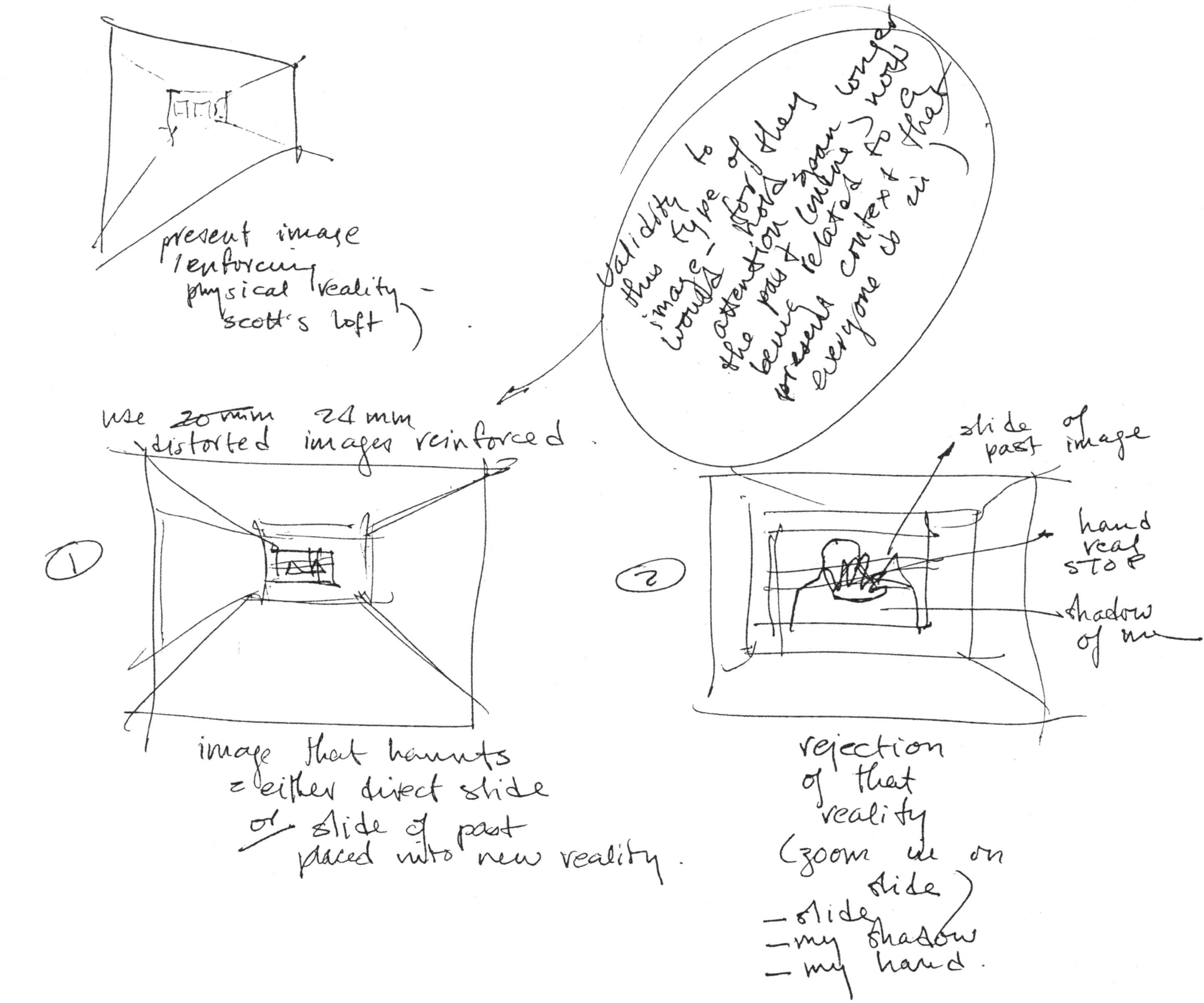

present image
reinforcing physical reality –
(scott's loft).
validity to thus type of image – for they no longer hold attention (span) – now the past relates to that being presents context in everyone
use ~~20 mm~~ 24 mm
distorted images reinforced.
1
image that haunts
= either direct slide
or slide of past
placed into new reality.
2
slide of past image
hand real STOP
shadow of me
rejection
of that
reality
(zoom in on
slide)
– slide
– my shadow
– my hand.

STEP (1)

presentation of
exact & of a physical
reality.

STEP (2)

presentation
of taking
that reality
and placing slide
within → representational
past

past image trying to
overcome present reality
(pulling back)

neurotic tendencies
depression + schizophrenia
time / space tendencies

the past is always coming back to haunt
(no, I won't go back —
physical into a state of mind

letting past come back to haunt
to impede growth — to
impede going on into future.

letting a flat image try to hold a physical space (wide & perspective of gallery you are in — trying to concentrate on and reinforce present space.

say only of gallery you are in — trying to hold onto present by establishing a physical reality from which to work from.

constant present

viewing zone.

past

(slides of what you don't want to go back to

what is pulling you back.

or simply a large white frame (painted on wall — going down to floor)

red bulbs where to stand (on - off blinker)

or without anything — just indicate where to stand.

maybe you must put on head phones here to hear tape or there is a

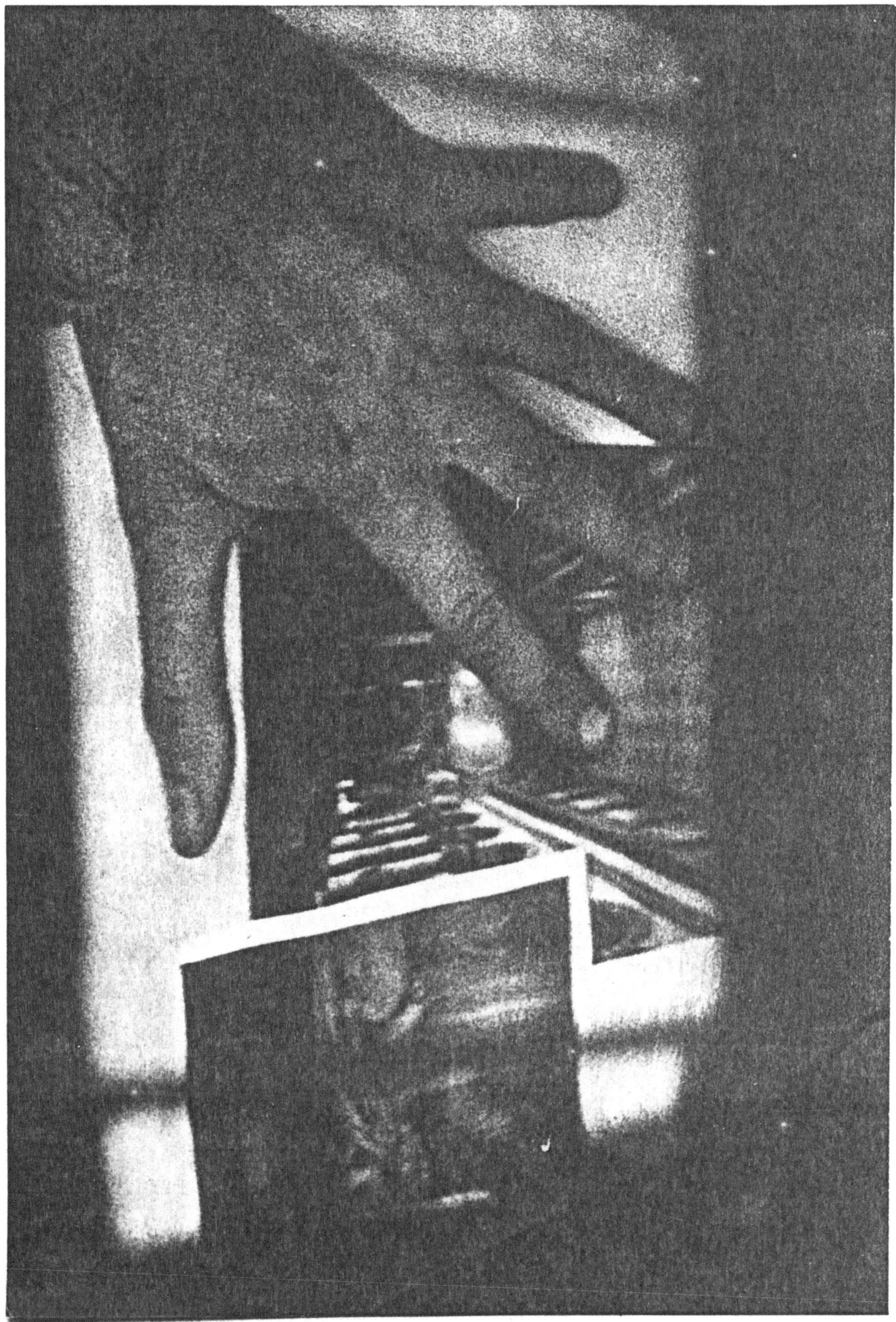

BACK PIECE
MAR 1975
NEW YORK CITY

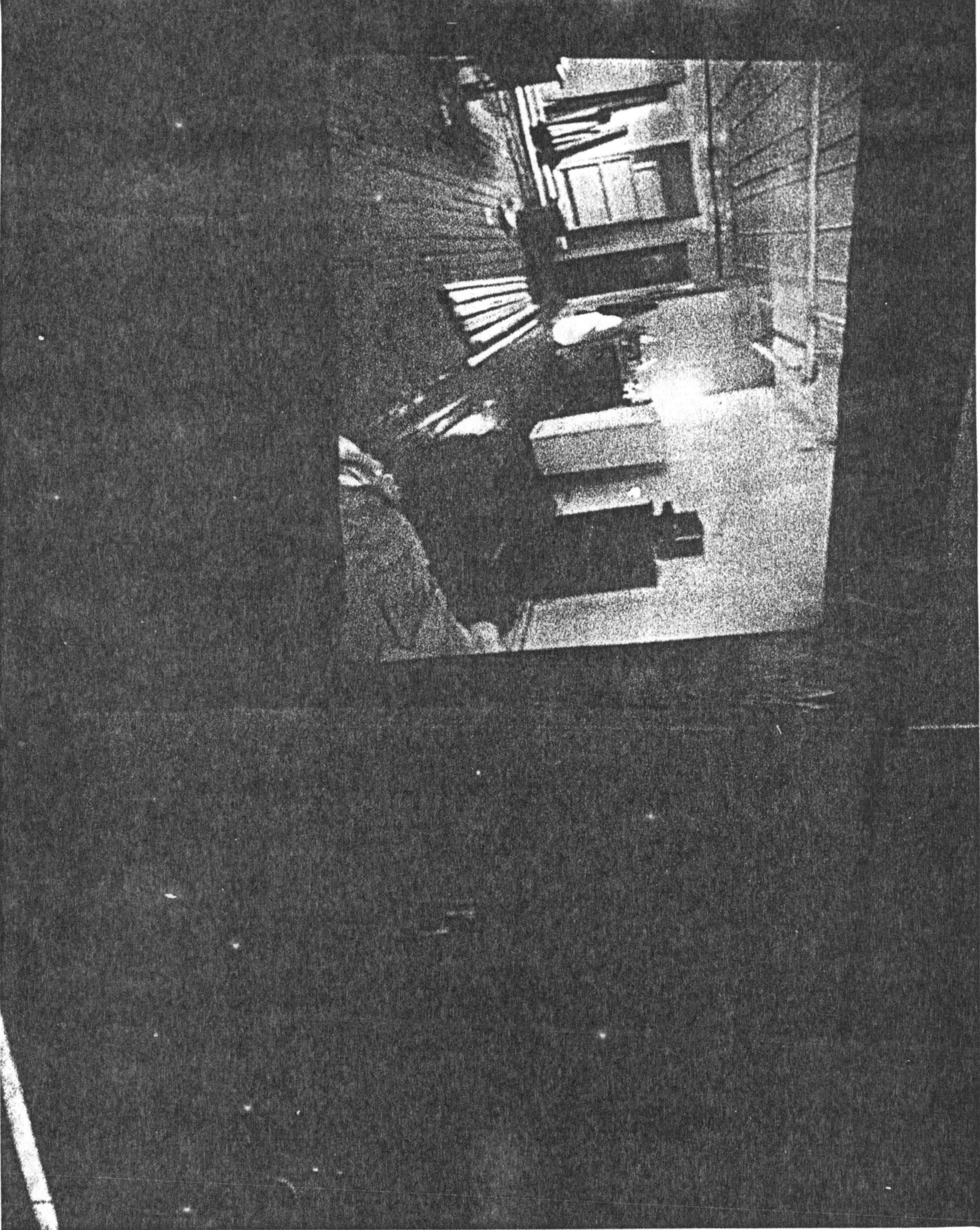

BACK PIECE
MAR   1975
NEW YORK CITY

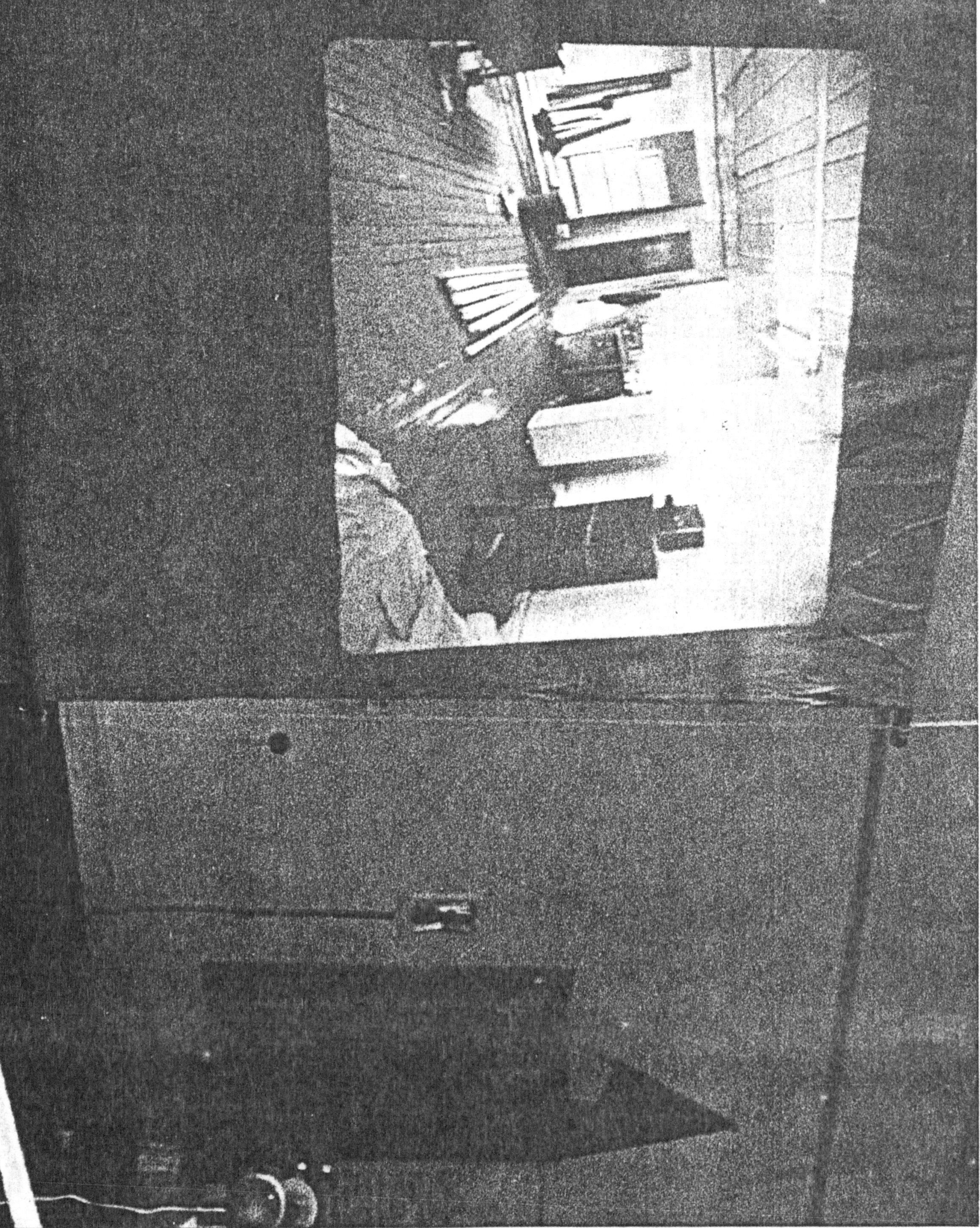

BACK PIECE
MAR 1975
NEW YORK CITY

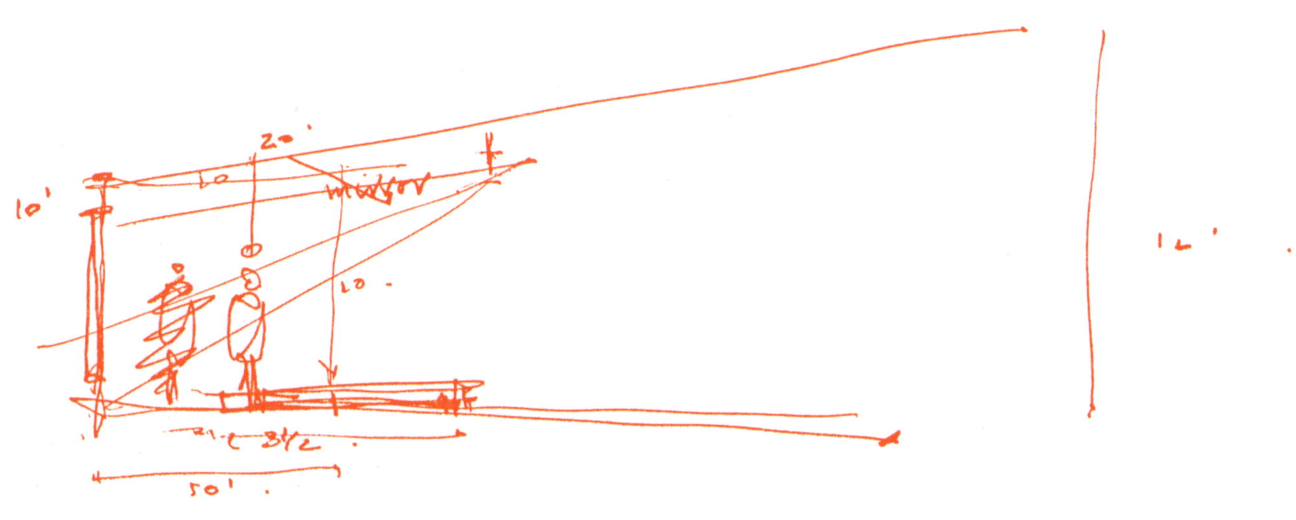

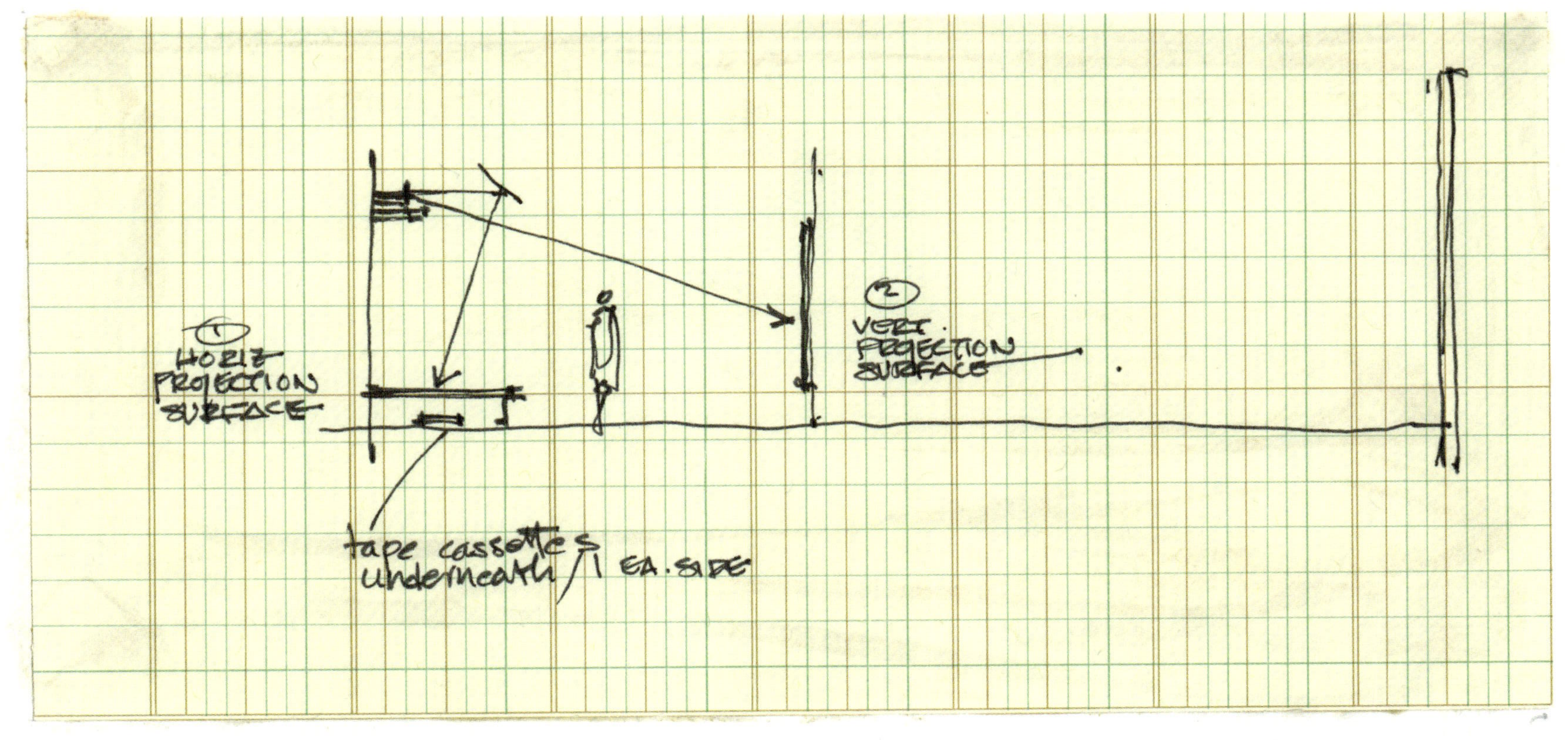

1
HORIZ
PROJECTION
SURFACE
tape cassettes
underneath / 1 EA. SIDE
2
VERT.
PROJECTION
SURFACE

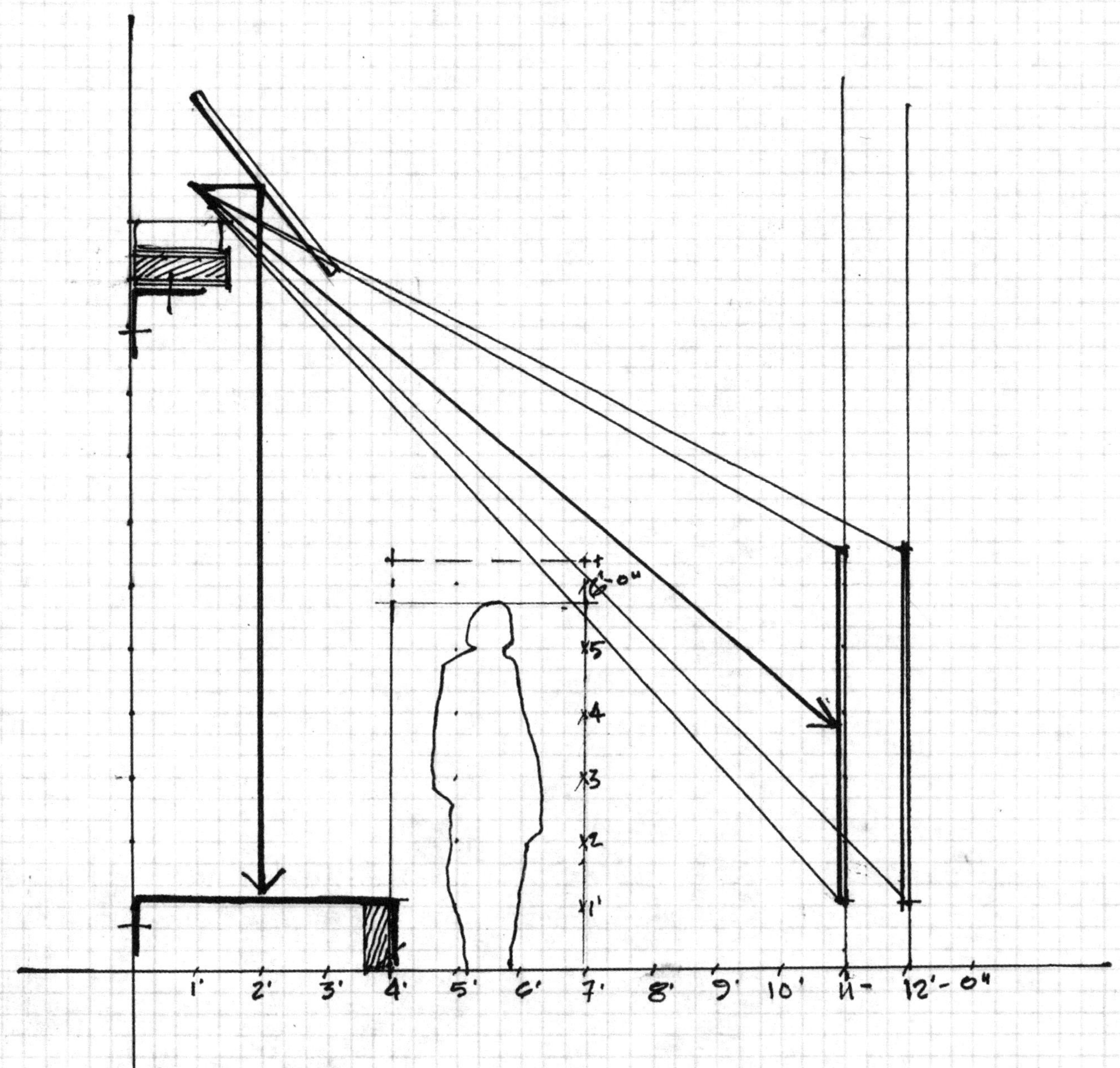

BACK PIECE
PROJECTION(S) DIAGRAM

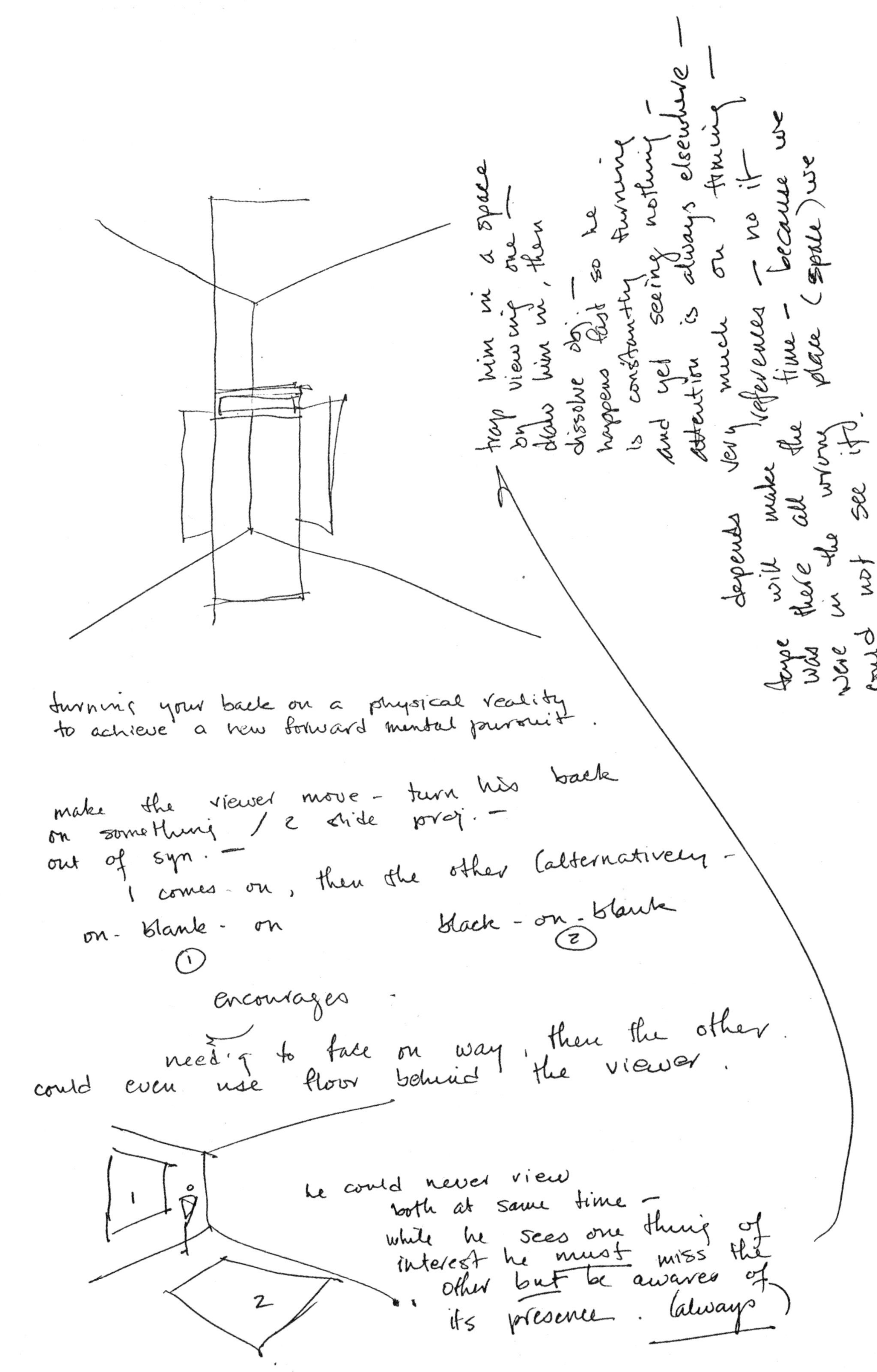
trap him in a space
on viewing one —
draw him in, then
dissolve obj. —
happens fast so he
is constantly turning
and yet seeing nothing —
attention is always elsewhere —
depends very much on timing —
tape will make references — no it
was there all the time — because we
were in the wrong place (space) we
could not see it.
turning your back on a physical reality
to achieve a new forward mental pursuit.
make the viewer move - turn his back
on something / 2 slide proj. —
out of syn. —
1 comes on, then the other (alternatively -
on - blank - on
1
black - on - blank
2
encourages
need'g to face on way, then the other
could even use floor behind the viewer.
1
2
he could never view
both at same time —
while he sees one thing of
interest he must miss the
other but be aware of
its presence. (always)

STEP ③

rejection slide
stop gap.
(closing in on past image + rejecting it).

---

① going to loft shooting wide & perspectives.
② recording exact locations where ~~shoot~~ ~~shots~~ shot from
i.e. by footprints.

①

③ going back @ sunset (some light to read space but also to read slide) and reshooting slide in that location.

maybe this could be done in a daylight hour all at the same time.

④ reshooting the ~~slide~~ (past image) with my shadow and hand.

or maybe white on white wall

1 present. of pres. / blank / ~~black~~ as if nothing ~~is there~~ / blank

2 blank (black) / pres. past / cancel reject

① presentation of present / blank /

this space would probably have to be white (paint / or material or paper for good proj.)

② ~~pr~~ blank / presentation of past

choices.

– pres. present / blank (A) *
– blank / present past.

– pres. present / blank / blank (B) *
~~– pres. past~~
– blank / present past / reject

– present present / blank / reject (C)
– blank / present past / reject

– present present / blank /re. present present (D)
– blank /present past / reject

needed 2 carosel projectors
that can have = speed
notations (ask Jerry –
help from Marcl or
Dennis / Bill's proj. –
will it match timewise w
kodak?

2 cassettes playing off ea. other

1 = intellectual approach

(a psychiatric explanation – clinical read of depression + relation to time – etc. as out of Beck's bk. / double binds, etc.

2 = emotional approach

tape of no, I won't go back
I can't –

resistance to this condition.
(emotional)

slides placed in loft picture destroys idea that if you are facing 1 thing – you must necessarily miss the other – again turning your back on one to go ahead w. the other.

What did you have to turn your back on to work yourself into this present situation? – i.e. your home backgr. / Europe / Calif. / arch. offices. etc.

pg. 251. Beck

157. spacial (distortion of) judgement.

→ PG. 29 – Escapism. Avoidance.

pg. 233 escapism
pg. 21 indecisiveness
21 – 25
25 on

what about linking tapes relating them?

PG. 25 / INDECISIVENESS / BECK

→ reading this into 1 tape system.

2nd system = all the manifestations of it (emotional) –
I can't go back – it might be the wrong decision —
I don't know if I can go back

PG. 27 . paralysis of will <<.

maybe make up own examples – more applicable to personnel hist.
decision to come back to NY from Europe.

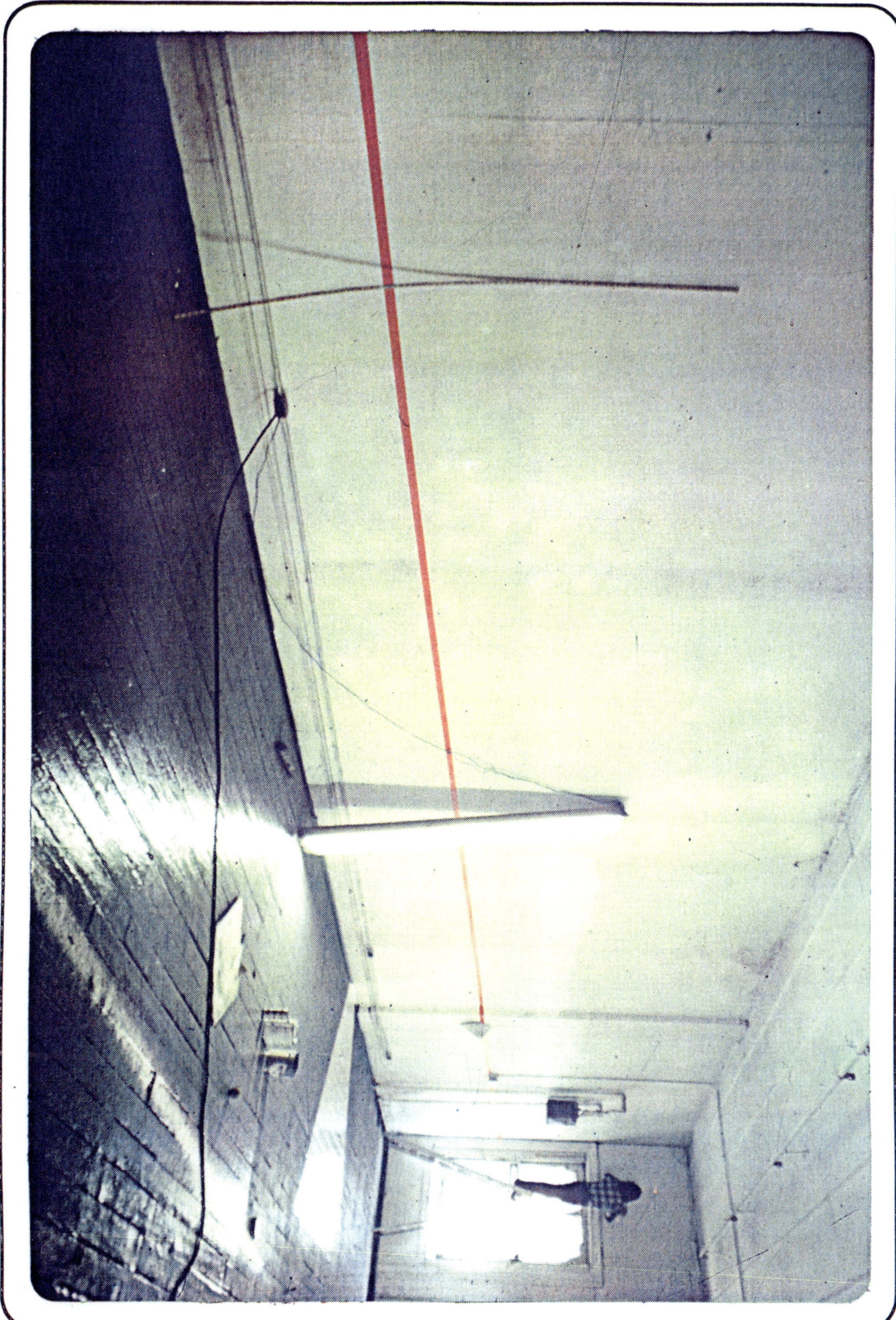

<u>BACK PIECE</u>
<u>MAR   1975</u>
NEW YORK CITY

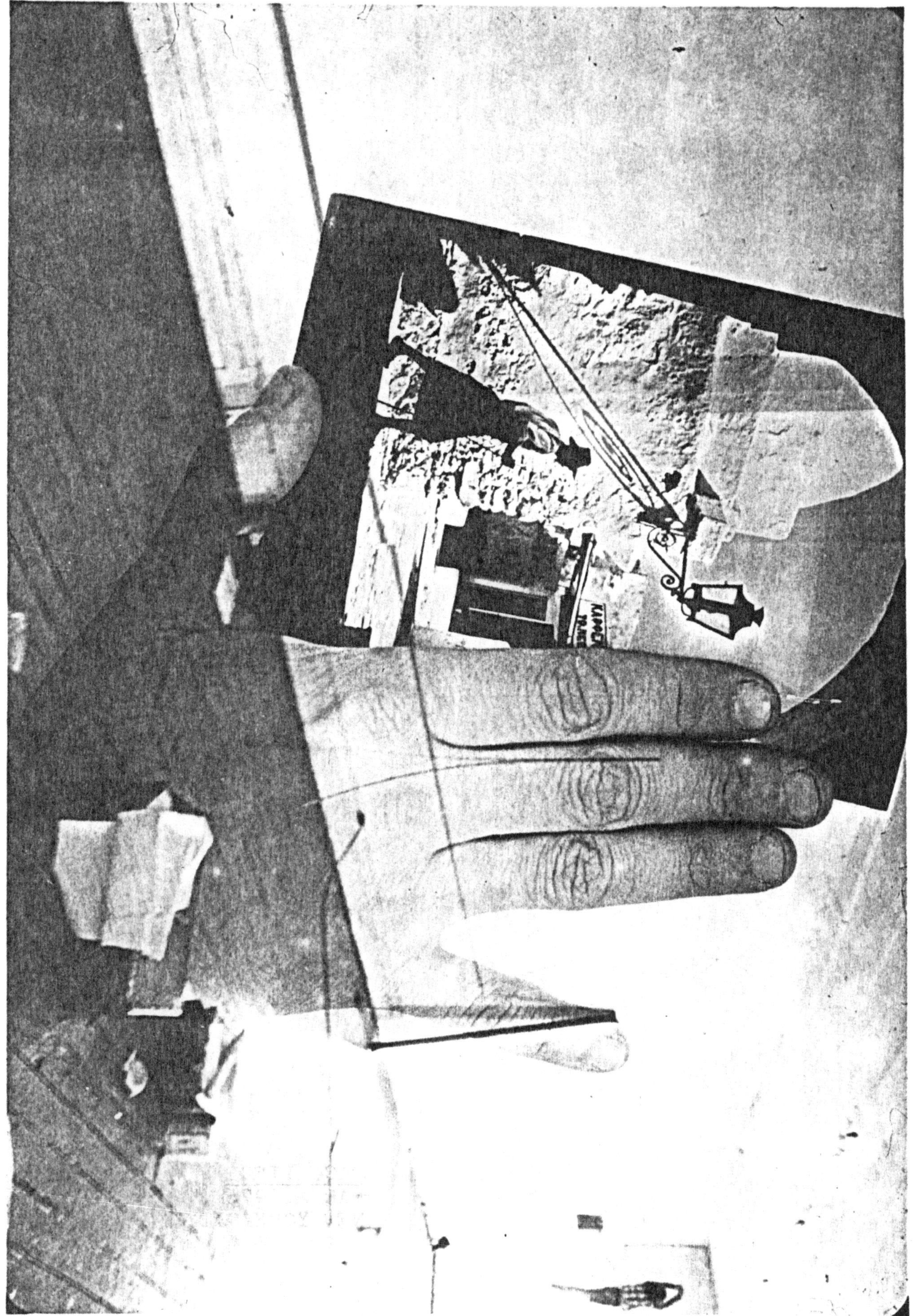

BACK PIECE
MAR 1975
NEW YORK CITY

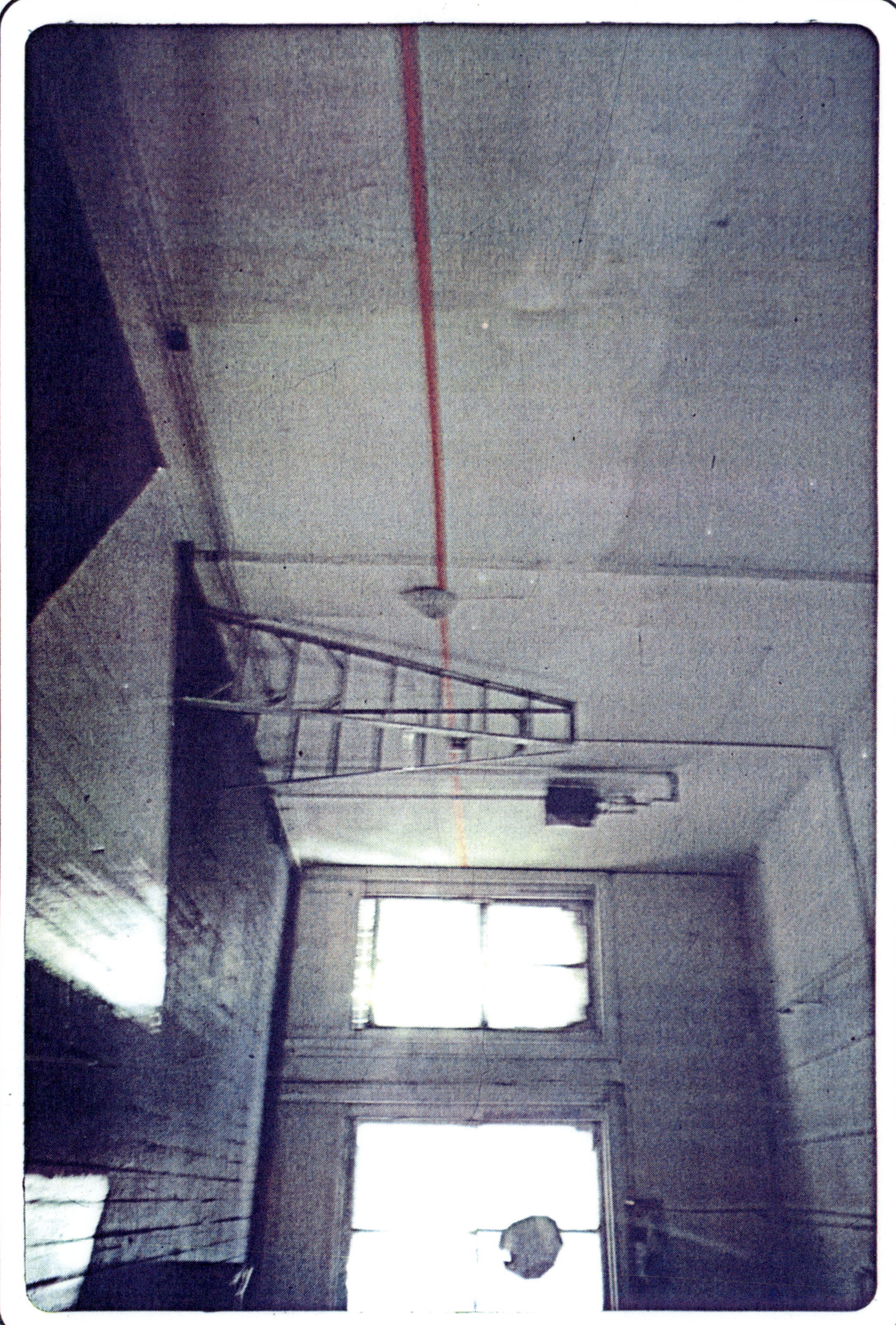

BACK PIECE
MAR 1975
NEW YORK CITY

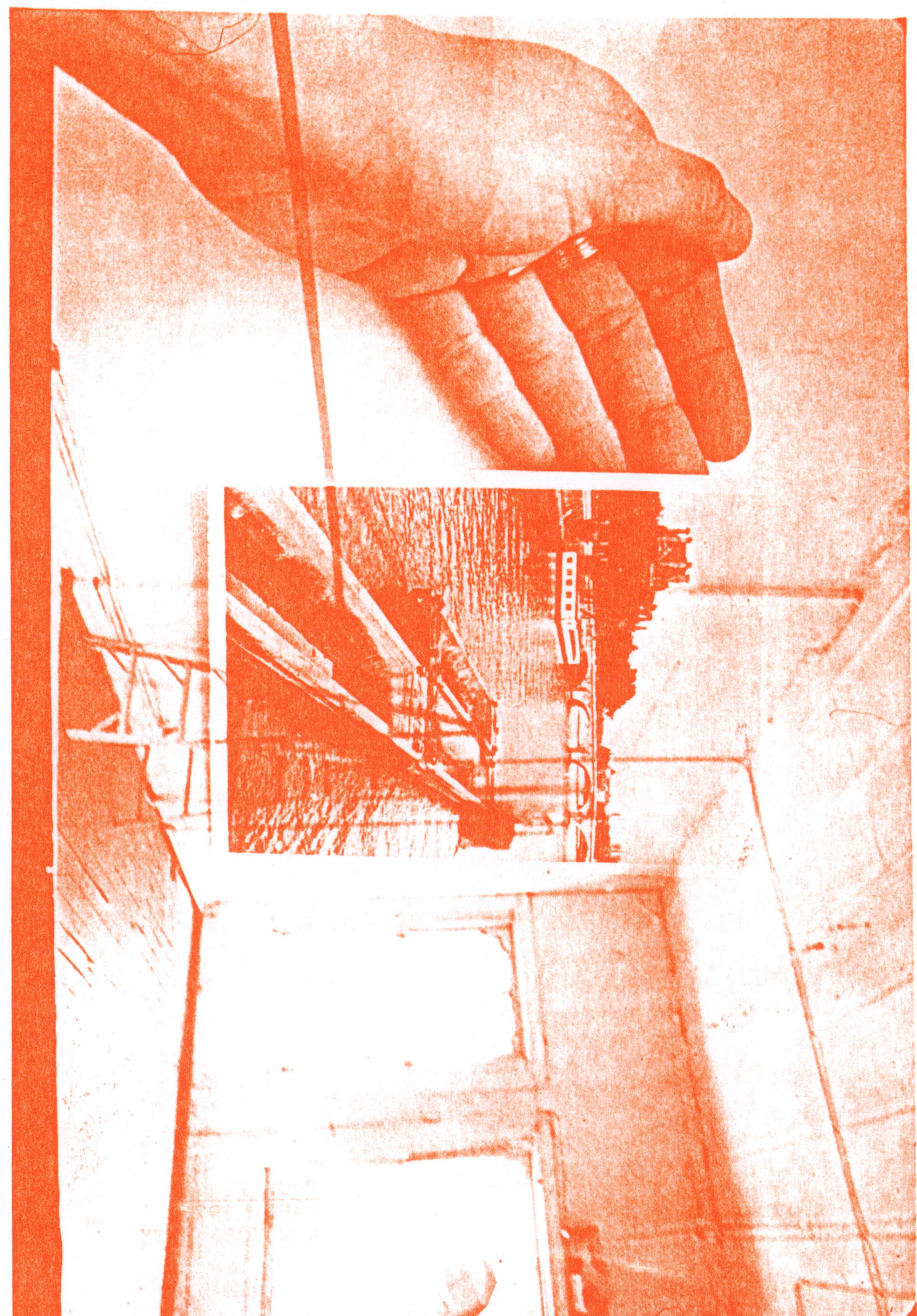

<u>BACK PIECE</u>
MAR 1975
NEW YORK CITY

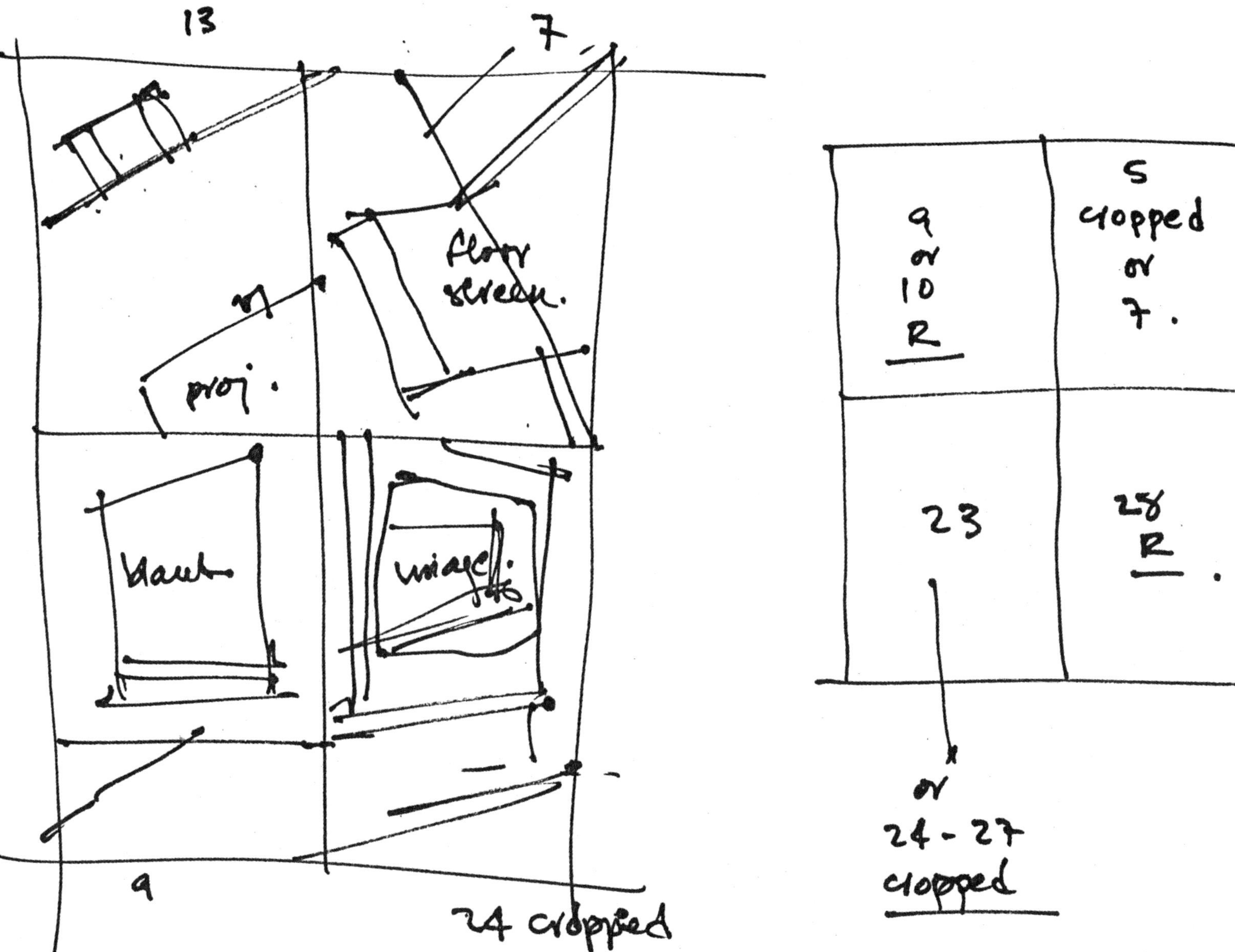
13
7
floor screen.
proj.
blank.
image.
9
24 cropped
9 or 10 R
5 cropped or 7.
23
28 R
or 24 - 27 cropped

for ~~installation~~ installation make 8x10 with combined 2-4 images – so intent of proj. better explained.

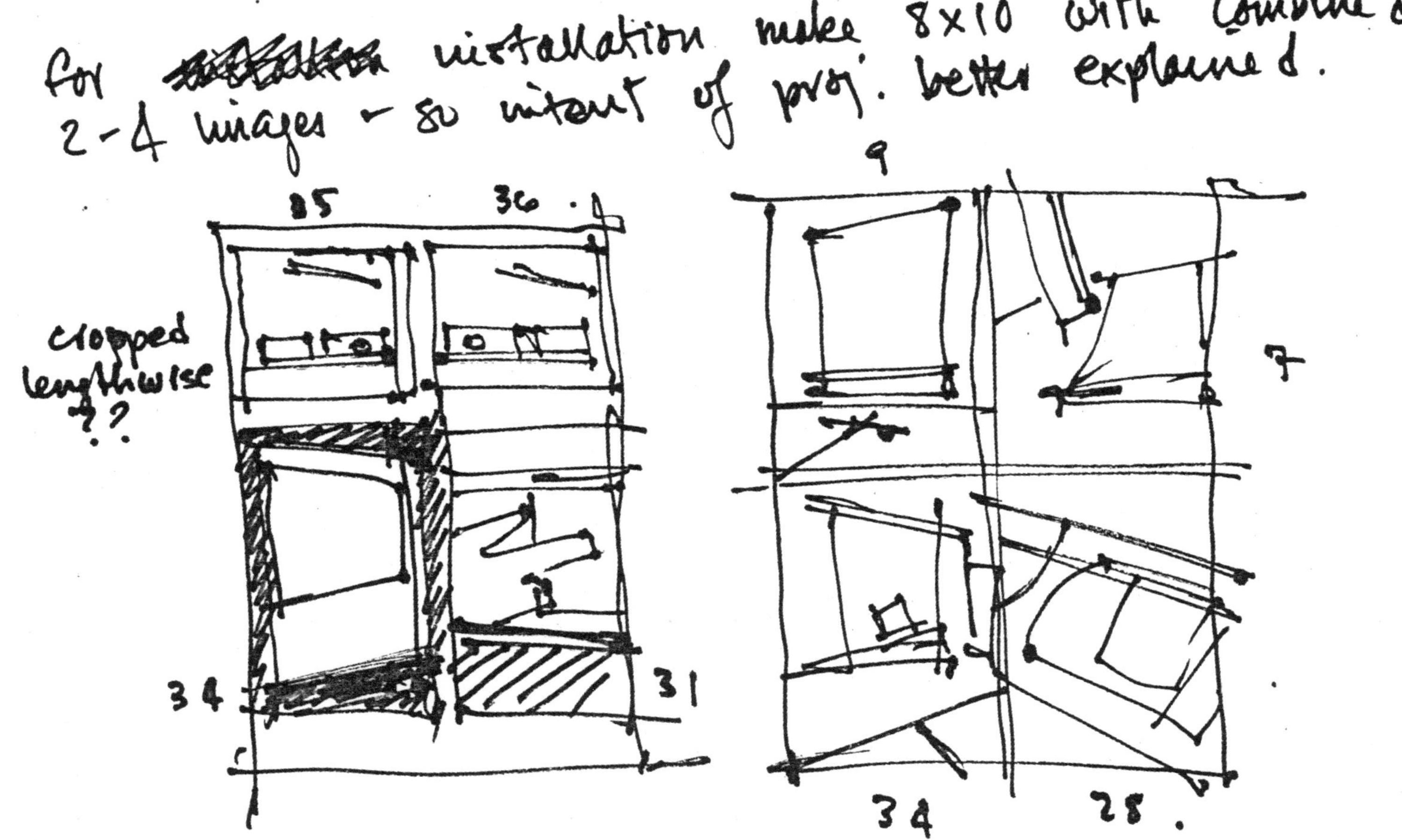

documentation of 'back piece' / 597 broadway

2 8 x 10 contacts
40 ea.
8 rows / 5 each.

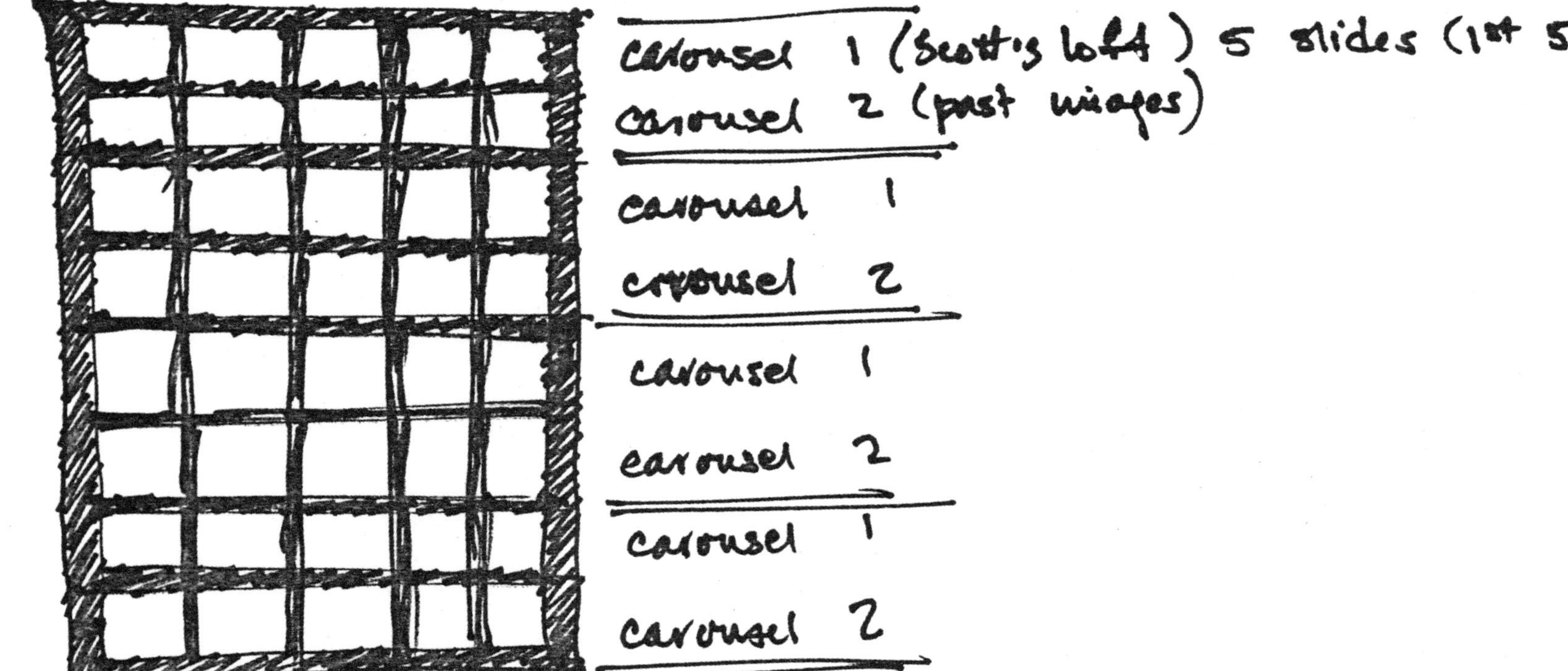

each contact will contain
20 slides from carousel 1
20 slides from carousel 2.

RE: CONCERNS (THAT TAKE ON / DEAL WITH)
STILL VS CONTINUOUS PROJECTION FORMAT(S)
SLIDE / FILM USAGE

IE: ATTACK PIECE
HALIFAX NS
AUG '75

ATTACK PIECE

HALIFAX, NOVA SCOTIA

ATTACK PIECE IS AN EXERCISE FROM A LARGER SERIES OF WORK CONCERNING ITSELF WITH APPROACH / AVOIDANCE ANXIETIES AND RELATED DEFENSE MECHANISMS (BUILT INTO PERSONALITY STRUCTURES). ATTACK ALSO INVOLVES ITSELF WITH A COMPETITIVE CONCERN BETWEEN THE INTRINSIC QUALITIES OF MOTION (MOVING) PICTURE VS STILL PHOTOGRAPHY (THUS, WE HAVE A PIECE EVOLVING OUT OF A DUAL-LEVEL COMPETITION: ONE PSYCHOLOGICAL; THE OTHER MECHANISTIC).

SET-UP: ONE PERSON (THE PERFORMER) TAKES THE ROLE OF DEFENSE (PROTECTOR: TO PROTECT). A PHYSICAL SPACE IS CHOSEN AS "HOME-GROUND". IT IS TO BE AN AREA THAT IS BASICALLY UN-COMFORTABLE TO THE PERFORMER: AN AREA IN WHICH SHE/HE FEELS ILL AT EASE (IE: DUE TO A PAST ANXIETY-PROVOKING SITUATION THAT MAY HAVE OCCURRED ON THIS SPOT OR ON A SIMILAR LOCATION). A GROUP OF PEOPLE (THAT ARE CONSIDERED OF AN APPROPRIATE FEEL-ING OF CLOSENESS) ARE ASKED TO MAKE AN "ATTACK" ON THIS PERSON WITHOUT COMING INTO DIRECT PHYSICAL CONTACT WITH HER/HIM. THEY ARE TO INTRUDE HER/HIS SENSE OF SPACE AND TO CONSIDER APPROACHING IN ANY WAY THAT THEY FEEL WOULD BE MOST UNCOMFORT-ABLE TO THE DEFENDER. THE PARTICIPANTS ARE "EQUIPPED"/"ARMED" WITH A SUPER-8 MOVIE CAMERA; THE DEFENDER BEING "EQUIPPED"/ "ARMED" WITH A STILL 35MM CAMERA. THUS, ANOTHER ADVANTAGE IS SET INTO PLAY.... STILL VS CONTINUOUS ACTION. THE "ATTACKER" ("CONTINUOUS") CAN CAPTURE ALL OF THE DEFENDER'S MOVEMENTS (SHE/HE IS CONTINUOUSLY IN VIEW). THE "DEFENDER", HOWEVER, CAN FIGHT BACK ONLY BY SINGLE ATTACKS AT ONE TIME (CAPTURING ONLY A PIECE AT A TIME THAT MUST BE MADE SELECTIVELY). THE "DEFENDER" (PROTECTOR) IS FURTHER DISADVANTAGED BY KEEPING HERSELF/HIMSELF PHYSICALLY "BLINDED" AND IN A PHYSICALLY DIS-ABLING POSITION. IE: SHE/HE DOES NOT PERMIT "STANDING" AS A POSSIBLE MOVEMENT THEREBY LIMITING IN NUMBER AND STRENGTH HER/HIS MOVEMENTS IN RELATION TO THOSE OF THE "OFFENSE". AC-CORDING TO THE MECHANISTICS OF THE TWO CAMERAS INVOLVED, THE "DEFENDER" WAS AGAIN AT A APPRECIABLE DISADVANTAGE. DUE TO THE PERIMETER OF THE CHOSEN PIECE OF LAND, THE SUPER-8 CAMERA COULD BE PRE-FOCUSED; THE 35MM CAMERA HAD TO BE FOCUSED BLINDLY ACCORDING TO "FEELINGS" DEVELOPED WITHIN THE "DEFENDER"/ "PROTECTOR" AS TO WHETHER THE "OPPRESSOR" WAS NEAR (AND HOW NEAR WAS OF EQUAL IMPORTANCE) OR FAR AWAY. THE SUPER-8 CAMERA HAD A WIDER ANGLE LENS AND WAS THERFORE MORE INCLUSIVE. THE MOVEMENT OF THE SUPER-8 IS, AS PREVIOUSLY MENTIONED, CONTINUOUS.

GENERAL REMARKS: FOR THIS PIECE, PARTICIPANTS MUST BE CARE-FULLY SELECTED. IT IS PREFERRABLE FOR THE PEROFRMER TO SELECT INDIVIDUALS WHOSE RELATIONSHIP TO HER/HIMSELF HAS EXISTED FOR A RELATIVELY SHORT DURATION AND YET HAS BEEN OF A RELATIVELY INTENSE NATURE. (IE: ONE WHERE A GREAT DEAL OF INFORMATION HAS BEEN EXCHANGED QUICKLY (IE: DURING LATE NIGHT DISCUSSIONS): USUALLY DISCUSSIONS OF A VERY PERSONAL NATURE WITH THE DEFENDENT "GIVING AWAY MORE OF HER/HIMSELF" THAN HER/HIS COMPANIONS.)

EACH PARTICIPANT ("ATTACKER") WAS ASKED TO REMEMBER AS MUCH AS HE/SHE COULD OF "REVEALED WEAKNESSES" WITHIN THE "DEFENDENT" AND TO USE THESE AGAINST HER/HIM IN THE ATTACK SITUATION. IT IS ALSO IMPORTANT THAT THIS PIECE HAVE THE QUALITY AND ESSENCE OF GAME TO IT. IT IS BELIEVED THAT THE IDEA OF SIMPLE GAME CAN AT TIMES DEVELOP MUCH FURTHER TOWARDS EXTRACTING DEFENSE MECHANISMS THAN SEEMINGLY LESS CONTROLLED SITUATIONS. THUS, THE "DEFENDER" MAKES UP HER/HER OWN DISADVANTAGES BASED ON PAST EXPERIENCES THAT WERE DECIDELY ANXIETY PROVOKING TO HER/ HIM. THESE MAY OR MAY NOT PROVIDE A STIMULUS TO THE INTERNAL STRUCTURES OF THE OTHER PARTICIPANTS CHOSEN AT THAT TIME. THUS, THE PROJECTED REALITY OF THE ONE MAY OR MAY NOT COINCIDE WITH THE PROJECTED REALITY OF THE OTHER. IT IS THIS VERY SPLIT THAT BECOMES THE ESSENCE OF THIS PIECE: "REAL" (INTERNAL REALITY) VS "UNREAL" (EXTERNAL / PROJECTED REALITY); MENTAL VS PHYSICAL ASSAULT; CONTINUOUS ACTION VS THAT OF A STATION-ARY NATURE (STILL); PSYCHOLOGICAL STRUCTURING VS MECHANISTIC STRUCTURING; ETC...

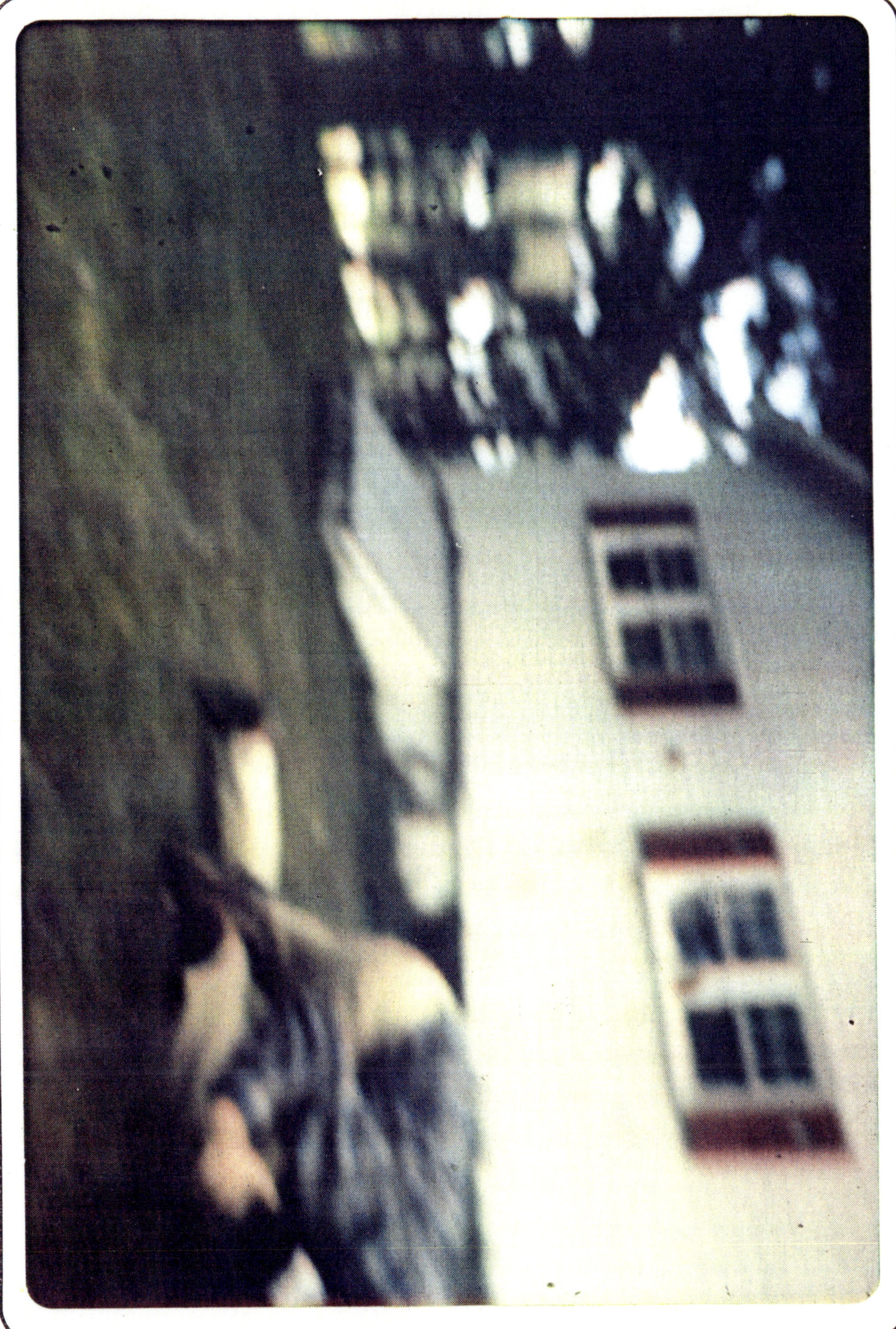

ATTACK PIECE
AUG 1975
HALIFAX, NOVA SCOTIA

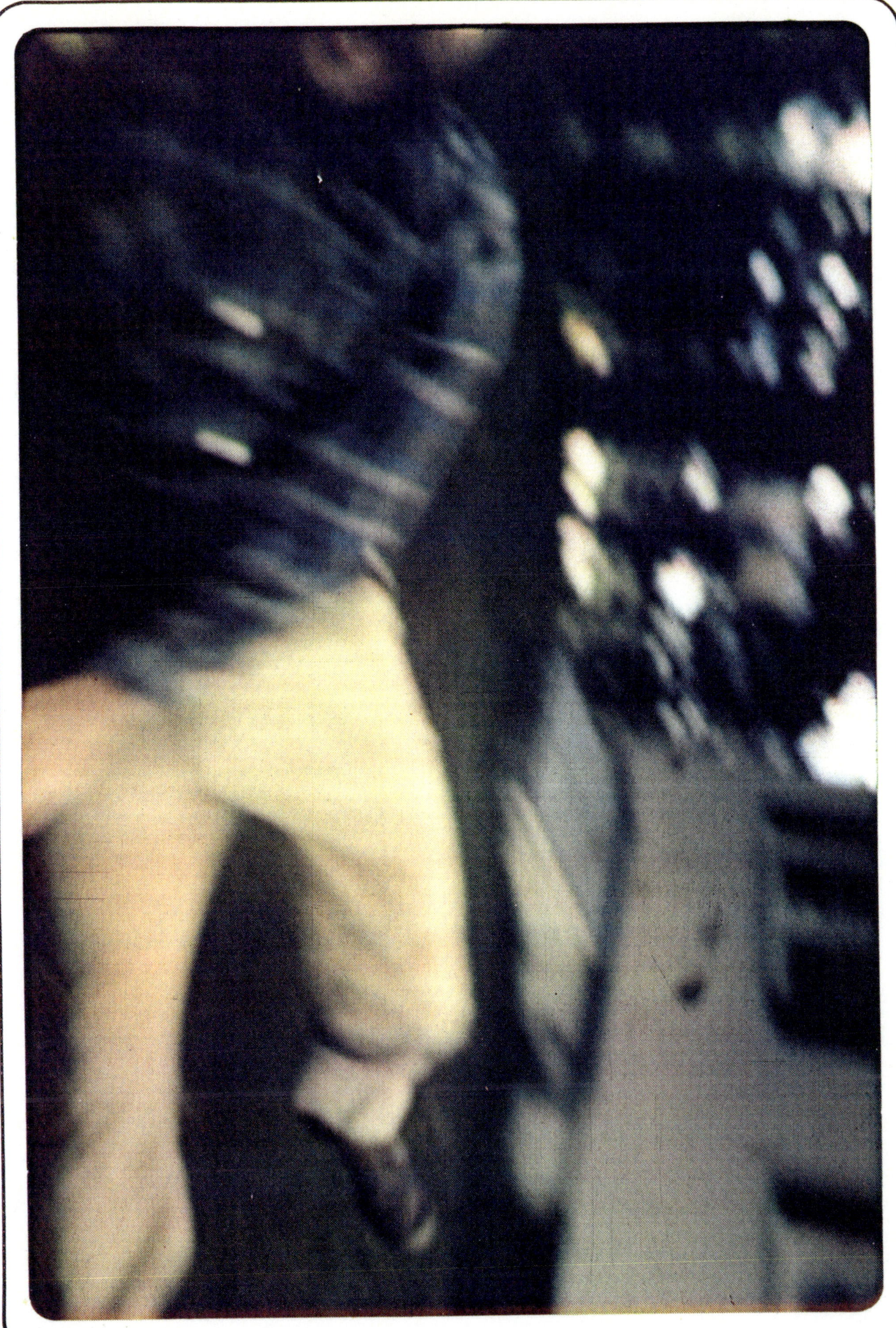

ATTACK PIECE
AUG 1975
HALIFAX, NOVA SCOTIA

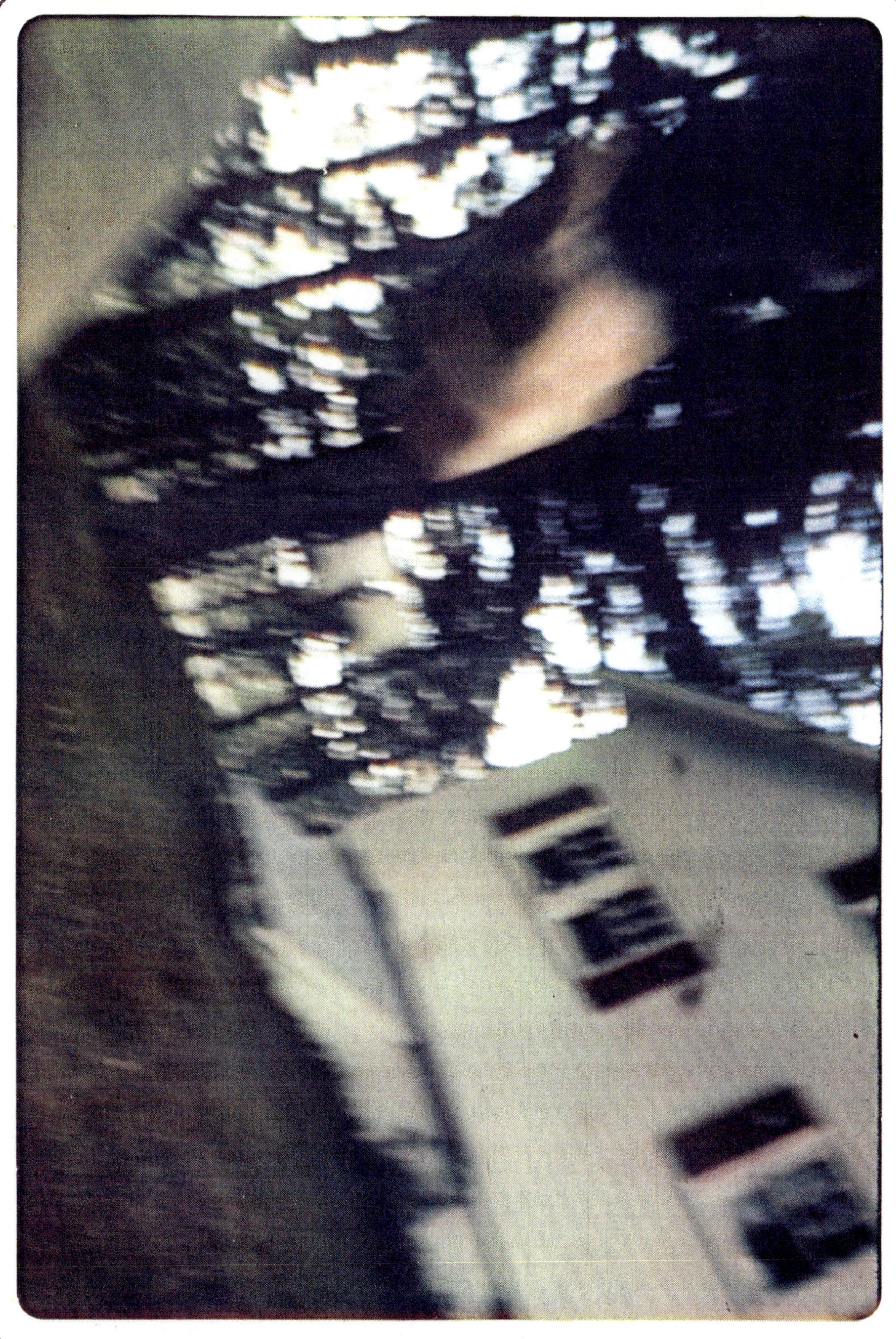

ATTACK PIECE
AUG 1975
HALIFAX, NOVA SCOTIA

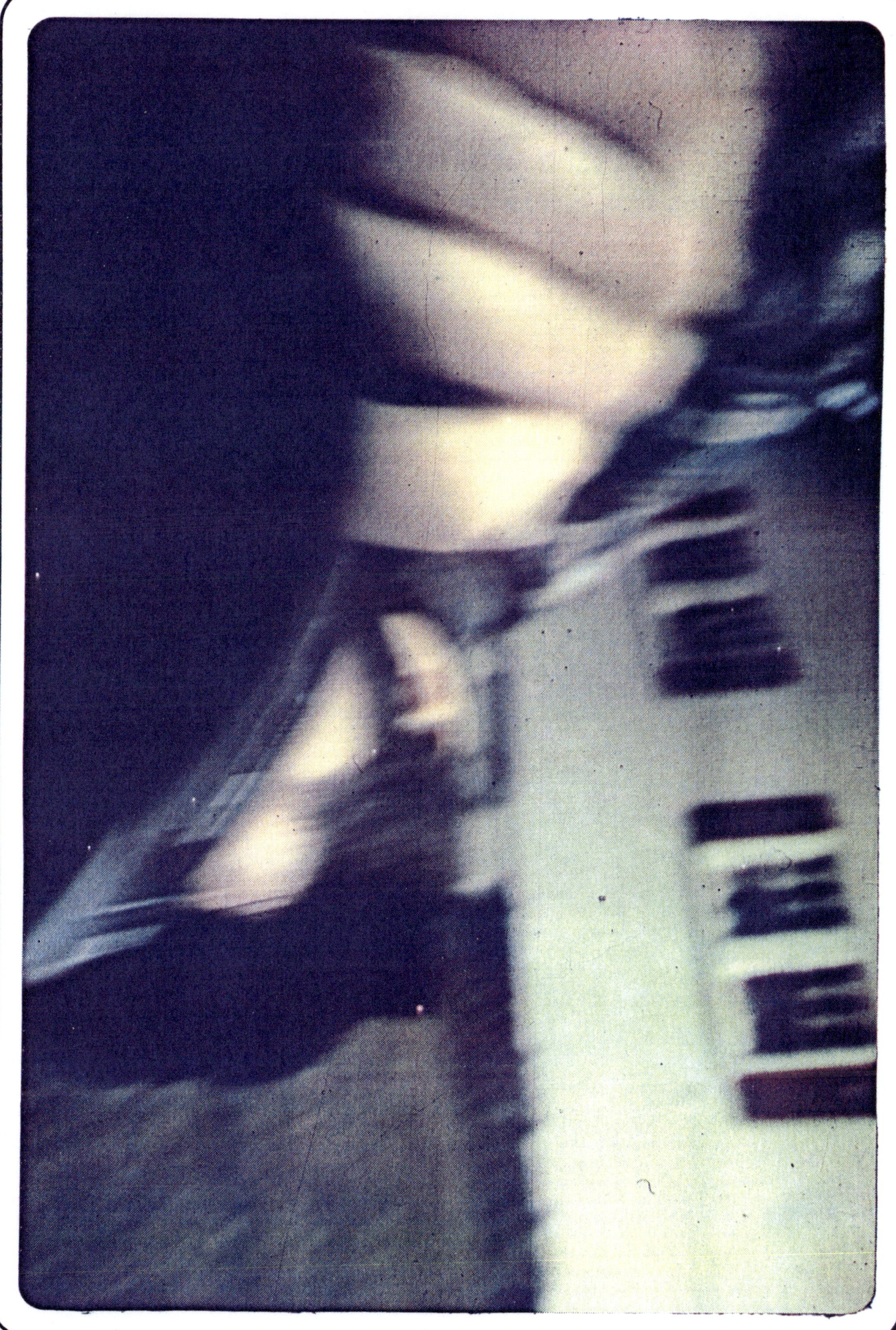

ATTACK PIECE
AUG 1975
HALIFAX, NOVA SCOTIA

NOTE(S)

VARYING METHODS OF APPROACH

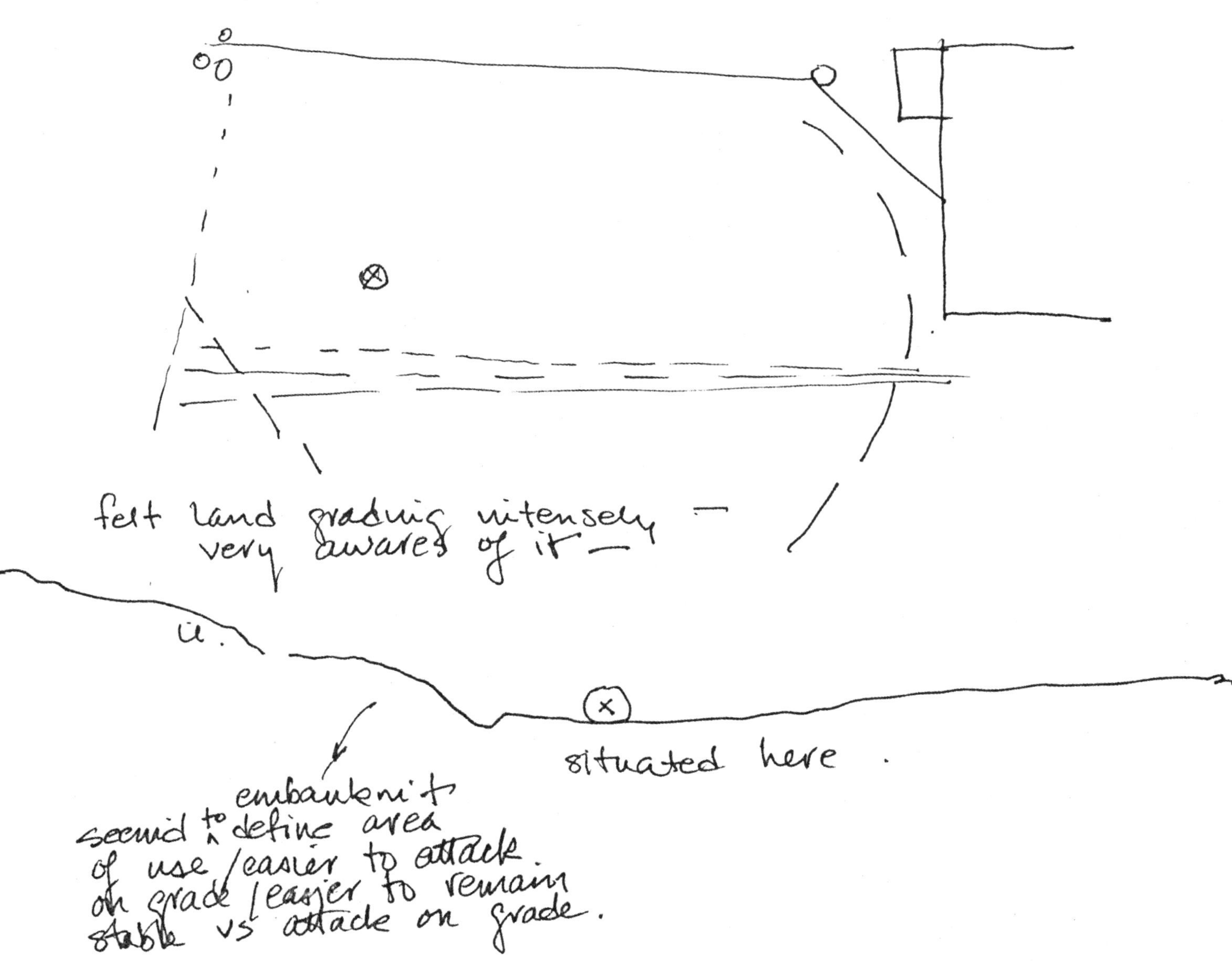

also:

embankment seemed to act as a buffer (to at least protect 1 side from possible attack — and allow concentration to rest on remain'g "open-ended" areas.

NOTE(S)

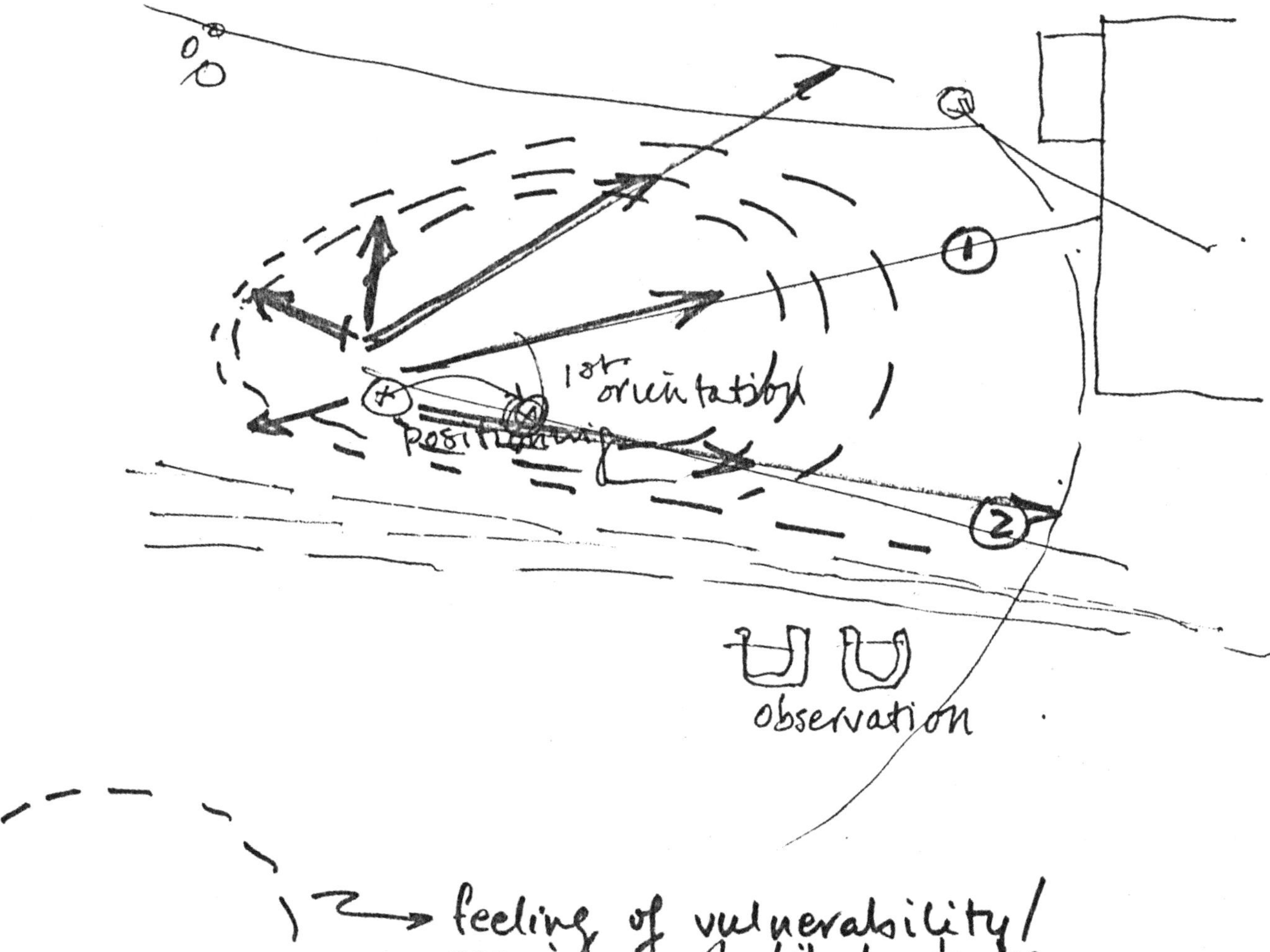

feeling of vulnerability / seem'd most likely to be attack-directions +

① + ② seem'd to be most likely areas from which attack would issue

main focus pt's

DAN GRAHAM

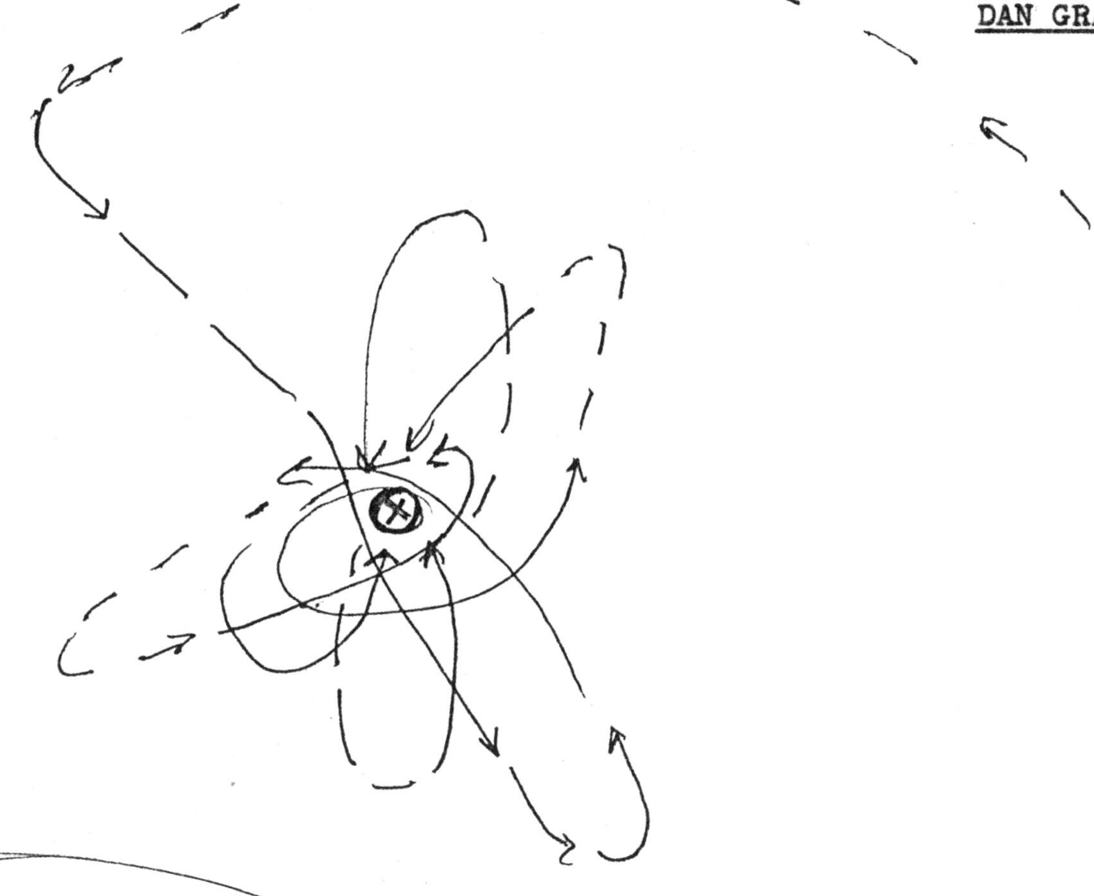

dan graham

a serces of running attacks — pulling back
slightly then running in to hoover over (very
on top of — esp. over head — buzzing in —
a plane zooming in to ~~boo~~ bomb — then staying
in tight — buzzing overhead / quick turns causing
sharp pivots by the "defender" / very fast pace /
in-tight a considerable amount of time — with
fast changes in orientation (— seemingly able from
camera being in tight over-head).

FIRST PARTICIPANT

sets trends / others watching — can observe /
assimilate / imitate / or reject approach —
also are already awares (become awares) of
some of the 'defender's reaction patterns) —
the 'attacker felt this 1st position to be a
disadvantage → having to be a "pace-setter" —
having to be spontaneous — did not see advantages
of situation (i.e. defender has built up no defense
mechanisms as yet — etc.)

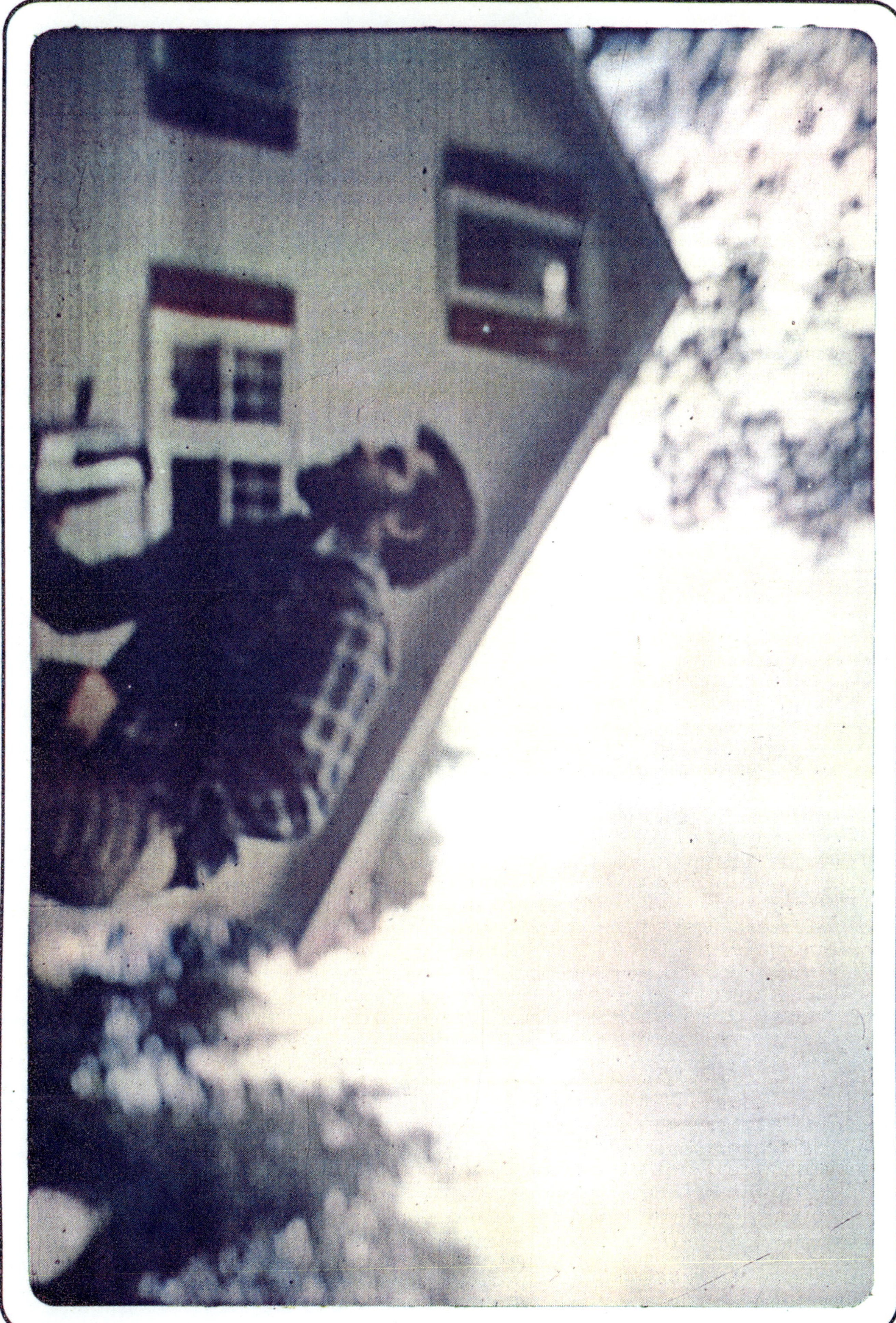

ATTACK PIECE
AUG 1975
HALIFAX, NOVA SCOTIA

IAN MURRAY

IAN MURRAY

(SECOND PARTICIPANT)

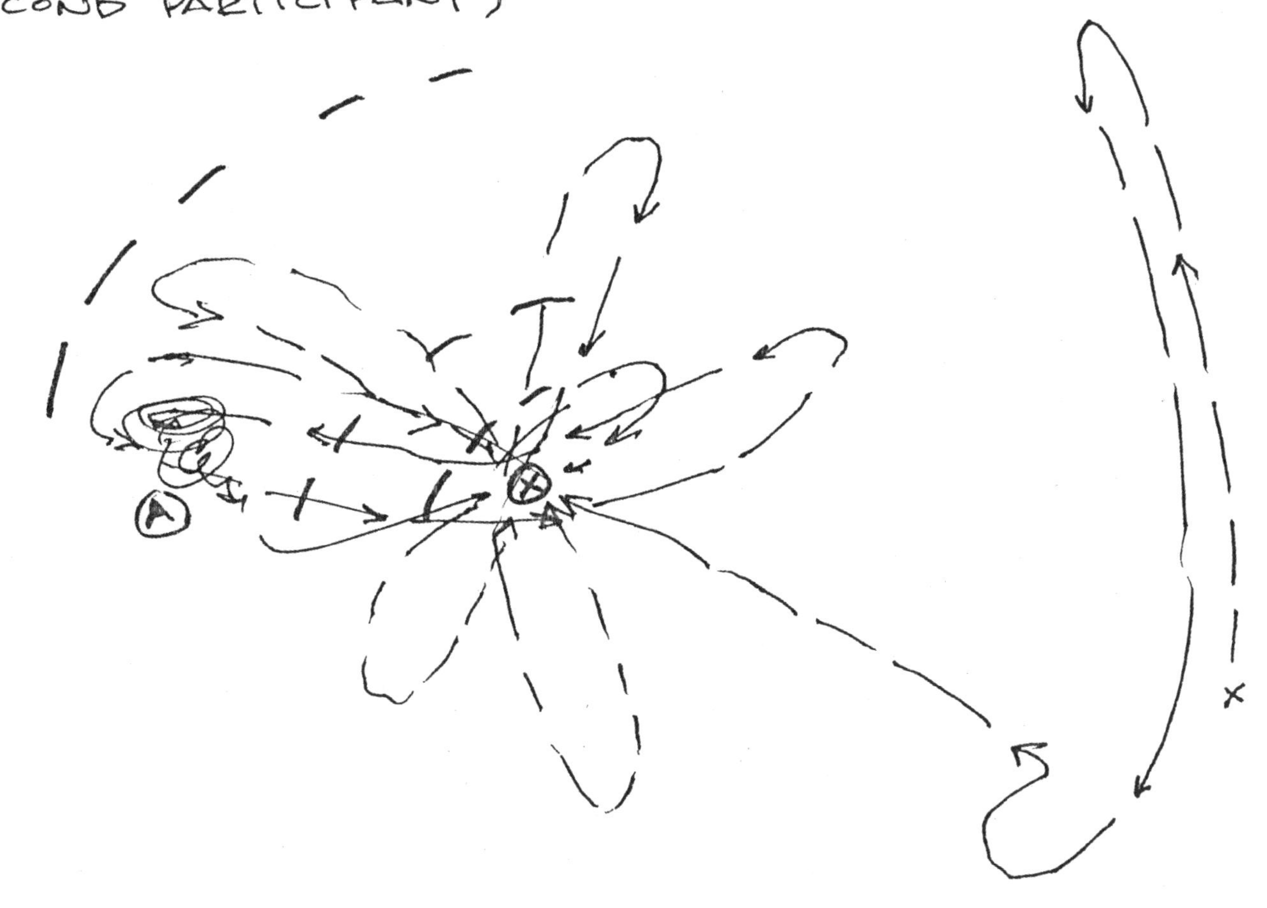

– – areas of concentrated attack

(A) confusion → seems that "attacker" is fallen /
laughing from observers causing same response /
in "defender" – adds humor to situation /
breaks mood somewhat – also realizing the
personality of 'attacker' rest of approach seems
not so serious – can now in my mind feel
that I am "safe" (will be left ~~unhurt~~ unhurt)
and enjoy this almost as a game).

again feel a dive-bombing technique — orientation
seems slightly concentrated more from what can
be adopted as a 'behind position → behind in the
sense of the original - first orientation becoming
"facing-front" or "facing forward".

IAN MURRAY (continued)

movement seems not quite as fast in some points – but again fast / perhaps seems "not as continuously fast – more modulation in speed /

orientation more biased (toward adopted 'behind')

again in-tight
fast pivot points

"falling moment" becomes turning point for awhile (in defender's attitude) → however seems to be very quick recovery → but "defender" can always recall this moment) (∴ seems to become crucial).

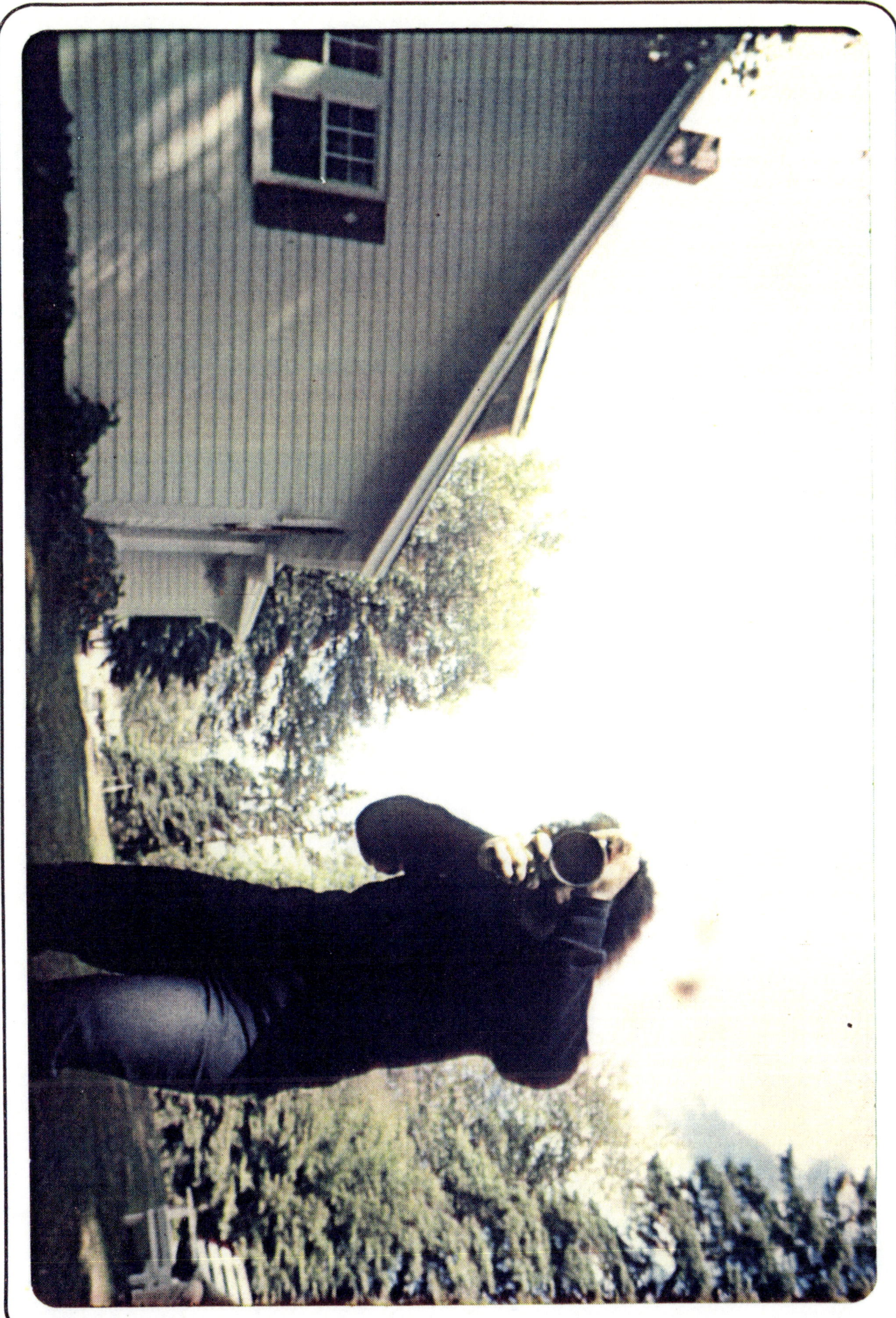

ATTACK PIECE
AUG 1975
HALIFAX, NOVA SCOTIA

CYNE COBB (THIRD PARTICIPANT)

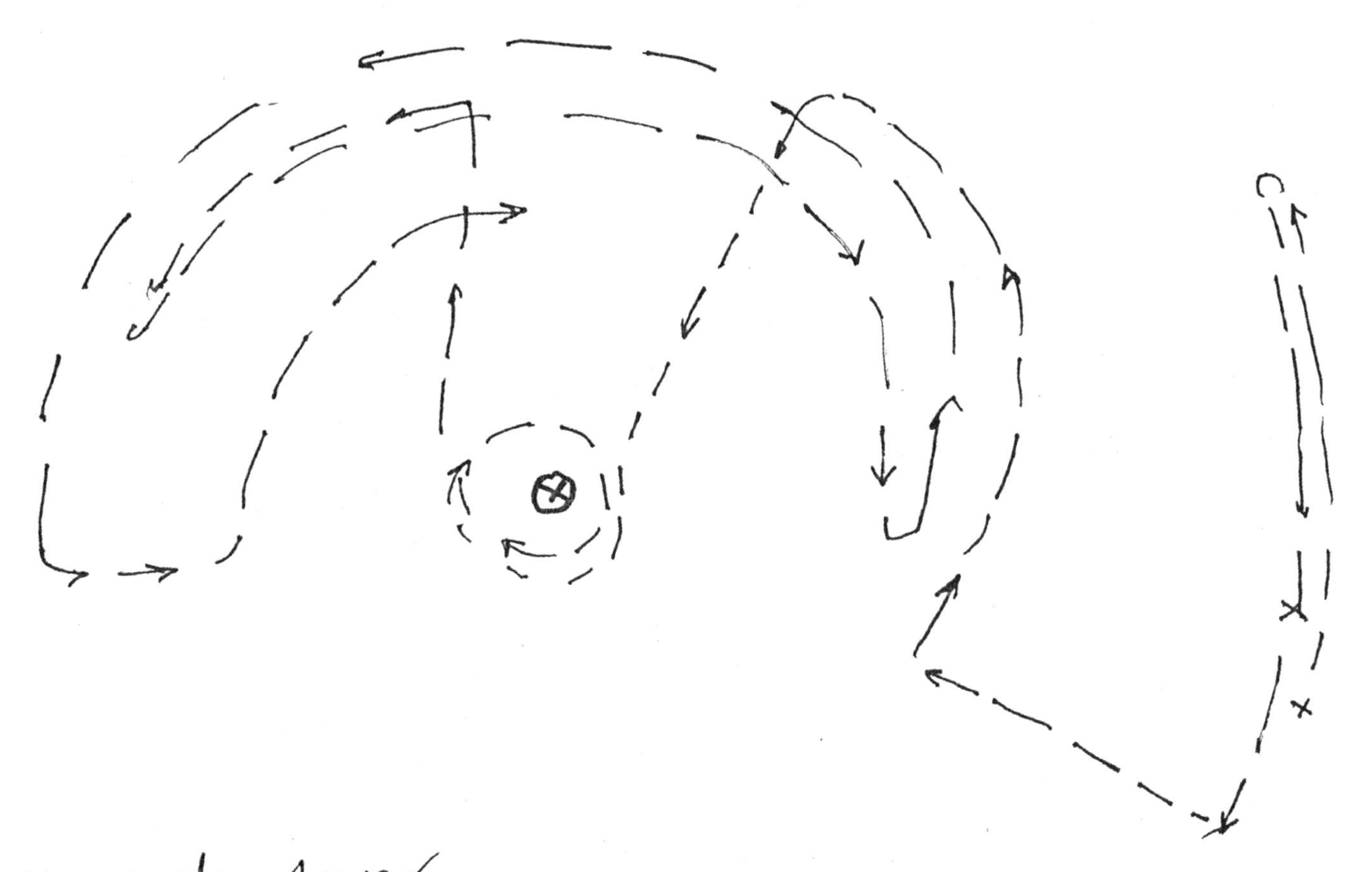

pace *much* slower
distance relationship changed considerably —
feeling that the attacker wishes to remain outside of —
(or beyond) a certain perifery —

the distance + pace is ~~now~~ now confusing to the defender / the distance ÷ being lengthened makes it harder to follow the sound of the camera / the pace being considerably slower seems as if there are actually breaks in the attacks — at times it seems as if there are (is) no attack underway (could almost be interpreted as if the attacker has given up — or just does not wish to see this as an 'attack' situation.

there could almost seem to be some sort of avoidance ((or insecurity about the movements of underway)).

CYNE COBB (continued)

These hesitancies give a feeling of strength to the defender — feelings of agression on the part of the defender are arouse(d) but also w. an almost immediate (but low level) guilt response to the aggressiveness within —

ie. (A)

(x) arousal of agression to a distant object that almost refuses to come in for attack.

(arousal is manifested by a change in position from sitting to rising high on one's knees or from squat to rising high — almost being forced to (wanting to stand erect on feet + then declining it)

(B)

(x) lowering (want'g to calm down / build strength if attack would occur) also lessen'g due to guilt of aroused desire to attack / want'g to achieve a calm — a moment of peace in midst of this hostile situation (note: defender in more hostile situation than any attacker — due not only to the position of defender but also defender undergoes 5 attacks in a row with a few minutes inbetween to calm down / others — undergo 1 attack ea. — but also note: most attackers became spectators for other attacks — this would tend to increase their hostile desires as well /. Note: cyne is the only attacker who choose not to observe any other attack — and seem to strongly desire not seeing any of the spectacle! / —

(C)

(x)(2) settling position / awaiting. (denial: again assuming role of defender / leave'g oneself quiet / await attack).)

CYNE COBB (continued)

after ~~see~~ settling several times giving the attacker ample opportunity to "rush-in" — and this response not occurring, the defendent almost seems to loose a certain interest — the situation is no longer threatening / nor is it a game / it plays itself out quickly / the defender's response (shooting back w still image-camera) is lessener —
it runs itself out and
almost leaves both parties a bit dissatisfied
or disappointed.

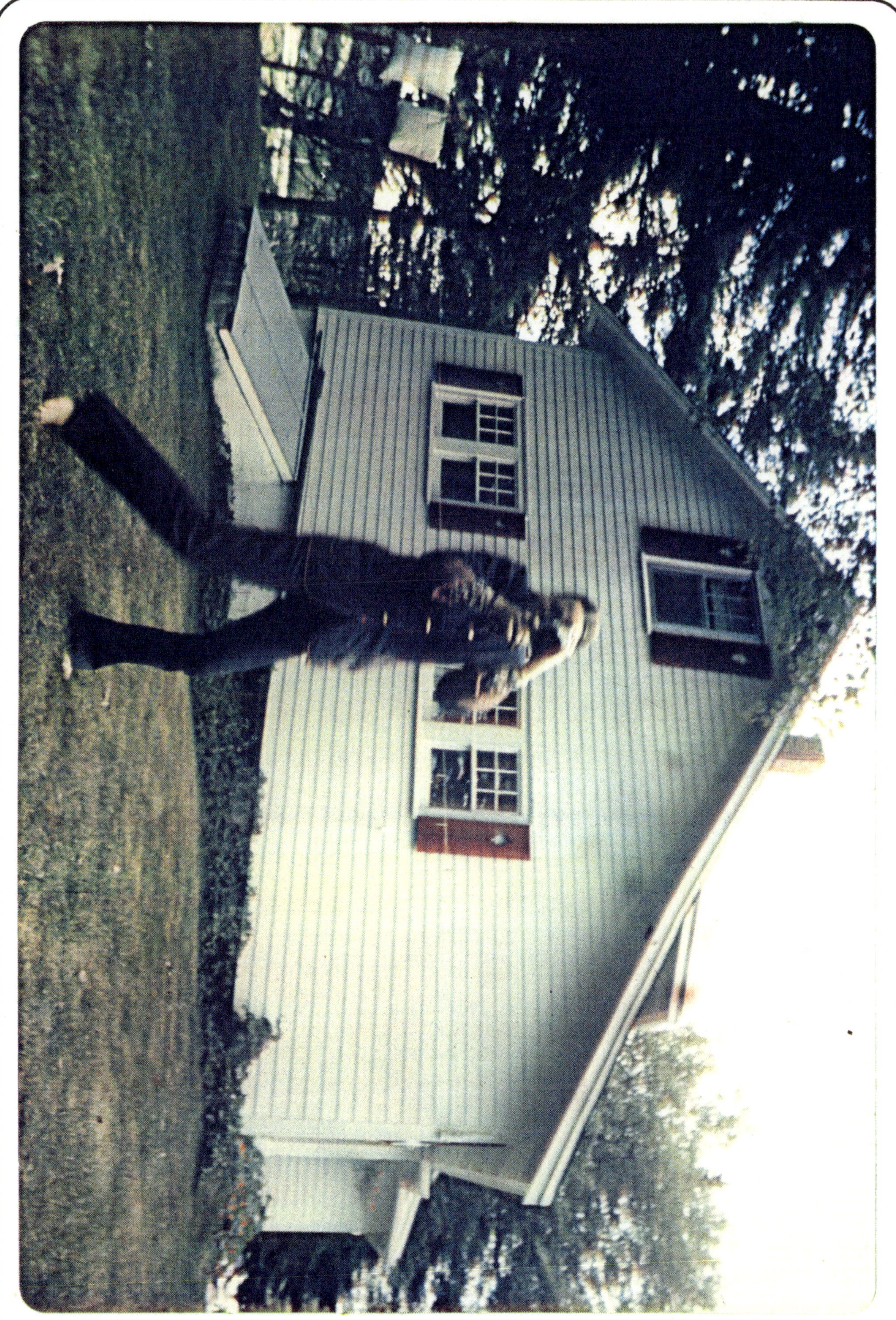

ATTACK PIECE
AUG 1975
HALIFAX, NOVA SCOTIA

DAVID ASKEVOLD (FOURTH PARTICIPANT)

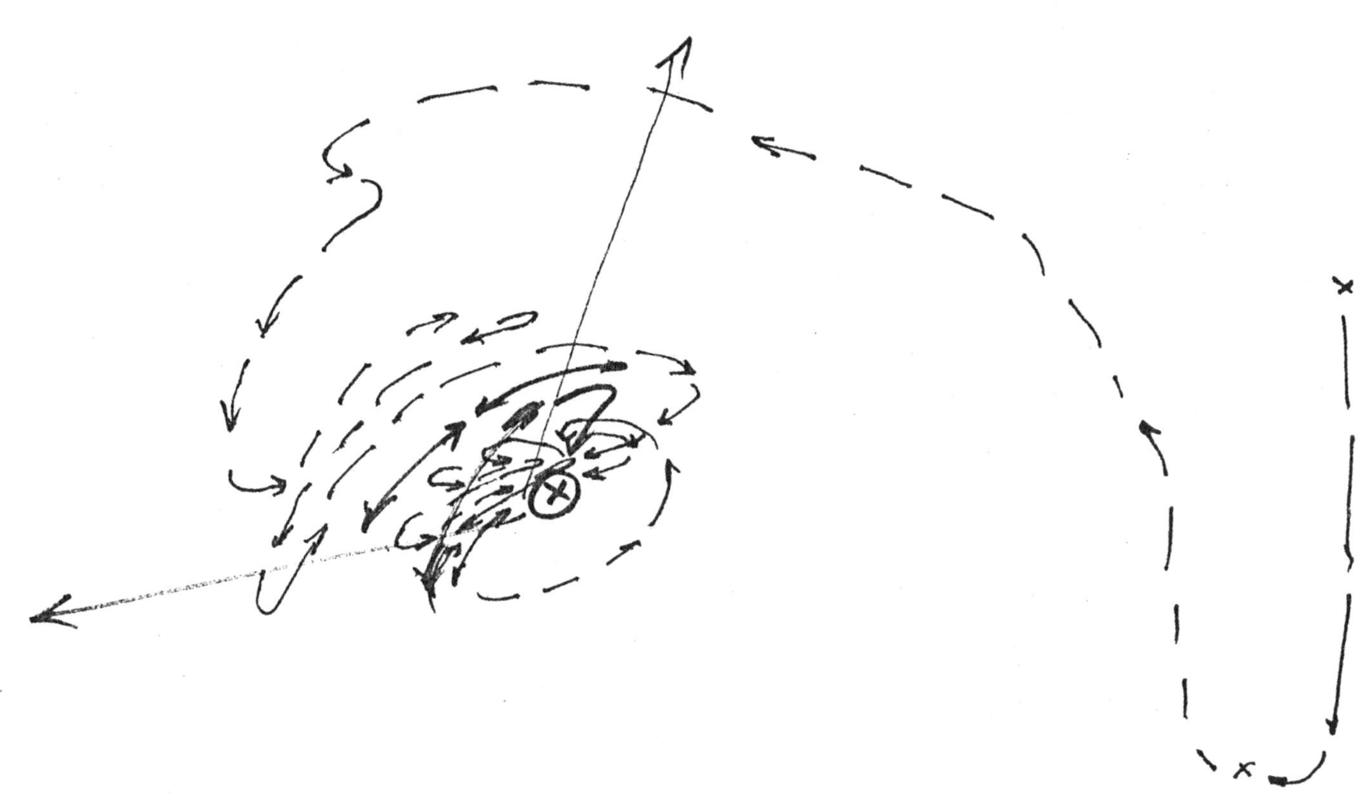

main areas of concentration.

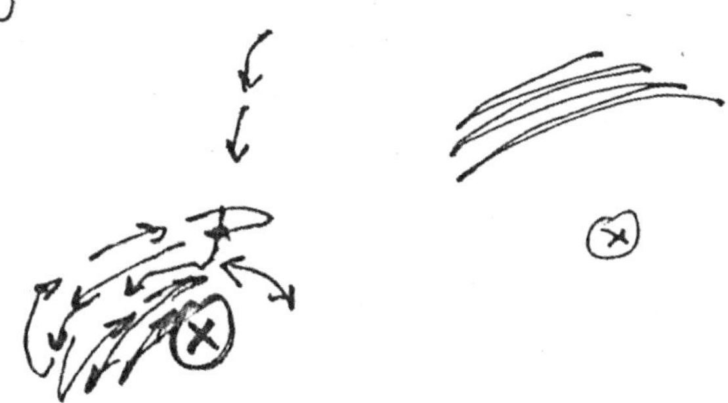

here again is a different approach / seemingly slow and steady — an immediate feeling of "tricky-ness" is the response /
there is confusing on the part of the defender — for though she feels the presense of the attacker in very tight the sound of the camera is not always evident and seems somehow to be mis-leading —

DAVID ASKEVOLD (continued)

there is the feeling that while the other attacks (esp. first 2 - dive-bomb'g) came in from a high angle — swooping down on the defender; *this* attack was like a "sneak" ground maneuver — crawling up under the defender / — "snake in the grass"

there were some *leaps* out — almost like a snake hissing — then a recoil — then slow — *very* calculated movement to see the most vulnerable of all spots to attack next.

the orientation was biased as shown.

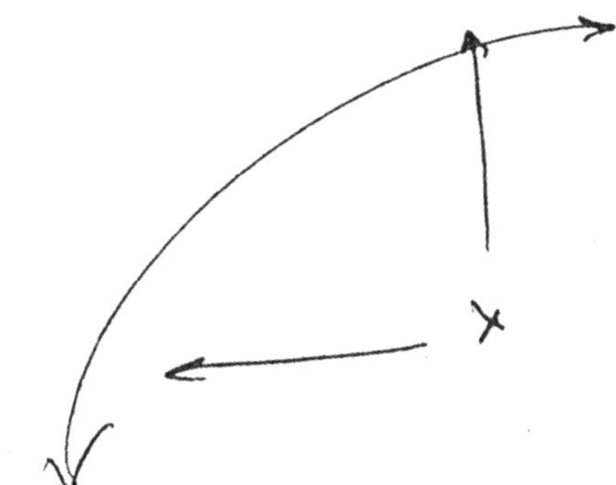

There were complete moments when the defender felt *extremely* vulnerable — esp. one that seemed zig-zag-d — where it was apparent that the attacker was in complete control of all his movements —

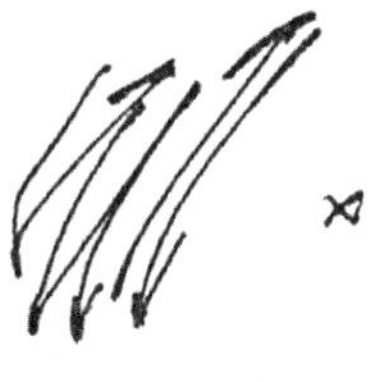

very confusing pace alternating but always quick — seemed that height of attack varied as well at this point.

(seems as if this occurred near the end).

DAVID ASKEVOLD (continued)

2 pt's. seemed abit crucial – the "zig-zag" and another, which seemed 1/2 way through (earlier) which seemed coming in low, slow, and very determined – to the leg area + the defender could imagine this as be'g directed 1st to the leg – but then to the ~~thigh~~ – thighs + then the vagina area – some sexual overtone – as if understand'g this defender as a woman + this being a weakened spot

NOTE: the idea of "this defender as woman" + thus perhaps vulnerable in some areas that carry sexual connotations did not occur in any other individuals attack pattern.

also note: perhaps this did occur – but as "repressed" desire – for the attacks of the men certainly differed from the women – in pace and esp in distance – women keeping far out of range most of the time (men keeping considerably in (in-tight on the defendent)).

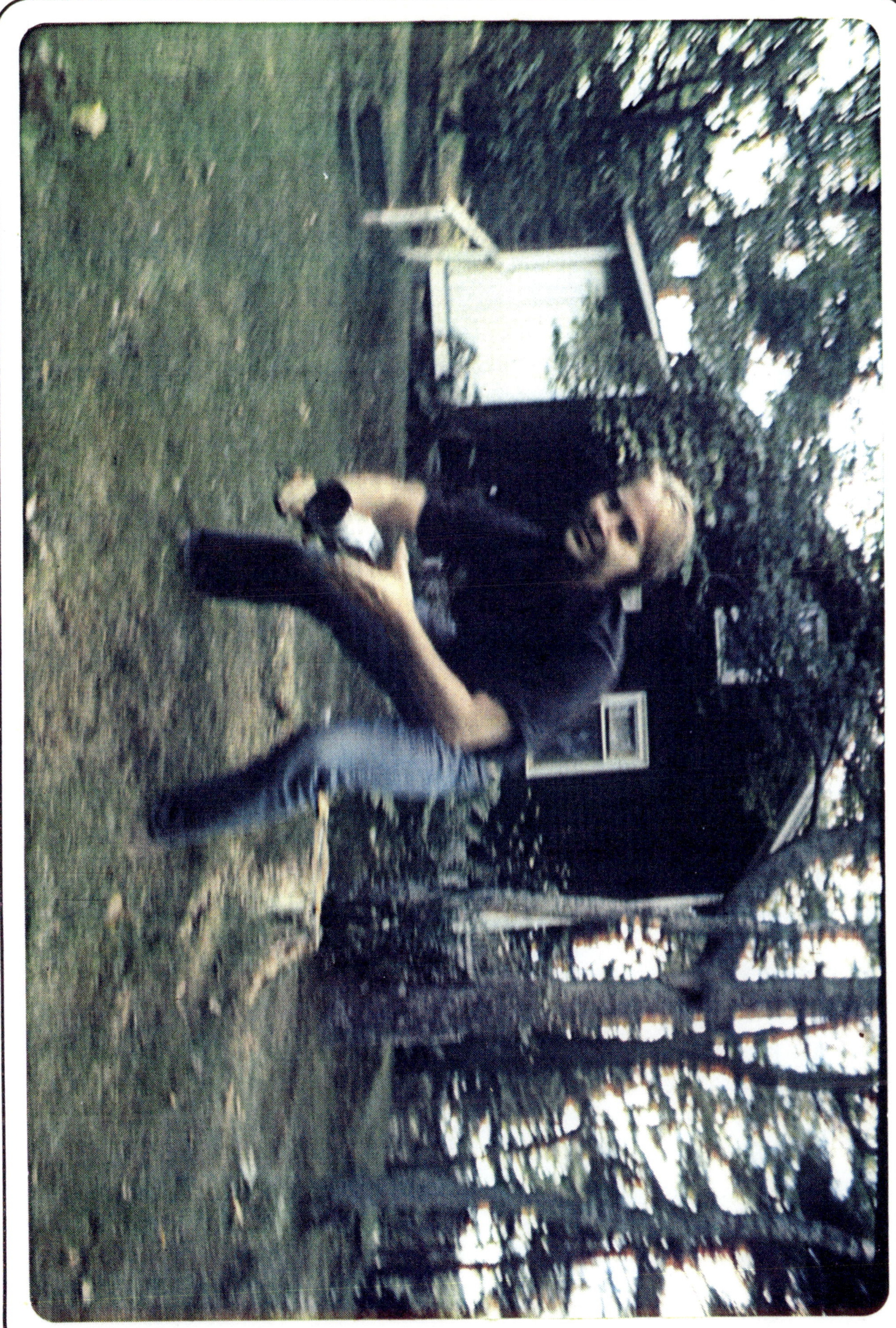

ATTACK PIECE
AUG 1975
HALIFAX, NOVA SCOTIA

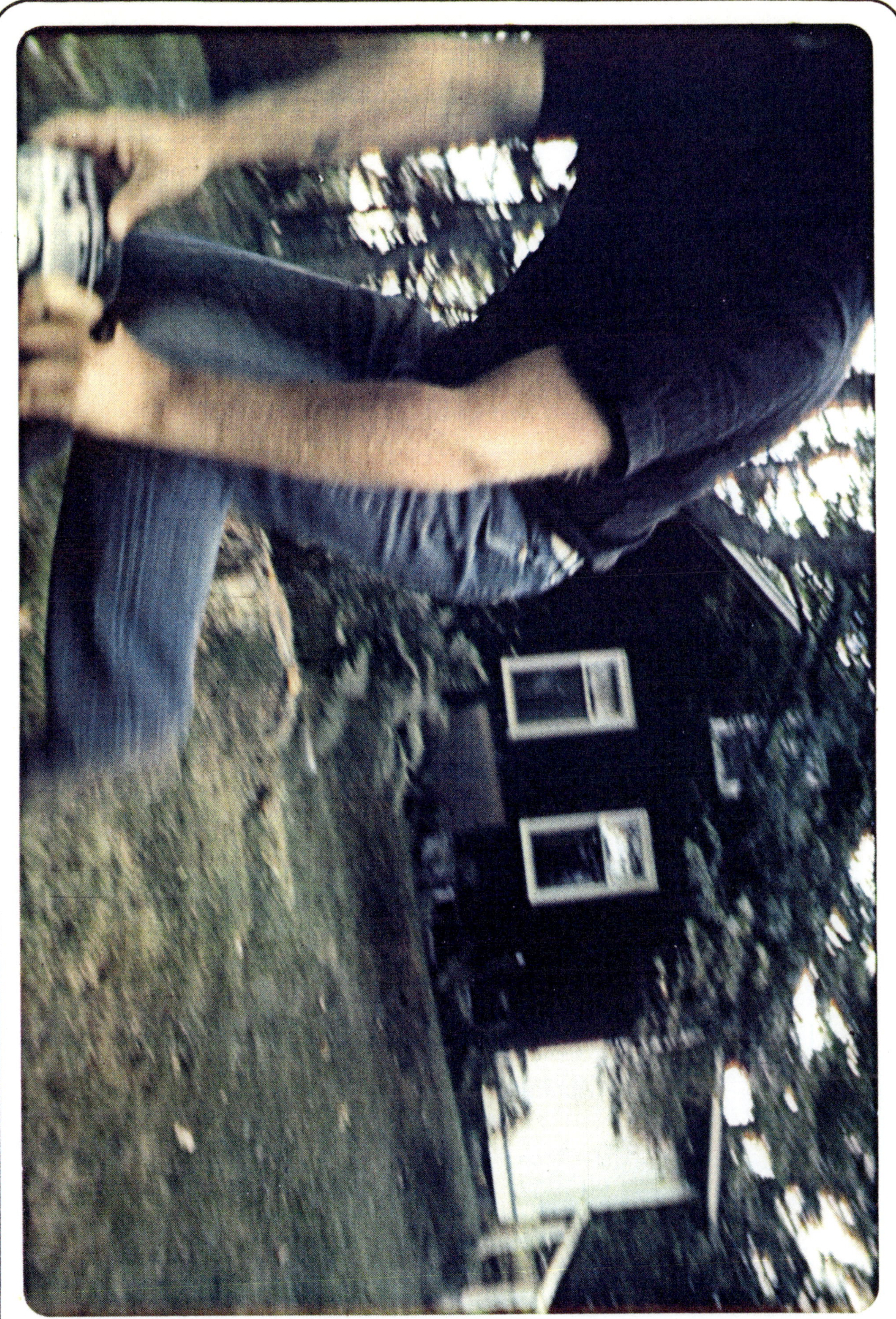

ATTACK PIECE
AUG 1975
HALIFAX, NOVA SCOTIA

CHRISTINA RITCHIE

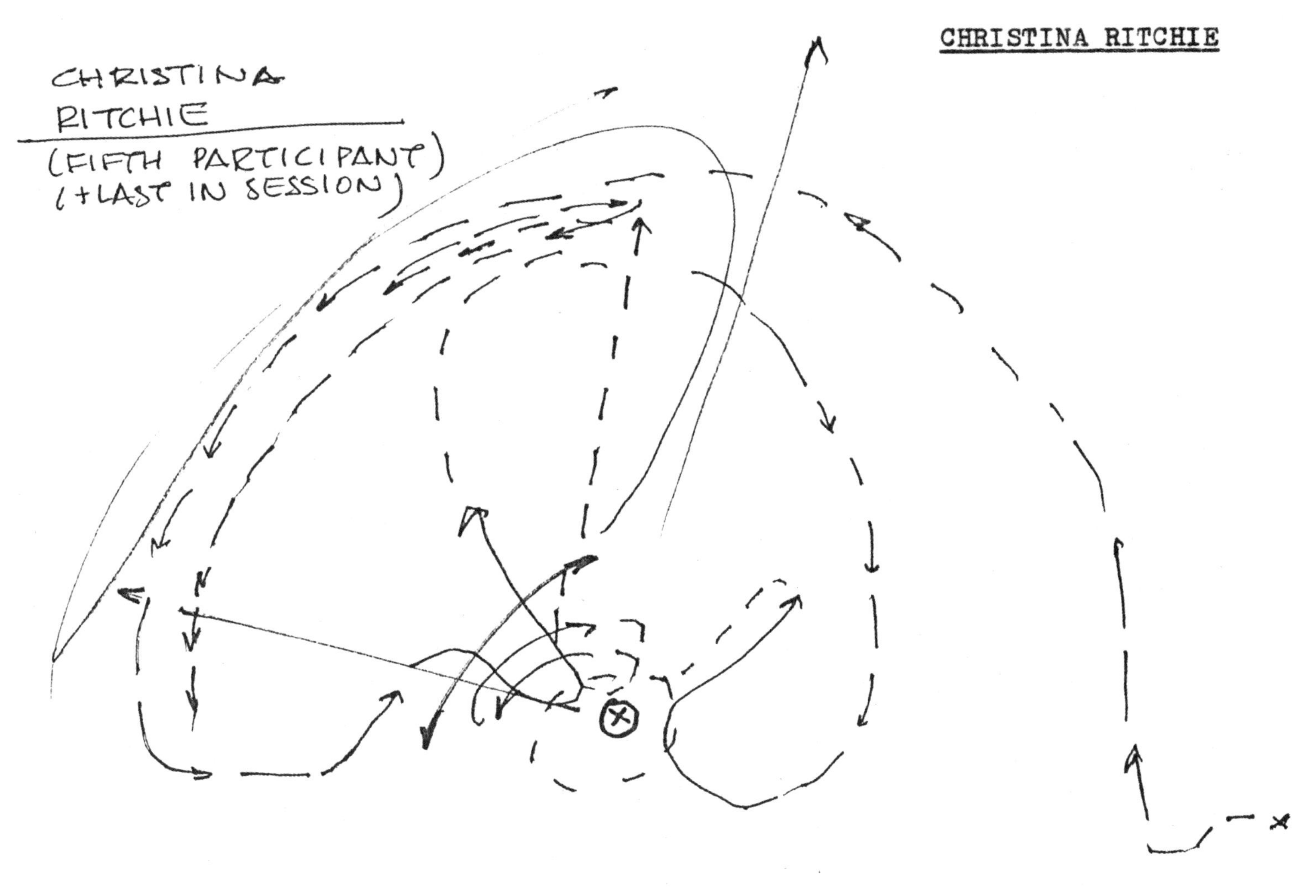

again, the pace slow — but seemingly cautious with great intent / again the feeling of "tricky-ness" or trickery very present / it seemed as if the distance was kept very far at the beginning — to really figure all this out and thus come in (in this case in an innovative way) in a vulnerable spot.

the distance → again confusion / much of the time the camera could not be heard → fear of unexpected attack / .

distance - arousing almost anger / (on the part of the defendent) & also a hostility + aggressiveness on the part of the defendent to attack first — this seemed to be mainly out of fear (i.e. that the time element was being used to figure out innovative, <u>effective</u> aggressive ~~all~~ action —

CHRISTINA RITCHIE (continued)

rather than as in Cyne's case an actual desire to remain passive.

in Cyne's case → aggressiveness on part of the defender due to desire to cause action – wanting to break the stillness – force the attacked into an action she otherwise would not take on her own.

in Christina's case → aggressiveness of defender to quicken the attack / to lessen the degree to which the aggressor could figure this out / more ~~of~~ out of fear of becoming more vulnerable as the time went on.

feeling of attributing to (the aggressor)
cunning
evasiveness
"sneaky"

feeling that the agressor was in tight a few times (but definitely not a majority of the time) —
at these times she was
"playing with" the victim
(i.e. playing w. her pray → i.e. the final
but would not make for
attack this way
would probably withdraw and then plunge in — come in high speed swooping —

"playing with" was kept @ neither a slow not fast pace but steady + moving.

CHRISTINA RITCHIE (continued)

toward the end, it seemed as if the attacker withdrew – but then almost disappeared into thin air –

this seemed to take a considerable am't. of time duration + ended this session –

at first the defender expected an ultimate rushed attack – but not knowing from where. However, the length of time lead to confusion + an ultimate frustration – feeling annoyed at this "seeming to hide out"

unfortunately there had been cross-communications with the participants – as to their intent or tactics or feelings about the piece – before these writings / however I have tried as very best I could to dis-regard these at this time + to reflect only upon my initial feelings while undergoing this experience / (this excercise) I do feel @ the time that I have been fairly successful in doing this – keep'g their thoughts + feelings separate from my own initial thoughts feelings. + reactions.

these notes were written on Sat. Aug. 30 12 noon to 2 PM in Cambridge – Boston. Mass. @ Bobby's

they are

"REFLECTIONS UPON BEING ATTACKED BY YOUR FRIENDS"

they are approx. the 3rd reflections upon the film'g although they are the first in a series of writings.

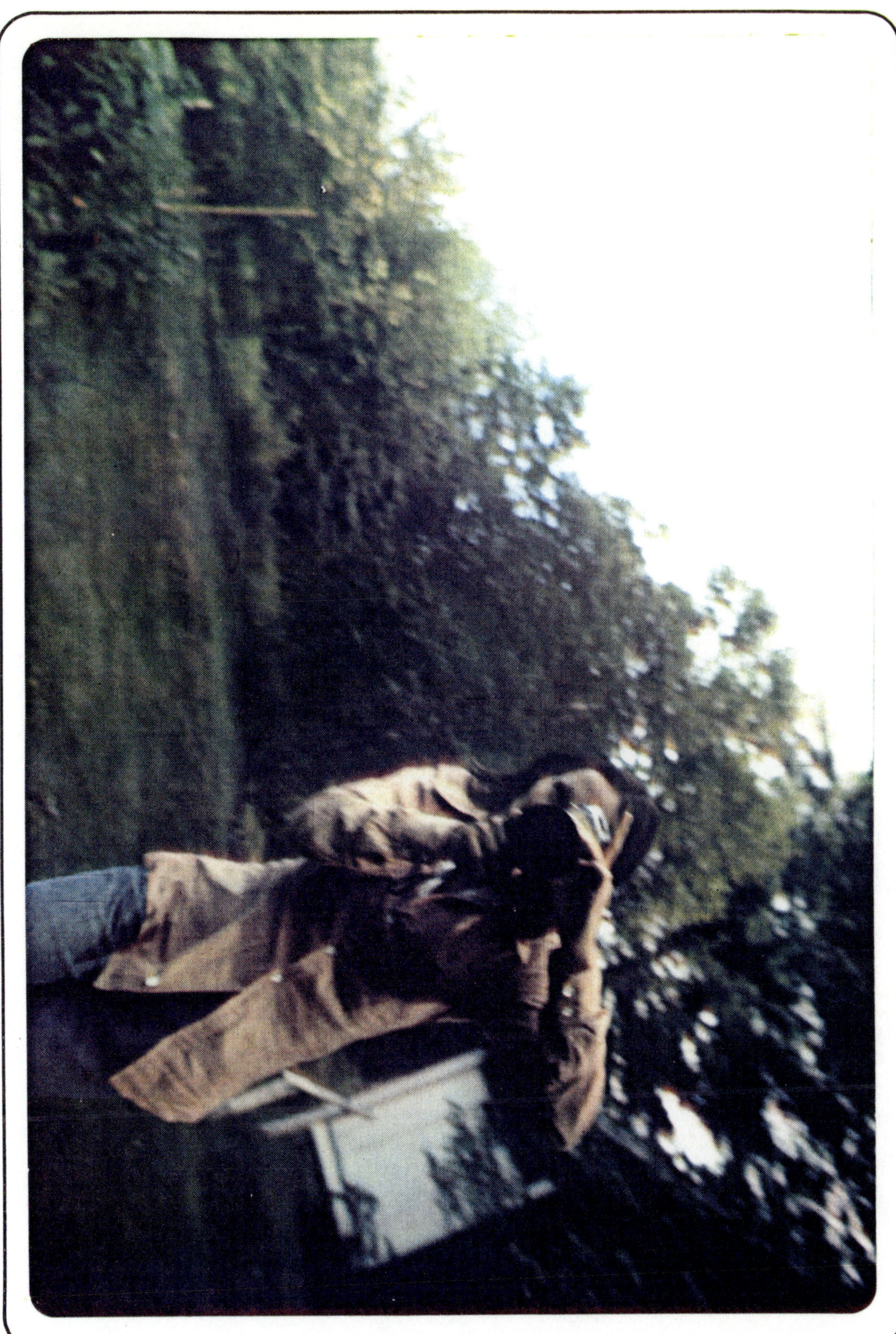

<u>ATTACK PIECE</u>
AUG 1975
HALIFAX, NOVA SCOTIA

NOTE:

This piece ("being attacked by ~~our~~ one's friends") was initially done 1 wk. ago today — in Bedford, Nova Scotia on Aug. 23rd / Saturday @ the home of Ian Murray

The participants at that time were:

Dan Graham, Ian Murray, Cyne Cobb, David Askevold, and Christina ~~Rich~~ Ritchie —

The participants chose to be spectators at ea. others' performances with the exception of Cyne Cobb who choose to be absent from all but her own.

— there was 1 time keeper for ea. performance — this was Ian Murray (except for his perf. when Dan Graham timed it). ea. performance lasted approx. 1 min. 15 sec. (film being shot @ 24 fps → approx 2 min 30 sec / role). Time was called approx. every 30 sec's — ie.

30 sec.

1 min — 1/2

15 sec. to go.

The no. of slides shot in this time varied with ea. new participant — from approx. 18 – 26 / ea.

No slide was ~~shoot~~ shot until it was felt that the film was started and the aggressor was already making an approach + coming into some sort of range!

RE: CONCERNS (THAT TAKE ON / DEAL WITH) VIDEO FORMAT

IE: MIRRORING
NYC 1975

PIVOT: TURNING AROUND SUPPOSITIONS
NYC 1976

LIBERTY: A DOZEN OR SO VIEWS
NYC 1976

MIRRORING

NEW YORK CITY, NEW YORK

1975

MIRRORING is a reductive 6 minute b+w video tape deriving in part from the "mirror phase" theories of Lacan (Stade du Miroir). It centers about a series of dance-like passes made between the video camera and a mirror, into which the camera is focused (Figure 1). Starting with the "mirrored self" of the performer in absolute focus, the passes evolve into a psychological competition between the two selves: the "mirrored self" (the "projected self"/ the self as "other") and the "Real". It is the continuous striving of the "Real" to overcome the "mirrored" - to at once strengthen itself and to obscure the other.

BASIC THEORY: In early stages of development, perceptual relationships to another of the same species is necessary in the normal maturing process. "Without the visual presence of others, the maturing process is delayed...
"The "mirror phase" derives its name from the importance of mirror relationships in childhood. "Through his perception of the image of another human being, the child discovers a form (Gestalt), a corporeal unity, which is lacking to him at this particular stage of his development. "...Lacan interprets the child's fascination with the other's image as an anticipation of his maturing to a future point of corporeal unity by identifying himself with this image."*

*WILDEN, Anthony, "Lacan and the Discourse of the Other," in: LACAN, Jacques, The Language of the Self / The Function of Language in Psychoanalysis, Delta Books, 1968.

In MIRRORING, we concentrate on a psychological shift in emphasis (from the "underdeveloped self" to the "matured self") as the camera performs a parallel mechanical shifting process. Between each successive pass, the focal distance of the camera is changed, slightly and intuitively by the performer, towards an exact focus on the "Real" self. The passes are made (checked by a slight viewing into the monitor) until the exact focus is achieved ((thus symbolizing the absolute recognition of "moi" (self) by the internalization of other through identification)).

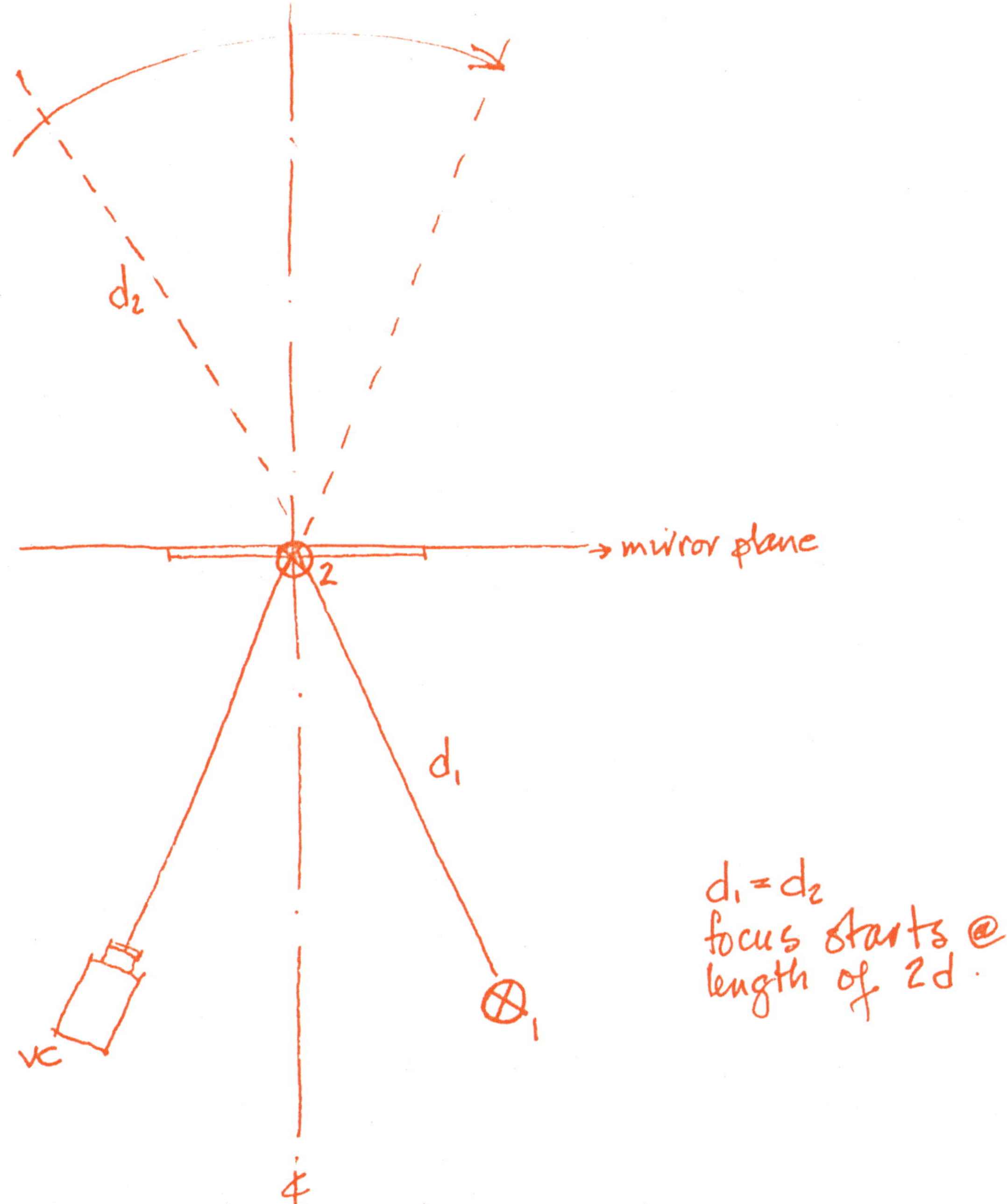

MIRRORING.

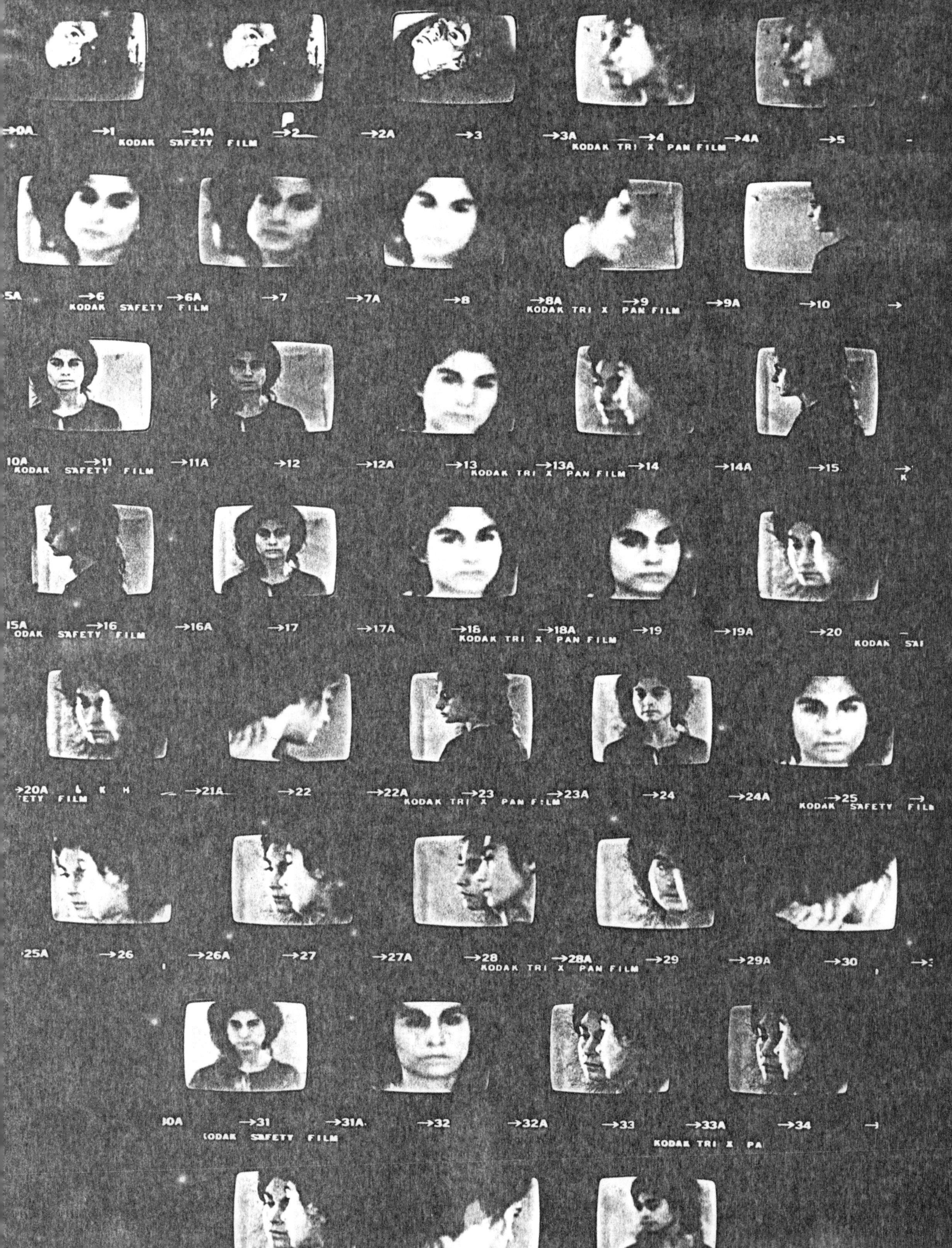
→1 KODAK SAFETY FILM →1A →2 →2A →3 →3A →4 KODAK TRI X PAN FILM →4A →5
→6 KODAK SAFETY FILM →6A →7 →7A →8 →8A →9 KODAK TRI X PAN FILM →9A →10
KODAK SAFETY FILM →11 →11A →12 →12A →13 →13A KODAK TRI X PAN FILM →14 →14A →15
→16 SAFETY FILM →16A →17 →17A →18 →18A KODAK TRI X PAN FILM →19 →19A →20 KODAK
→20A FILM →21A →22 →22A →23 KODAK TRI X PAN FILM →23A →24 →24A →25 KODAK SAFETY FILM
→26 →26A →27 →27A →28 →28A KODAK TRI X PAN FILM →29 →29A →30
→31 KODAK SAFETY FILM →31A →32 →32A →33 →33A →34 KODAK TRI X PA

MIRRORING
OCT 1975
NEW YORK CITY

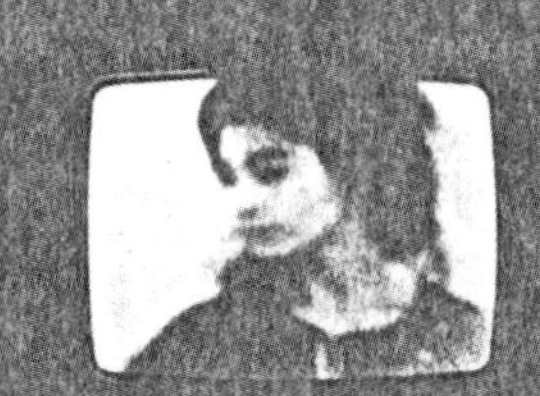

→6
→6A

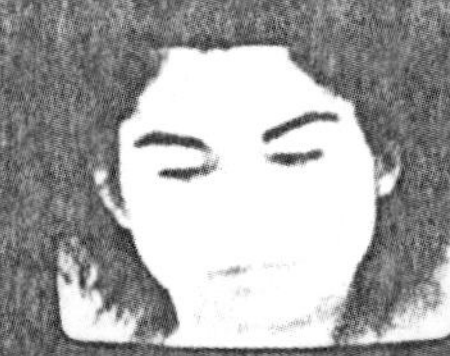

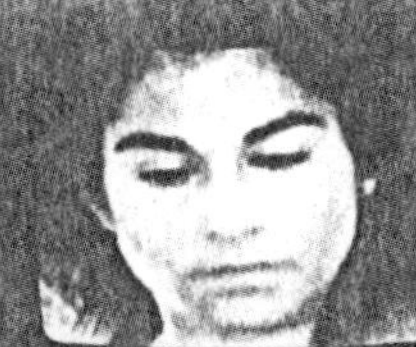

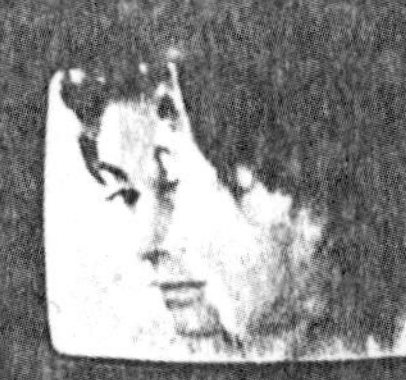

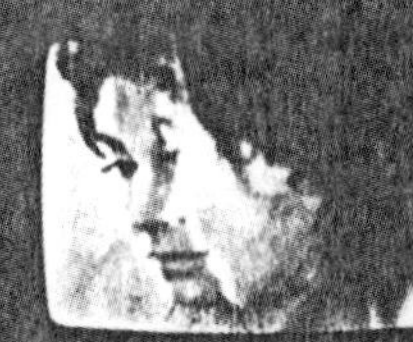

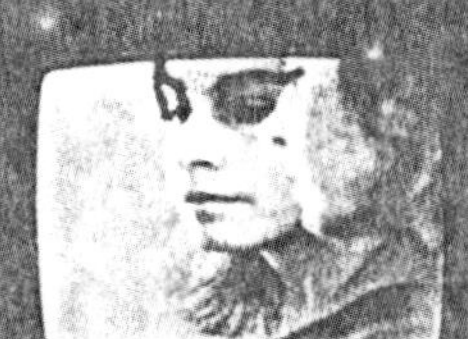

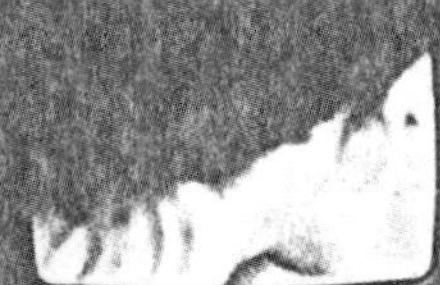

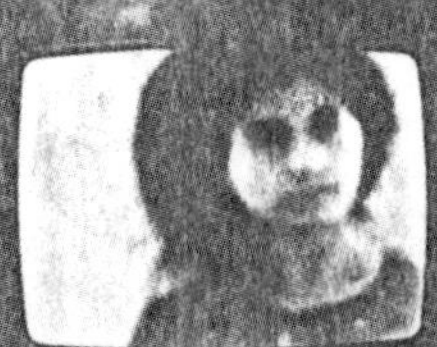

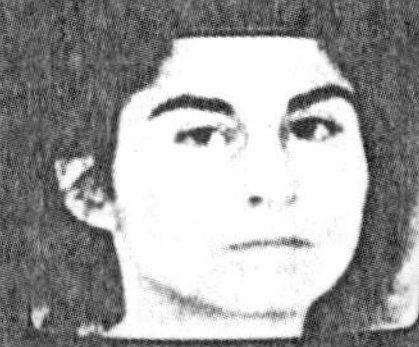

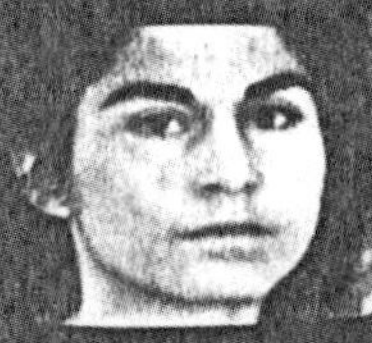

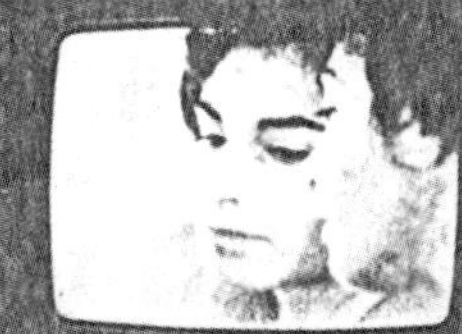

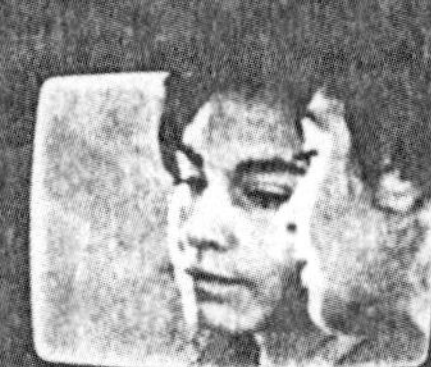

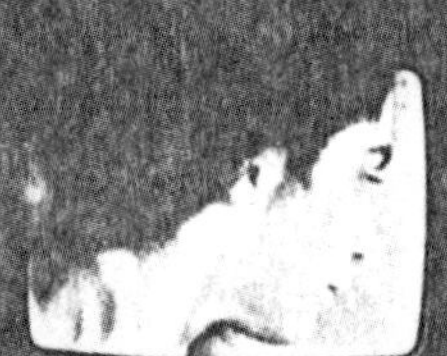

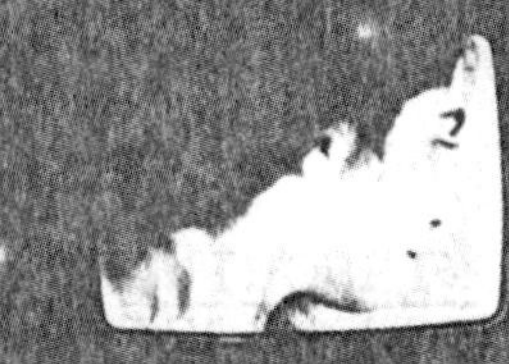

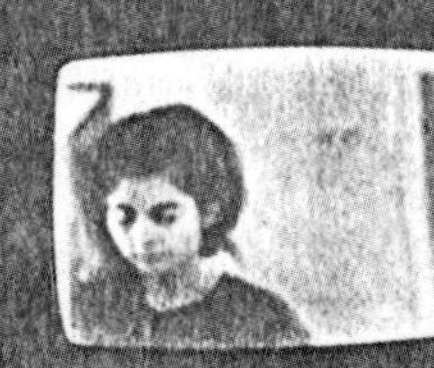

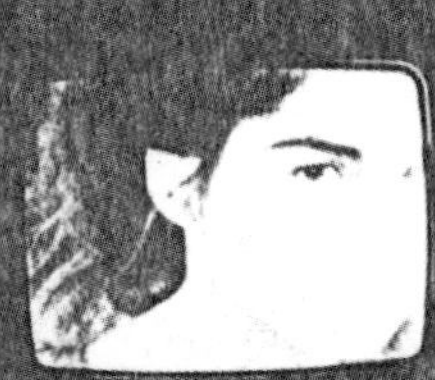

<u>MIRRORING</u>
OCT 1975
NEW YORK CITY

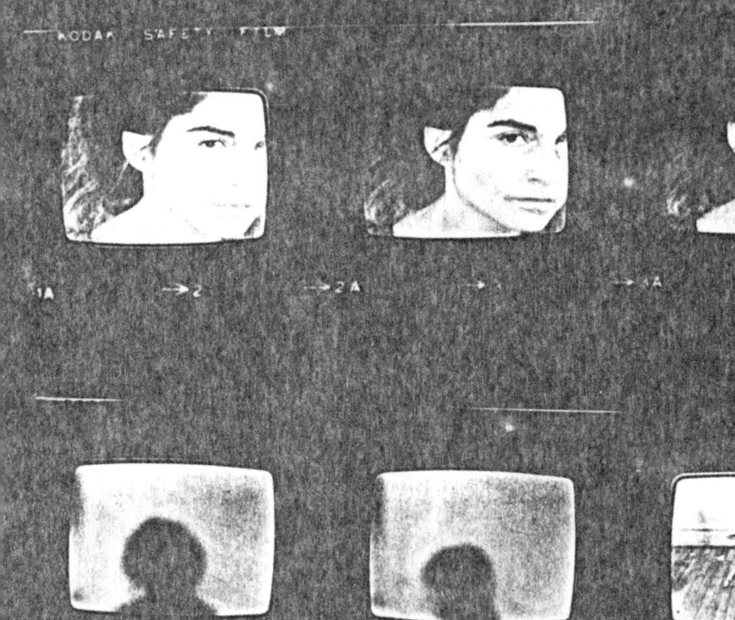
KODAK SAFETY FILM
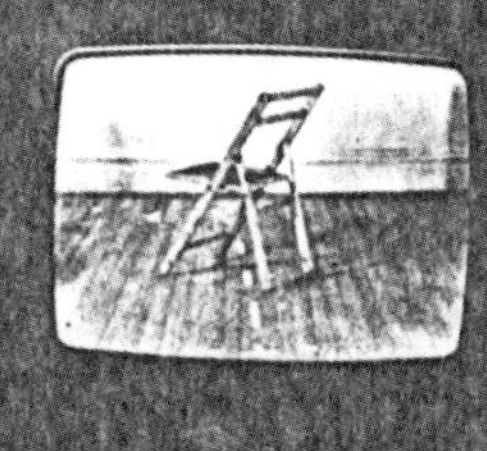
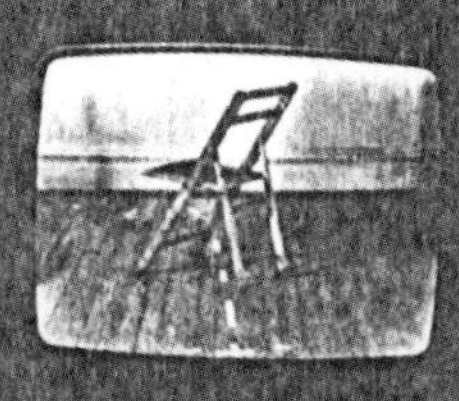
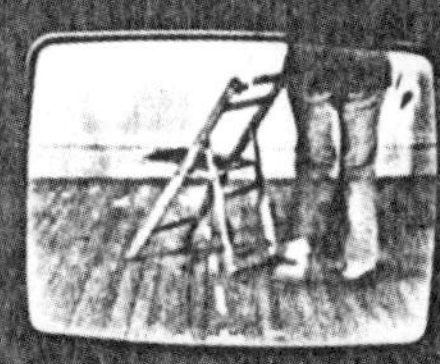
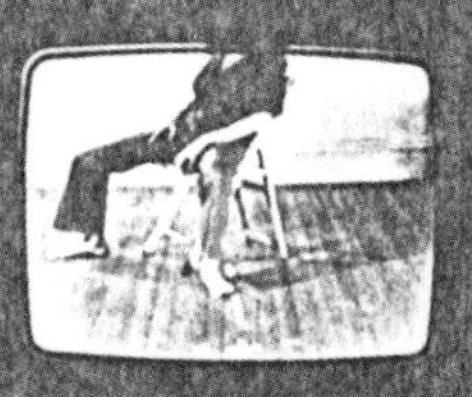
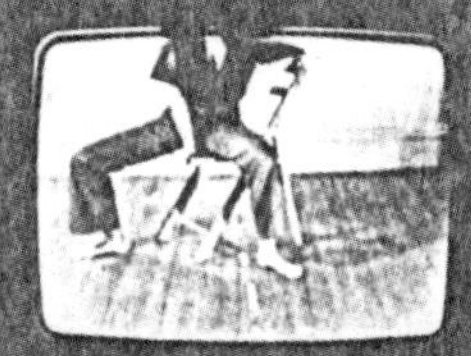
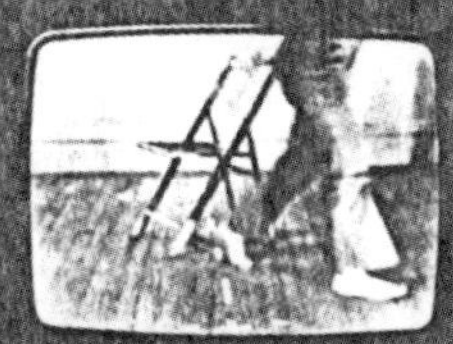
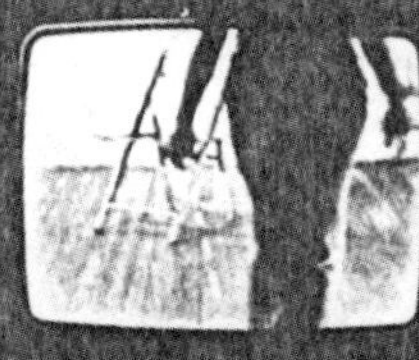
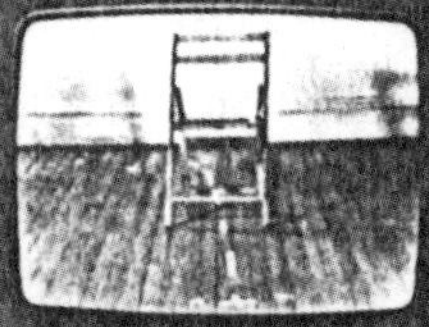
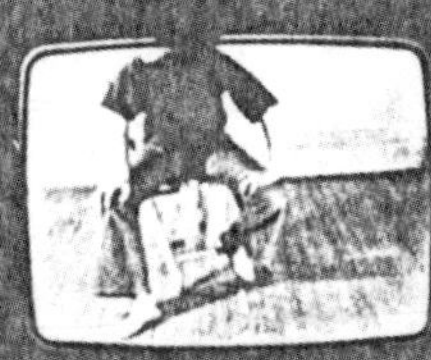

→17 →17A
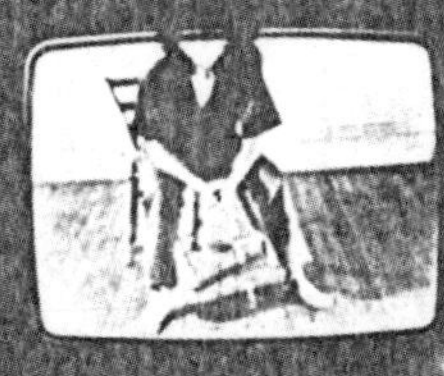
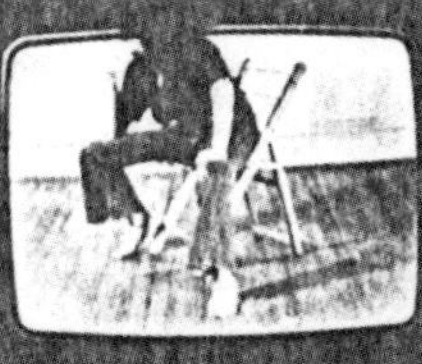
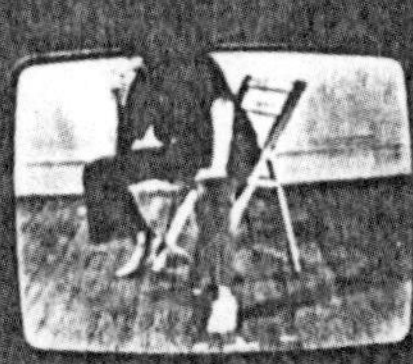
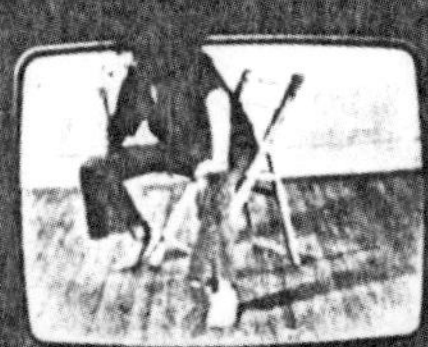

MIRRORING /
THE REJECTION SERIES:
CHAIRED ANXIETIES -
ABANDONED

OCT / NOV 1975
NEW YORK CITY NY

MIRRORING (NOTES)

OPENING SHOT: FOCUSED ON "MIRRORED SELF" / FULL FRAME
COME ABOUT: REPLACE WITH "REAL"

IE: TRYING TO BE MORE WHOLE THAN, MORE TOGETHER THAN "MIRRORED SELF"

THE ATTRACTION TO MIRROR IMAGE BECOMES THE CONFLICT
REAL BACK VS MIRROR FRONT
CAMERA CAN NOW VIEW BOTH

(SUR-)
(SUB-)COME BY ALLOWING "MIRROR" SELF TO REPLACE WHOLE

WALK OUT - LEAVING THE MIRRORED SELF TO REPLACE "REAL"

DEALING ALSO WITH ROLE REPLACEMENT
WITH CONTROLLING AND BEING CONTROLLED BY

THE MEDIA (IE: CAMERA) IS DETERMINING THE "LIMIT OF SCOPE" THE PERFORMER MUST REMAIN WITHIN A GIVEN SPACE TO BE SEEN - TO CONTINUE THIS STRUGGLE.

THE MEDIA (IE: VTR CAPACITY) IS DETERMINING A "LIMIT OF TIME" - YOU HAVE ONLY SO LONG A PERIOD (DEFINITE / + REAL TIME USAGE) IN WHICH TO MAKE A STATEMENT.

THE MEDIA (IE: CAMERA / LIGHTING CONDITIONS) IS DETERMINING A LIMIT TO THE "DEPTH OF FIELD" - YOU MUST REMAIN WITHIN A CERTAIN PLANAR FIELD TO REMAIN AS "CLEAR" AS DESIRED.

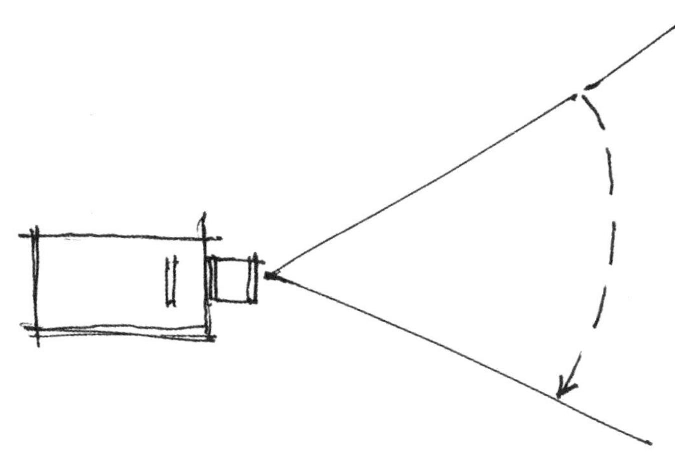

MIRRORING (NOTES)

(3) THREE TYPES OF OBLITERATION POSSIBLE:
1- CONFRONTING IMAGE (COVERING WITH BACK)
2- REPLACING IMAGE (COVERING FACING THE CAMERA)
3- COMPETING VS IMAGE (IE: TRYING TO BE ...
BETTER THAN (OUTPERFORM)
"REALER" THAN
"MORE WHOLE" THAN
MORE EXPRESSIVE
MORE SINCERE

(at this time it becomes important to note the treatment given to the mirrored image due to camera location - there should be shots established through positioning that allow the mirrored self an equally strong chance at representation)

ie: facing sideways - so that the mirror image is also at that moment facing sideways

ie: if facing the camera directly (at all times) the mirrored self can only show "back" - notice: also see this as a type of "strategy move" with the possibility of being used as such later on

pacing: to extend time in one position (over the other) would seem to indicate a preference for this "self" (or role, etc) / it could be taken as an affirmation of this position.

to "quicken" the pace - as in moving out of a position relatively "quickly" would seem to indicate a desire to be out of this "self" / a removal / and thus, it could be taken as a rejection (or negation) of this position(ing).

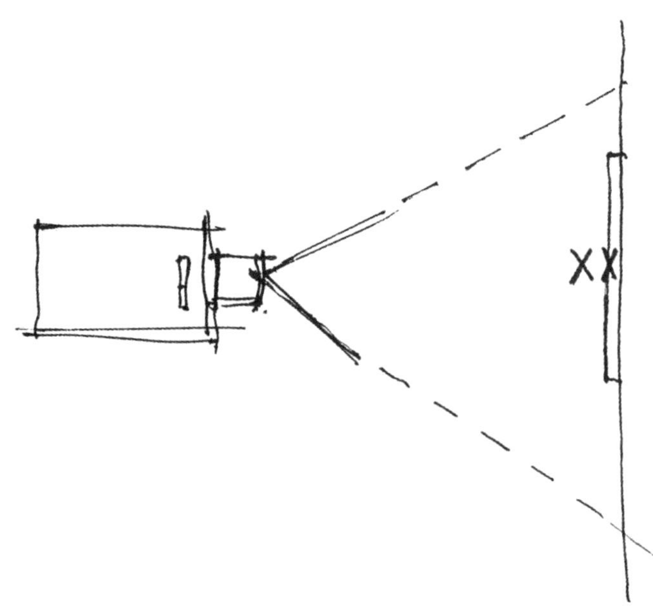

In MIRRORING we concentrate on a psychological shift in emphasis (from the "undeveloped self" to the "matured individual" - as the camera performs a similar (parallel) mechanical shifting process. Between each successive pass the focal distance of the camera is changed, slightly and intuitively by the performer - towards an exact focus on the "Real" self. The passes are made (checked by a slight viewing into the monitor) until the exact focus is achieved (thus symbolizing the absolute recognition of (and unification with) "MOI" (self) by the internalization of OTHER through identification).

It is a series of dance-like passes made between the video camera and a mirror placed some 9 feet away (in opposition). These movements become the vehicle of a competition that (physically / then psychologically) unfolds between the 2 images (the mirrored self / the self as "other" / the self as projected image - and - the "real"self).

It is a continuous striving of the "Real" to overcome the mirrored - to at once strengthen itself and obscure the "Other"

According to Lacan, the mirror fixation process develops within the infant personality structure during the period that the mirrored image of the individual is seen as "more whole, more together", and functioning on a more refined level than the "Real" can at that time. This perception has a reality bases in the fact that the visual and motor facilities of the perceiving individual at such a young (or undeveloped) age are more developed (advanced) than are the perceptual and cognitive processes.

theory

(B) increase differing of action within the space - showing an improvement - greater control over the action

MATURATION (gaining greater control over the situation)

strength (of character vs physical strength)

ie. as a child in the space

physical manifestation

crawling -
showing impaired movement
weakened movement
lack of strength.

⇨ learning
youthful
position

more assertive
posture
position(ing)
movement

ie. - in repose
sitting well
within a space
but relatively
inactive.

⇩

more active
adult-like

assertive moves
becoming more
positive -
no longer in repose
but walking through
a space -
* slowly - cautiously - but
deliberately *.

⇨ "full adult"
fully assertive
positive moves that
over-power - are in
full control -

(C) AVOIDANCE

making one's self unavailable
turning one's back on the space (+ the situation)

(D) DEMANDING SYMPATHY OR EMPATHY

establishing DIRECT CONTACT with "audience" (viewer) and through emotional moods - ask for a shift of focus towards yourself -

emotional impact
direct contact
through feelings of

GUILT | PAIN (evident) | DESPAIR

NERVOUSNESS | PSYCHOTIC ATTACK - DISTURBANCE READILY EVIDENT

• PSYCHOLOGICAL REFERENCE(S) PT. OF VIEW

---

take over
through manipulation of technical means available —

TECHNICAL MANIPULATION
(media control)

— using the advantages of video - ie. using f stops making the slide backgr. faint - ie. barely visible - but the person entering the space is very visible - in detail -
— or too dark - but when person enters spotlight would light face and make it clear - way over background.

manipulation of
1. lighting (spot person may place himself in)
2. f stop on video camera backgr. too light
** 3. focus (focal length) on video camera person may step in intermintantly and interrupt picture + be more in focus - rival (as in mirroring) try this
4. concentrating on slide projector —
(A) time system (black-whites/image/negative)
(B) also focus (also autofocus → in + out running in replacing taking advantage of when out of focus.)

try this

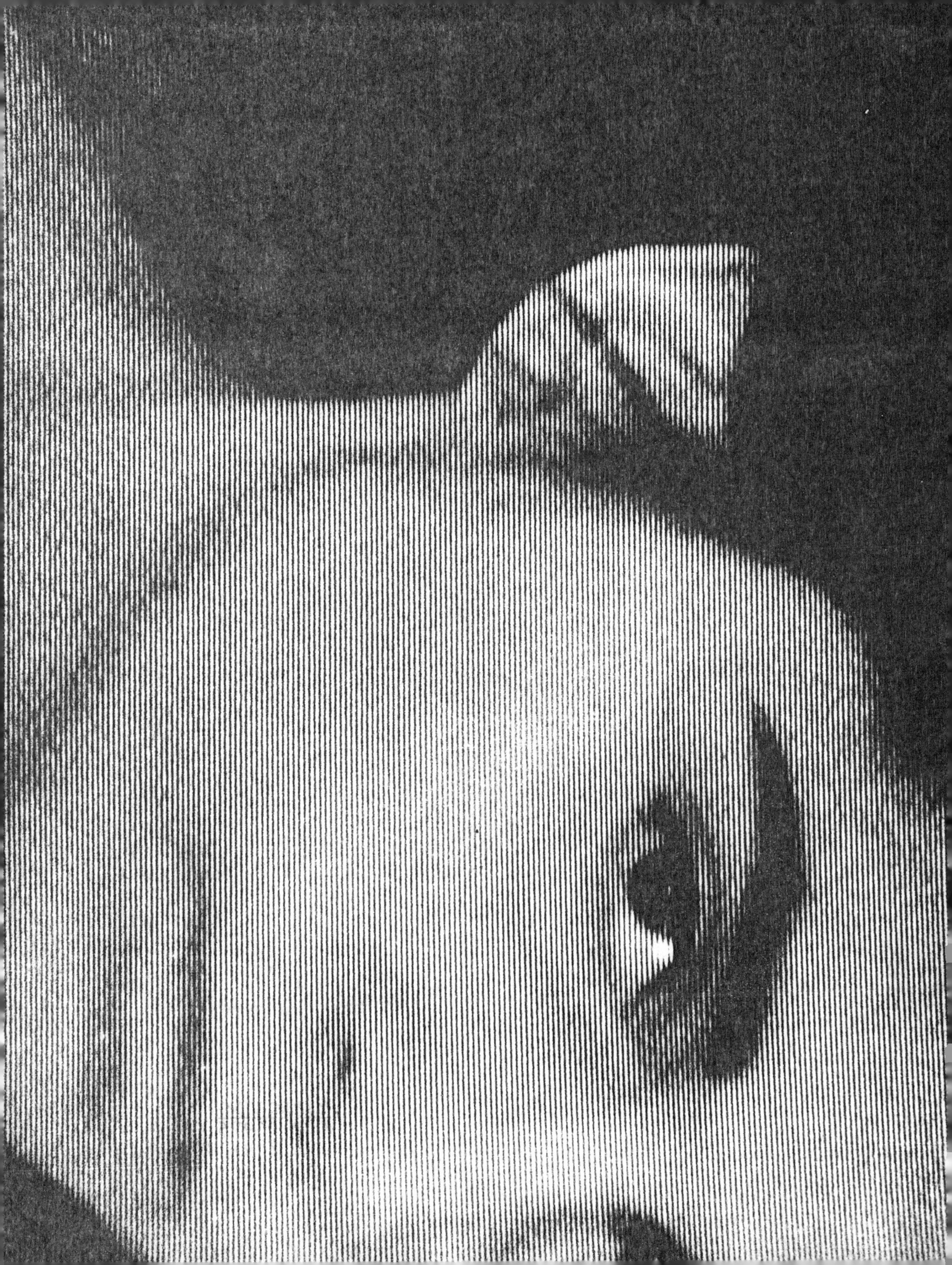

MIRRORING
OCT 1975
NEW YORK CITY

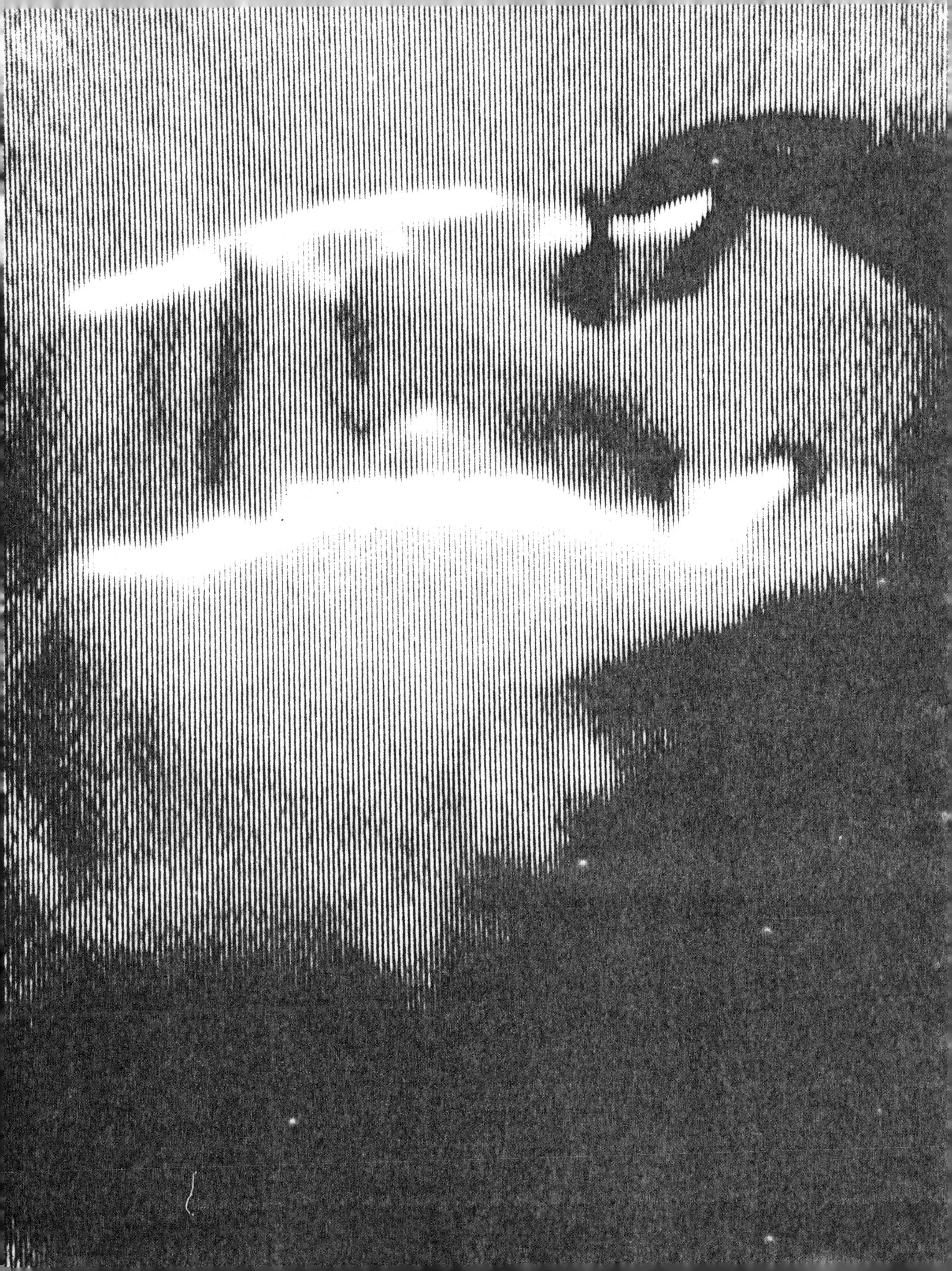

MIRRORING
OCT 1975
NEW YORK CITY

PIVOT: TURNING AROUND SUPPOSITIONS

NEW YORK CITY, NEW YORK

PIVOT: TURNING AROUND SUPPOSITIONS

PIVOT IS AN INVESTIGATIVE EXERCISE ALLOWING ONE A BETTER UNDERSTANDING OF THE OPENNESS AND LIMITATIONS PRESENT WHEN ADOPTING A CHOSEN ROLE IN THE FILM / OR VIDEO MAKING PROCESSES. THE SUPPOSITIONS ARE DAILY CONVERSATIONAL EXTRACTIONS ALTHOUGH IT MAY EASILY BE SEEN THAT IN THEIR VERY EXTRACTION THEY BECOME EXAGGERATED (OR LARGER THAN LIFE). THUS, THERE IS A GREAT FREEDOM INVOLVED IN INTERPRETATION. THIS OCCURS BOTH IN THE PROJECTED PSYCHOLOGY OF THE CAMERAMAN AND IN THE INNER PSYCHOLOGY OF THE PERFORMER. THE STRENGTH OF THE PIECE DERIVES FROM THE VISIBLE MANIFESTATIONS OF EACH PARTICIPANT'S REACTION (IN THEIR EXPRESSED SIMILARITIES AND DIFFERENCES DUE TO DIFFERENT PSYCHOLOGICAL INTERPRETATION AND STRESS). IT IS TO BE NOTED THAT DURING CAMERA PIVOT ONLY THE CAMERA MAY MOVE / THE PERFORMER MUST REMAIN STATIONARY. WHEREAS, DURING PERFORMER PIVOT, ONLY THE PERFORMER MAY MOVE AND THUS, THE CAMERA NO LONGER HAS ANY FREEDOM OF MOVEMENT (AND IS STATIONARY).

EXERCISES WITH A (VIDEO) CAMERA:
PIVOT: TURNING AROUND SUPPOSITIONS

THIS PIECE CONSISTS OF TWO PARTS, EACH 100 SECS LONG (1 MIN 40 SECS). TOTAL RUNNING TIME IS 200 SECS (3 MINS 20 SECS).

PART ONE: CAMERA PIVOT

SET-UP: THERE IS ONE PERFORMER THROUGHOUT THE ENTIRITY OF THE PIECE. HE IS STANDING ERECT, LOCATED SOME 6 FEET FROM A NON-DESCRIPT WALL (THIS WALL MAY OR MAY NOT CONTAIN A WINDOW AREA/ IT SEEMS AS THOUGH A BLANK WALL WOULD BE PREFERABLE FOR IT WOULD ALLOW MORE VARIATION IN LIGHTING TECHNIQUE). THERE ARE NO VISIBLE PROPS. THERE IS NO SOUND RECORDING MECHANISM DUE TO THE FACT THAT ALL SOUND WILL LATER BE DUBBED ONTO THE VISUAL IMAGE DURING POST PRODUCTION.

PERFORMANCE DESCRIPTION: THE PERFORMER IS AND MUST STAY STATIONARY AND STANDING. THERE IS NO BODY MOVEMENT OTHER THAN SIMPLE INHERENT CHANGES; SUCH AS WEIGHT SHIFTS. THE CAMERAWOMAN/MAN IS PRESENTED WITH A LIST OF TEN GENERAL SUPPOSITIONS ABOUT THE PERFORMER - THEY ARE EXTREMELY GENERALIZED AND MAY OR MAY NOT BE IN AGREEMENT WITH ONE ANOTHER. THE CAMERAWOMAN/MAN MUST RESPOND TO EACH "PSYCHOLOGICAL" STATEMENT WITH WHAT IS FELT TO BE AN APPROPRIATE "PHYSICAL" CAMERA STATEMENT. IN OTHER WORDS, EACH STATEMENT WILL DETERMINE IN THE CAMERA'S "MIND"/"EYE" AN APPROPRIATE REACTION TOWARDS VIEWING THE PERFORMER. THERE ARE 10 STATEMENTS PRESENTED. THIS ALLOWS THE CAMERAWOMAN/MAN 10 SECONDS FOR EACH REACTION.

CAMERA LIMITATIONS: THE CAMERA MAY PIVOT ENTIRELY AROUND THE PERFORMER. PROPS MAY BE USED BY THE CAMERA TO CHANGE VIEWING HEIGHT AND ANGLE. LIGHTING IS ENTIRELY AN OPEN DECISION - FOR THIS REASON THE PERFORMER HAS BEEN PLACED CLOSE TO A WALL OR ROOM CORNER TO ALLOW A MAXIMUM NUMBER OF VARIATIONS. ALL MECHANISMS BUILT INTO THE CAMERA UNIT ARE TO BE CONSIDERED AS AIDES (IE: TELEPHOTO CAPABILITY; FOCUS; DEPTH OF FIELD; ETC.). THE CAMERA TO BE USED IS ANY VARIATION OF THE SONY ½" PORTAPAK SYSTEM.

SAMPLE SUPPOSITIONS:
1. YOU ARE MY FRIEND
2. YOU ARE MY LOVER
3. YOU REALLY MUST BE THE DEVIL....
4. YOU TREAT BADLY THE PEOPLE YOU KNOW THE BEST
5. NO ONE CAN GET CLOSE TO YOU
6. YOU ARE ALWAYS OPEN TO MEETING NEW PEOPLE
7. YOU ARE ALWAYS THERE WHEN NEEDED
8. ALL ONE HAS TO DO IS TO REACH OUT TO GET HELP FROM YOU

9. YOU NEVER SPEAK TO PEOPLE DIRECTLY
10. YOU DON'T KNOW HOW TO CONFRONT NEW SITUATIONS

THE CAMERA MAY MOVE WITHIN EACH SEQUENCE OR CHOOSE TO REMAIN STATIONARY. HOWEVER, THE PERFORMER MUST ADOPT ONE, DIRECTED POSITION THROUGHOUT THE FIRST 1 MIN 40 SECS..

PART TWO: SUBJECT (PERFORMER) PIVOT

CAMERA LIMITATIONS: THE CAMERA NOW TAKES THE PLACE OF "PERFORMER". IT IS SET STATIONARY ON A TRI-POD AND ITS DIRECTION IS DETERMINED BY BOTH PARTICIPANTS (NOTE: BY DIRECTING THE CAMERA TOWARDS THE WALL, LIGHTING CONDITIONS WILL AGAIN BE MORE VARIABLE BUT THE PERFORMER'S WORKING SPACE WILL BE LIMITED. IE: HIS DISTANCE FROM CAMERA LENS CAN NEVER EXCEED 6 FEET.) THE CAMERA LENS IS ADJUSTED TO EYE HEIGHT. FOCAL LENGTH AND DEPTH OF FIELD ARE PRE-SELECTED. THESE WILL BOTH BE MADE KNOWN TO THE PERFORMER.

PERFORMANCE DESCRIPTION: AGAIN THE SUPPOSITIONS WILL BE GONE THROUGH - BEING READ ALOUD TO THE PERFORMER. SHE/HE NOW HAS 10 SECS TO MAKE A RESPONSE TO EACH OF THE SUPPOSITIONS THUS READ. HER/HIS PSYCHOLOGICAL REACTION TO A STATEMENT CONCERNING ONE'S SELF MUST BE TRANSFERRED TO A PHYSICAL REACTION THAT CAN BE RECORDED BY THE CAMERA'S "MIND"/"EYE". IE: THESE REACTIONS MAY VARY FROM AVOIDANCE (STAYING OUT OF CAMERA FRAME) TO DIRECT CONFRONTATION (FILLING CAMERA FRAME) TO TAKING ADVANTAGE OF CAMERA LIMITATIONS (BLURRING ONE'S OWN IMAGE THROUGH DEPTH OF FIELD LIMITATIONS). THE PERFORMER MAY USE PROPS TO CHANGE VIEWING HEIGHT, LIGHTING CONDITIONS OR TO OBSTRUCT THE CAMERA'S DIRECT LINE OF VISION.

GENERAL REMARKS: IT IS HOPED THAT THIS PIECE WILL BECOME AN INVESTIGATIVE EXERCISE ALLOWING ONE A BETTER UNDERSTANDING OF THE OPENNESS AND LIMITATIONS PRESENT WHEN ADOPTING A CHOSEN "ROLE" IN THE FILM MAKING PROCESS. THE SUPPOSITIONS ARE DAILY CONVERSATIONAL EXTRACTIONS - ALTHOUGH IT MAY BE EASILY SEEN THAT IN THEIR VERY EXTRACTION THEY MAY BECOME EXAGGERATED OR "LARGER THAN LIFE". (IE: 3. YOU REALLY MUST BE THE DEVIL..../ COULD HAVE BEEN EXTRACTED FROM AN (OVERLY ROMANTIC LOVERS') ARGUMENT ??/ ...."YOU REALLY MUST BE THE DEVIL TO BE DOING THIS TO ME...") THUS, IN PIVOT: TURNING AROUND SUPPOSITIONS, THERE IS A GREAT FREEDOM INVOLVED IN INTERPRETATION. THIS OCCURS BOTH IN THE PROJECTED PSYCHOLOGY OF THE CAMERAWOMAN/MAN AND IN THE INNER PSYCHOLOGY OF THE PERFORMER. THE STRENGTH OF THE PIECE DERIVES FROM THE VISIBLE MANIFESTATIONS OF THE PARTICIPANTS (IN THEIR EXPRESSED SIMILARITIES AND DIFFERENCES) DUE TO DIFFERENT PSYCHOLOGICAL INTERPRETATIONS AND STRESS.

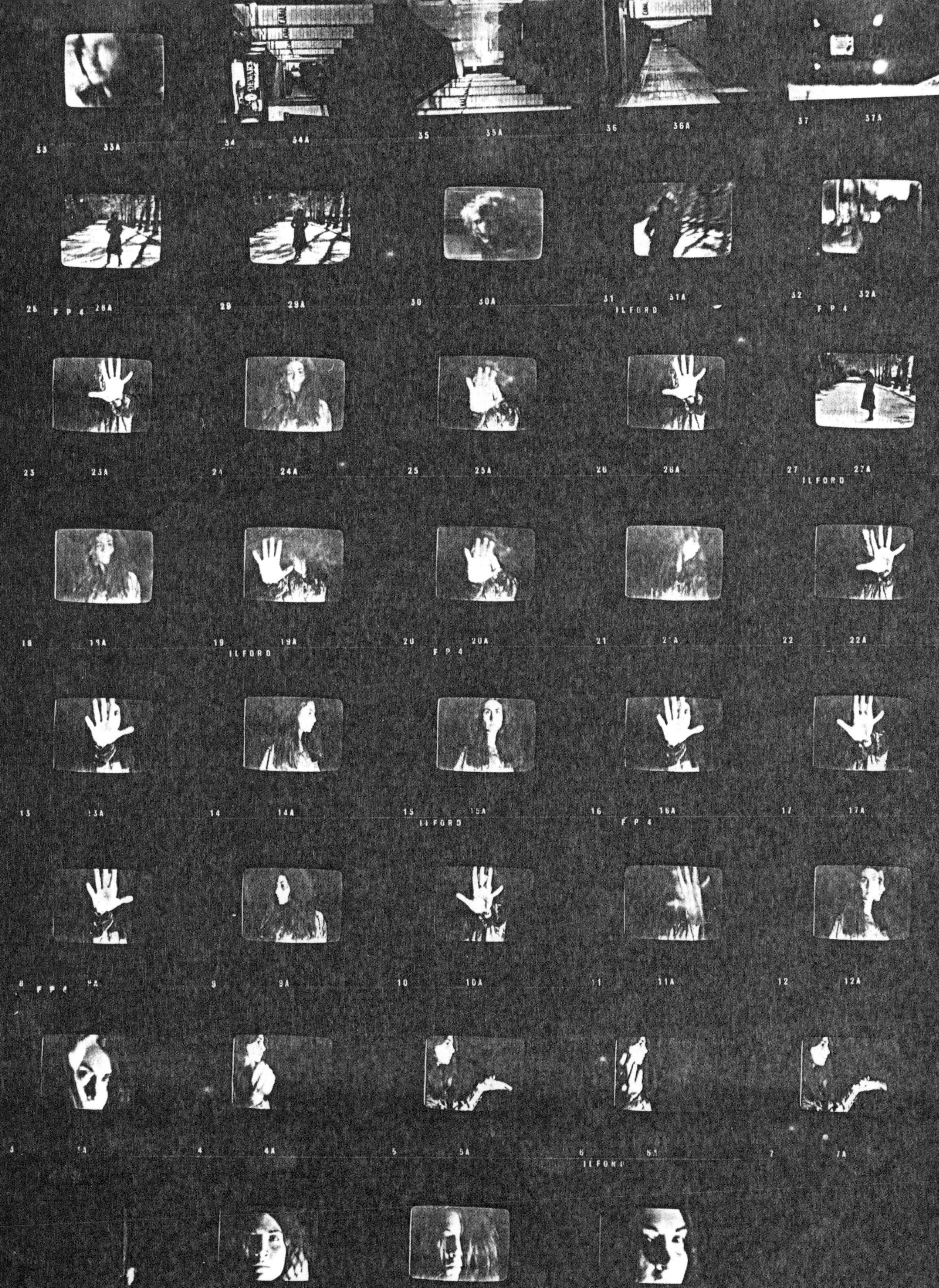

PIVOT:
TURNING AROUND SUPPOSITIONS

MAR 1976
NYC NY

NOTES

PIVOT:

AMERICAN MOVIE ROLES (ROLE-PLAYING)

the good / bad girl GILDA
long black glove strip act

> the promiscuity was only to make him jealous.

the BIG SLEEP (paying blackmail / protecting the innocent sister)

better than she seemed (THE STRANGE LOVE OF MARTHA IVERS) - stealing the fur coat or is it given by a boyfriend??

EXTRACT THE CLICHES ...
ISOLATE THE DIALOGUE...
ISOLATE THE ROLE(S) PLAYED / ROLE•PLAYING ....
ISOLATE THE MOVEMENTS

SPLIT

" you treat badly the people you know best "
" no one can get close to you "

GET (10) suppositions: daily conversational extractions (relate to the GRADE-B AMERICAN FILM - the American LATE SHOW).

The person is stationary standing / the camera must pivot around him - it can use props - to change viewing ht. / lighting (person should be in close approximation to wall & yet leave room for camera to be able to ⊀ all sides) - closeness - zooms / - sound?
Repeat allowing the camera to be stationary + the person to move around it - changing positions / ht. / lighting / etc.

I will make 10 statements about myself
you (camera) will react as you see the statement
as a psychological distance ÷ us.
you can manipulate my moves but not
my distance (that movement is up to you).
i.e. turn towards me. 1' 30"

I will make 10 statements about you
you (camera) will react as you see the statement
made as a psychological reaction on my part
towards you i.e. a rejection of you (your
character / personality etc. I you may
chose to move away – or turn your back
on me (through the mechanism of the camera
("cool video") as I have reacted psychologically
to you ("warm video")).

you will react physically towards me
as you psychologically project your reactions
to my psychologically revealing myself.

PIVOT:

(A)

3

4

2

1

CAMERA PIVOT -

4

(B)

2

1

3

PERFORMER PIVOT:

NOTE: DUR'G PERFORMER PIVOT, THE PERFORMER MAY CHOSE TO STAY 'OUT OF FRAME' (POS. 2)

1

2

AS A POSSIBLE ALTERNATIVE - INDICAT'G HE/SHE IS UNABLE TO FACE DIRECTLY (WISHES TO AVOID) THE STATEM'T MADE . . .

SUPPOSITIONS:

1. YOU ARE MY FRIEND

1. CMAERA MOVES IN CLOSE CONCENTRATING ON THOSE PARTS OF THE BODY OPEN TO FRIENDSHIP IE: STRONG HANDS / STRONG BACK IE: I'LL BE THERE TO BACK YOU UP / DIRECT ANGLES HINTING AT I'LL NEVER TURN ON YOU.

2. YOU ARE MY LOVER

2. CONCENTRATE ON EXTREME CLOSE-UPS ONLY AT THE DIST. A LOVER IS NORMALLY ALLOWED CONCENTRATE ON PRIVATE PARTS OF THE BADY.

3. YOU REALLY MUST BE THE DEVIL

3. EXAGGERATED. LOOKING EXTREMELY UP AT THE FIGURED FRIGHTENED/ LOOKING EXTREMELY DOWN AT THE FIGURE / CONDEEM - ING. KEEP SLIPPING OUT OF FOCUS OBSCURED.

4. YOU TREAT BADLY THE PEOPLE YOU KNOW BEST

4. RAPID TRANSITIONS. STILL SIDE VIEW THEN CUT STRAIGHT CUT TO OTHER SIDE / IE YOU ALWAYS TURN ON PEOPLE NEVER FACE DIRECTLY.

5. NO ON E CAN GET CLOSE TO YOU

5. LONG SHOTS THAT ARE BLOCKED FROM DIRECT CAMERA VIEW BY OBJECTS GETTING IN THE WAY.

6. YOU ARE ALWAYS OPEN TO MEETING NEW PEOPLE

6. looking for direct openings into the person - eyes opened / mouth - a smile or open breathing.

7. you are always there when needed.

7. mid shots / full personage - short cuts - full 1 ∡, quick cut to second ∡ - always an affirmations of presence.

8. all one has to do is reach out to get help from you.

8. zoom into hand slow pan up to face - camera ∡ approaches from low to coming up onto face

SCRIPT I

PIVOT: TURNING AROUND SUPPOSITIONS

THIS PIECE CONSISTS OF TWO PARTS, EACH 100 SECS LONG (1 min 40 SEC). TOTAL RUNNING TIME IS 200 secs (3 min 20 sec).

PART ONE: CAMERA PIVOT

SET-UP: THERE IS ONE PERFORMER THROUGHout THE ENTIRITY OF THE PIECE. HE IS STANDING ERECT, LOCATED SOME 6 FEET FROM A NON-DESCRIPT WALL (THIS WALL MAY OR MAY NOT CONTAIN A WINDOW AREA/ IT SEEMS AS THOUGH A BLANK WALL WOULD BE PREFERABLE FOR IT WOULD ALLOW MORE VARIATION IN LIGHTING TECHNIQUE). THERE ARE NO VISIBLE PROPS. THERE IS NO SOUND RECORDING MECHANISM DUE TO THE FACT THAT ALL SOUND WILL LATER be DUBBED ONTO THE VISUAL IMAGE during post production

PERFORMANCE DESCRIPTION: THE PERFORMER IS AND MUST STAY STATIONARY AND STANDING. THERE IS NO BODY MOVEMENT OTHER THAN inherent CHANGES SUCH AS WEIGHT SHIFTS. THE CAMERA-MAN/WOMAN IS PRESENTED WITH A LIST OF TEN GENERAL SUPPOSITIONS ABOUT THE PERFORMER - THEY ARE EXTREMELY GENERALIZED AND MAY OR MAY NOT BE IN AGREEMENT WITH ONE ANOTHER. THE CAMERAMAN/WOMAN MUST RESPOND TO EACH "PSYCHOLOGICAL" STATEMENT WITH WHAT IS FELT TO BE AN APPROPRIATE "PHYSICAL" CAMERA STATEMENT. IN OTHER WORDS EACH STATEMENT WILL DETERMINE IN THE CAMERA'S "MIND"/"EYE" AN APPROPRIATE REACTION TOWARDS VIEWING THE PERFORMER. THERE ARE 10 STATEMENTS PRESENTED. THIS ALLOWS THE CAMERA-MAN/WOMAN 10 SECONDS FOR EACH REACTION.

CAMERA LIMITATIONS: THE CAMERA MAY PIVOT ENTIRELY AROUND THE PERFORMER. PROPS MAY BE USED BY THE CAMERA TO CHANGE VIEWING HEIGHT AND ANGLE. LIGHTING IS ENTIRELY AN OPEN DECISION - FOR THIS REASON THE PERFORMER HAS BEEN PLACED CLOSE TO A WALL OR ROOM CORNER TO ALLOW A MAXIMUM NUMBER OF VARIATIONS. ALL MECHANISMS BUILT INTO THE CAMERA UNIT ARE TO BE CONSIDERED AS AIDES (IE: TELEPHOTO capabilities/ FOCUS/ DEPTH of field/ ETC.) THE CAMERA TO BE USED IS ANY VARIATION OF THE SONY ½" PORTAPAK SYSTEM.

SAMPLE SUPPOSITIONS:

1. YOU ARE MY FRIEND
2. YOU ARE MY LOVER
3. YOU REALLY MUST BE THE DEVIL....
4. YOU TREAT BADLY THE PEOPLE YOU KNOW BEST
5. NO ONE CAN GET CLOSE TO YOU
6. YOU ARE ALWAYS OPEN TO MEETING NEW PEOPLE
7. YOU ARE ALWAYS THERE WHEN NEEDED
8. ALL ONE HAS TO DO IS TO REACH OUT TO GET HELP FROM YOU

9. YOU NEVER SPEAK TO PEOPLE DIRECTLY
10. YOU DON'T KNOW HOW TO CONFRONT NEW SITUATIONS

THE CAMERA MAY MOVE WITHIN EACH SEQUENCE OR CHOOSE TO REMAIN STATIOARY. HOWEVER, THE PERFORMER MUST ADOPT ONE, DIRECTED POSITION THROUGHOUT THE FIRST 1 MIN 40 SEC.

PART TWO: SUBJECT (PERFORMER) PIVOT

CAMERA LIMITATIONS: THE CAMERA NOW TAKES THE PLACE OF "PERFORMER". IT IS SET STATIONARY ON A TRI-POD AND ITS DIRECTION IS DETERMINED BY BOTH PARTICIPANTS (NOTE: BY FACING THE WALL LIGHTING CONDITIONS WILL AGAIN BE MORE VARIABLE BUT WORKABLE SPACE WILL BE LIMITED ~~TO THE PERFORMER.~~ IE: HIS DISTANCE FROM CAMERA LENS ~~MAY~~ NEVER EXCEED 6 FEET.) THE CAMERA LENS IS ADJUSTED TO "EYE HEIGHT". FOCAL LENGTH AND DEPTH OF FIELD ARE PRE-SELECTED. THESE WILL BOTH BE MADE KNOWN TO THE PERFORMER.

directing the camera towards

the performer's

PERFORMANCE DESCRIPTION: AGAIN THE SUPPOSITIONS WILL BE GONE THROUGH - BEING READ ALOUD TO THE PERFORMER. HE/SHE NOW HAS 10 SECS(~~FOR EACH SUPPOSITION~~)TO MAKE A RESPONSE. to ea. of the suppositions then read. HIS/HER PSYCHOLOGICAL REACTION TO A STATEMENT CONCERNING ONE'S SELF MUST BE TRANSFERRED TO A PHYSICAL REACTION THAT CAN BE RECORDED BY THE CAMERA'S "MIND"/"EYE". IE: THESE REACTIONS MAY VARY FROM AVOIDANCE (STAYING OUT OF FRAME) TO DIRECT CONFRONTATION (FILLING CAMERA FRAME) TO TAKING ADVANTAGE OF CAMERA LIMITATIONS (BLURRING ONE'S OWN IMAGE THROUGH DEPTH OF FIELD LIMITATIONS). THE PERFORMER MAY USE PROPS TO CHANGE VIEWING HEIGHT, LIGHTING CONDITIONS, OR TO OBSTRUCT THE CAMERA'S DIRECT LINE OF VISION.

GENERAL REMARKS: IT IS HOPED THAT THIS PIECE WILL BECOME AN INVESTIGATIVE EXERCISE ALLOWING ONE A BETTER UNDERSTANDING OF THE OPENNESS AND LIMITATIONS PRESENT WHEN ADOPTING A CHOSEN "ROLE" IN THE FILM MAKING PROCESS. THE SUPPOSITIONS ARE DAILY CONVERSATIONAL EXTRACTIONS - ALTHOUGH IT MAY BE EASILY SEEN THAT IN THERE VERY EXTRACTION THEY ~~MAY BECOME~~ COME EXAGGERATED OR "LARGER THAN LIFE" (IE: "YOU MUST BE THE DEVIL ... / ... YOU MUST REALLY BE THE DEVIL TO BE DOING THIS TO ME ....." COULD BE EXTRACTED BY AN (OVERLY ROMANTIC LOVER'S) ARGUMENT...?) THUS, THERE IS A GREAT FREEDOM INVOLVED IN INTERPRETATION. THIS OCCURS BOTH IN THE PROJECTED PSYCHOLOGY OF THE CAMERA (man/woman) AND IN THE INNER PSYCHOLOGY OF THE PERFORMER. THE STRENGTH OF THE PIECE DERIVES FROM THE VISIBLE MANISFESTATIONS ~~(AND THERE DIFFERENCES)~~ DUE TO DIFFERENT PSYCHOLOGICAL INTERPRETATIONS AND STRESS.

have

in pivot: turning around suppositions,

of the participants (in ~~the developed~~ their expressed similarities + differences)

<u>LIBERTY: A DOZEN OR SO VIEWS</u>

NEW YORK CITY, NEW YORK

SW: Do you see artworks as political — not necessarily expressing a particular ideology — but as instruments of influence over other people?
DB: It has to do with responsibility. Artists have always reflected their culture. In the last two years some groups here have been discussing Marxist premises in art. I agree with them that you are responsible for the statements you make. I'm not sure if artists can determine the course of history, but at least they would be conscious of what they're reflecting. The French posters in 1967 — it seems as if those artists wanted themselves to be tools of a movement.
SW: What are the responsiblities in video specifically?
DB: I'm interested in the extent to which video can be controlled by the artist, and how much the artist is controlled by video's techniques and vocabulary. the artist is responsible to society. When film and video came into artists' hands, they could affect more people in a shorter length of time.

Video is very seductive. It has a warm side, personal, familiar. Then it has a cool side, manipulative. In *Liberty* I explored this problem. I let tourists on the boat to the Statue of Liberty handle the camera. Their vision was expanded and they could see the object in a new way. But I had pre-set and pre-focused the camera for distance and zoom. So their sense of intimacy with the object was predetermined. With video, you can give someone freedom, but qualify it — hold them, but at a distance. In *Liberty* I relinquished camera control to control referential viewpoint.
SW: And the news on broadcast TV?
DB: Propaganda. When the newsreels went from film to video, the image had a greater sense of depth. Film lies flatter on the screen. You also know with video that you can watch events anywhere in the world as they're happening. With the image quality and the immediacy, you can be convinced you're seeing the reality of the moment.

LIBERTY: A DOZEN OR SO VIEWS

IN *LIBERTY*, EACH PARTICIPANT WAS CHOSEN WHILE ALREADY VIEWING A SELECTED OBJECT (THE STATUE OF LIBERTY). HE/SHE WAS ASKED TO DISRUPT THEIR NORMAL VIEWING PROCESS IN ORDER TO ASSERT A VIDEO CAMERA BETWEEN THEIR LINE OF SIGHT AND THE CHOSEN OBJECT. THIS ALLOWS A NEW (SEEMINGLY EXPANDED) FIELD OF VISION FOR EACH PARTICIPANT. HOWEVER, UPON CLOSER EXAMINATION, IT IS ACTUALLY A NARROWING OF ONE'S POINT OF VIEW. THE ARTIST GAINS CONTROL OVER THE REFERENTIAL VIEWPOINT OF THE OTHER THROUGH MANIPULATION OF THE MECHANISTIC QUALITIES OF THE MEDIA. THE CAMERA HAS BEEN PRESET TO TELEPHOTO USE (THE NARROWEST OF THE POSSIBLE FIELDS OF VISION) AND PRE-FRAMED. DURING EACH ENSUING INTERVIEW THE INFORMATIONAL EXCHANGE IS ALSO KEPT ON THE LEVEL OF "COOL VIDEO" - A REDUCTION OF FACTS TO PURE PHYSICAL DESCRIPTION INSTEAD OF ALLOWING A MORE NORMAL "INTIMATE" (PSYCHOLOGICAL) DEVELOPMENT TO OCCUR.

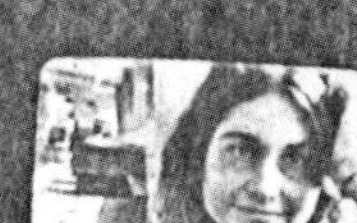
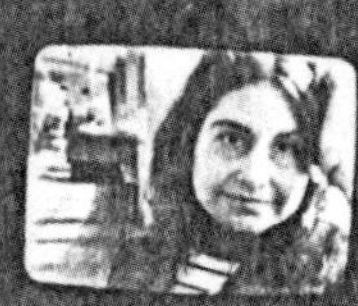
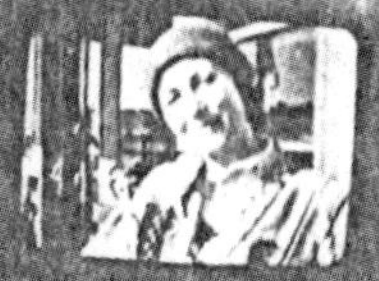
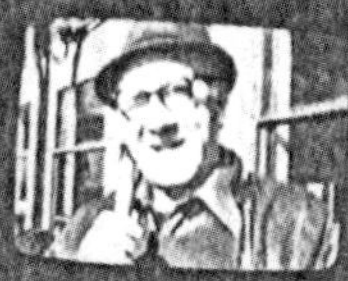
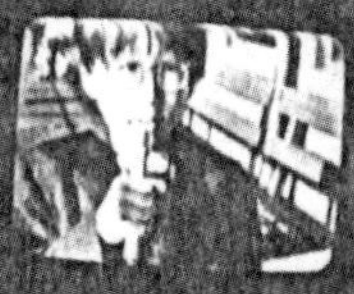
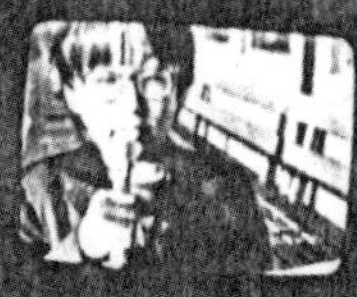
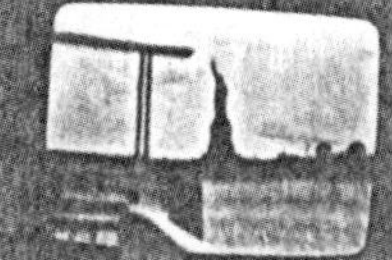
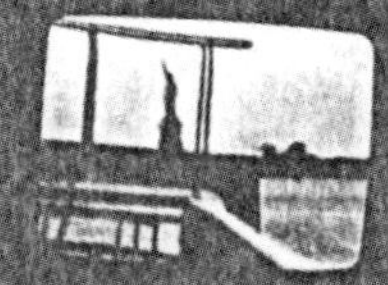
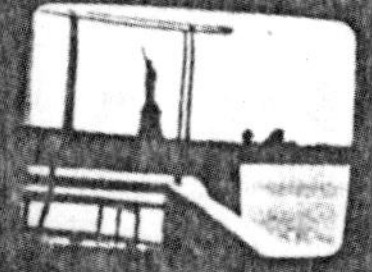
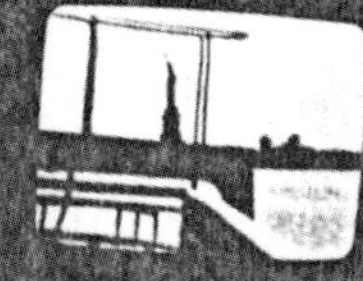
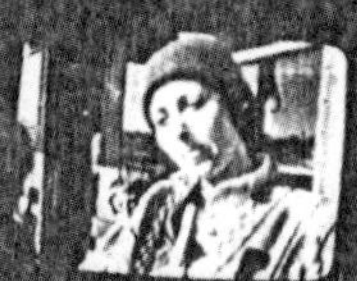
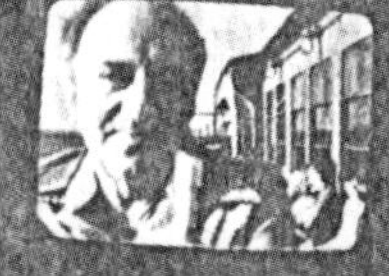
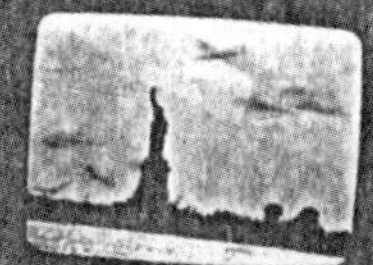
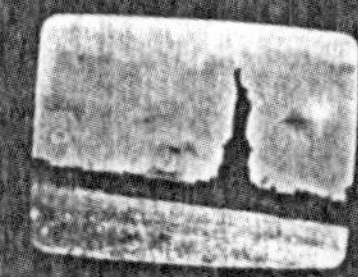
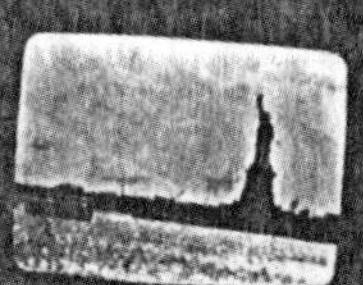
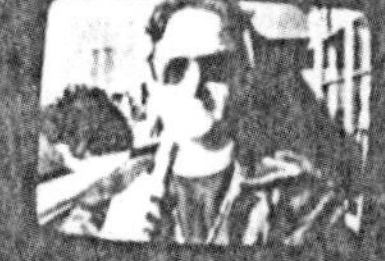

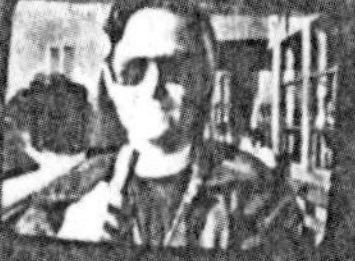
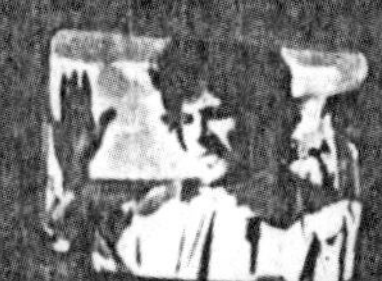
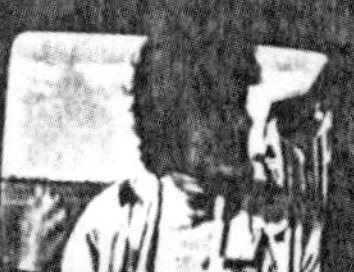
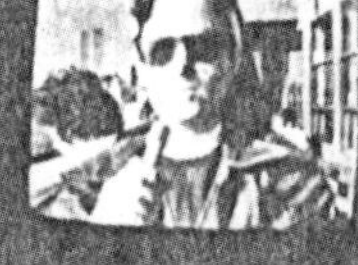
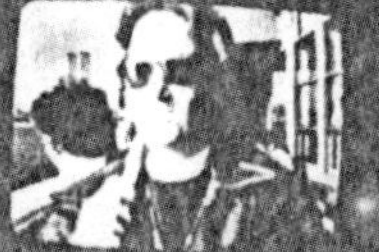
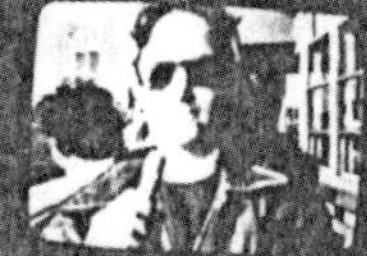
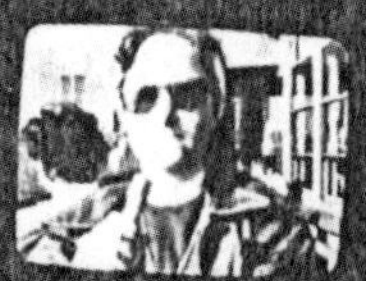
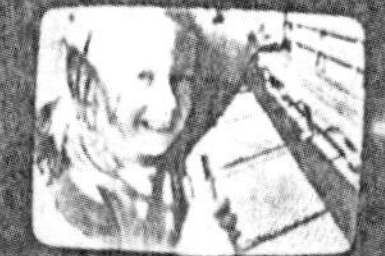
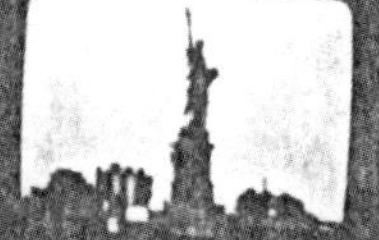
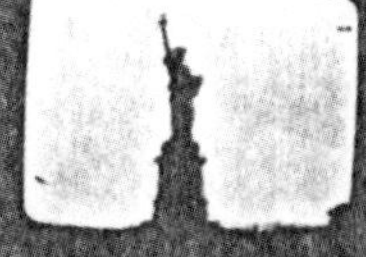
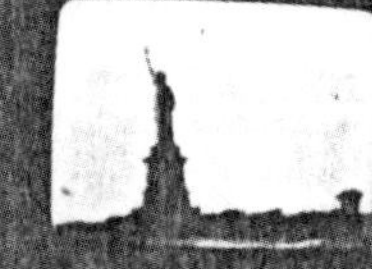
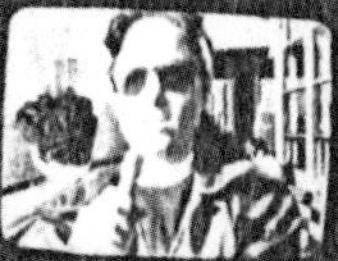
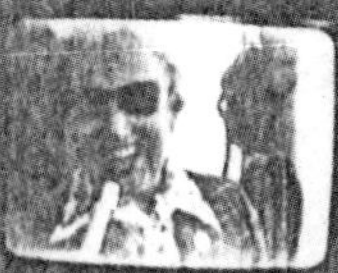
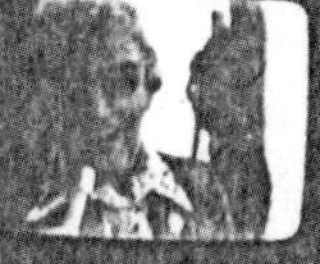
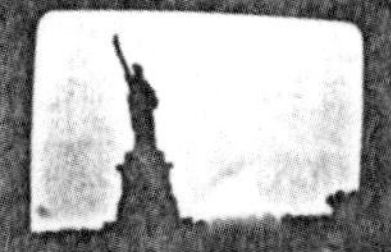
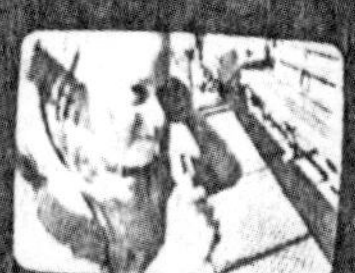
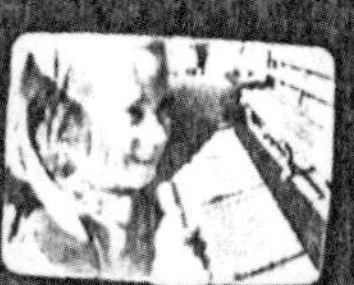

<u>LIBERTY:</u>
<u>A DOZEN OR SO VIEWS</u>
<u>MAY 1976</u>
NYC NY

LIBERTY PIECE

MAY 1976

A DOZEN (OR SO) ASSORTED VIEWS OF LIBERTY

(ROUGH EDIT FOR GLOBAL)

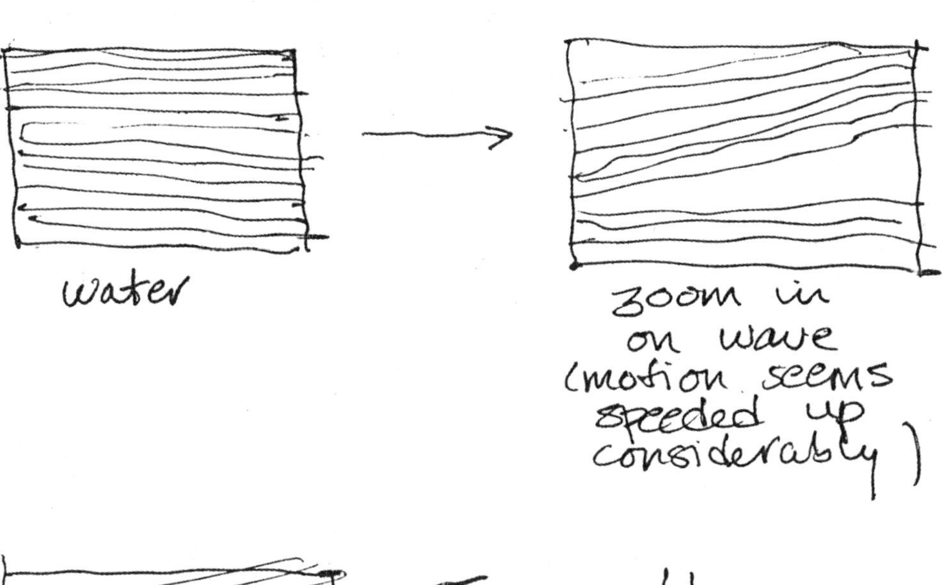

water

zoom in on wave (motion seems speeded up considerably)

zoom in complete so speeded up seems like jet stream / wipe's out picture

CUT

voice dubbed under: title recited.

straight cut directly into 12 very short 'freeze frames' of tight shots of statue . . .

OR

GRAY

GRAY

(more snap-shot like . . . emphasises still shots)

portrait interview

view of statue

cut

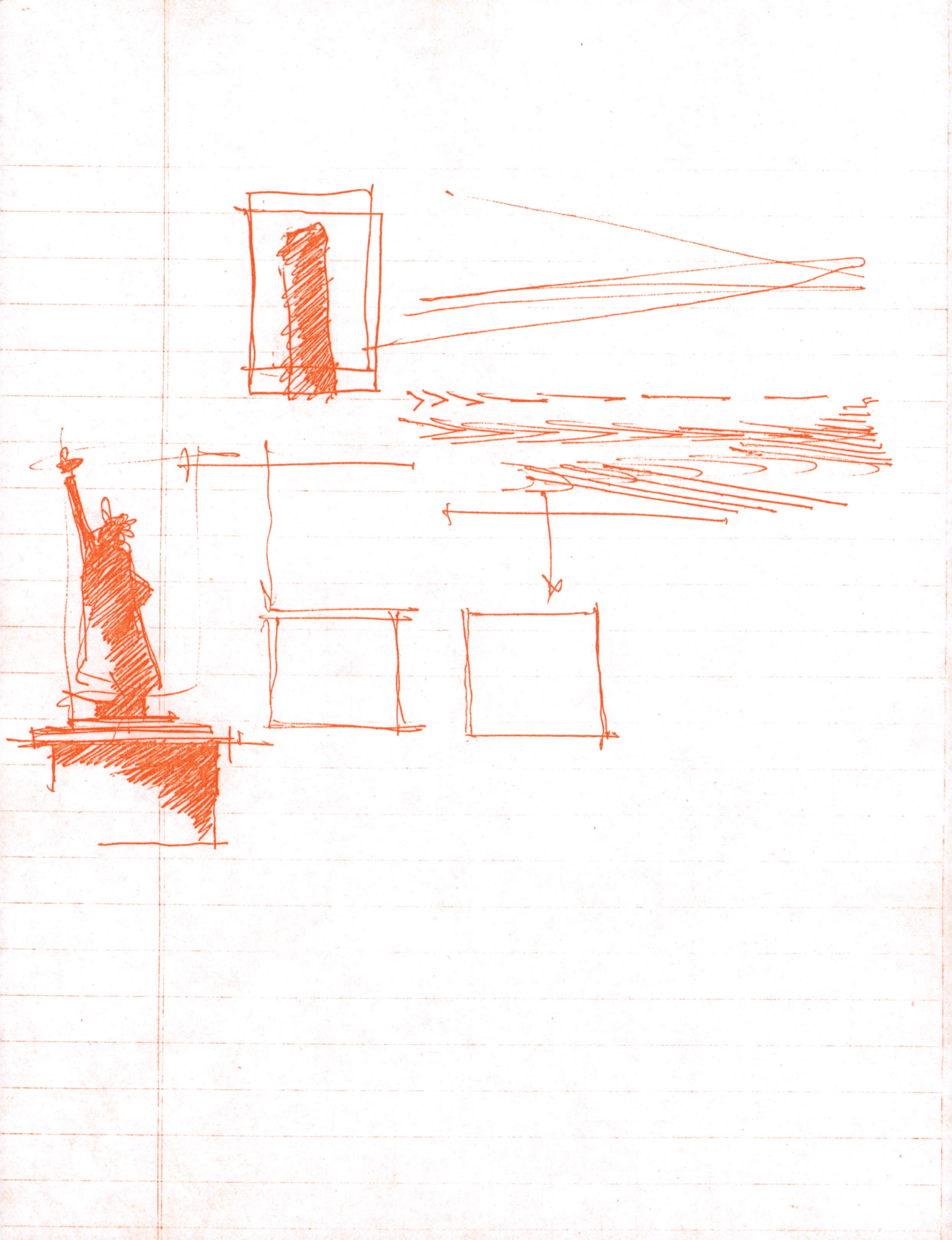

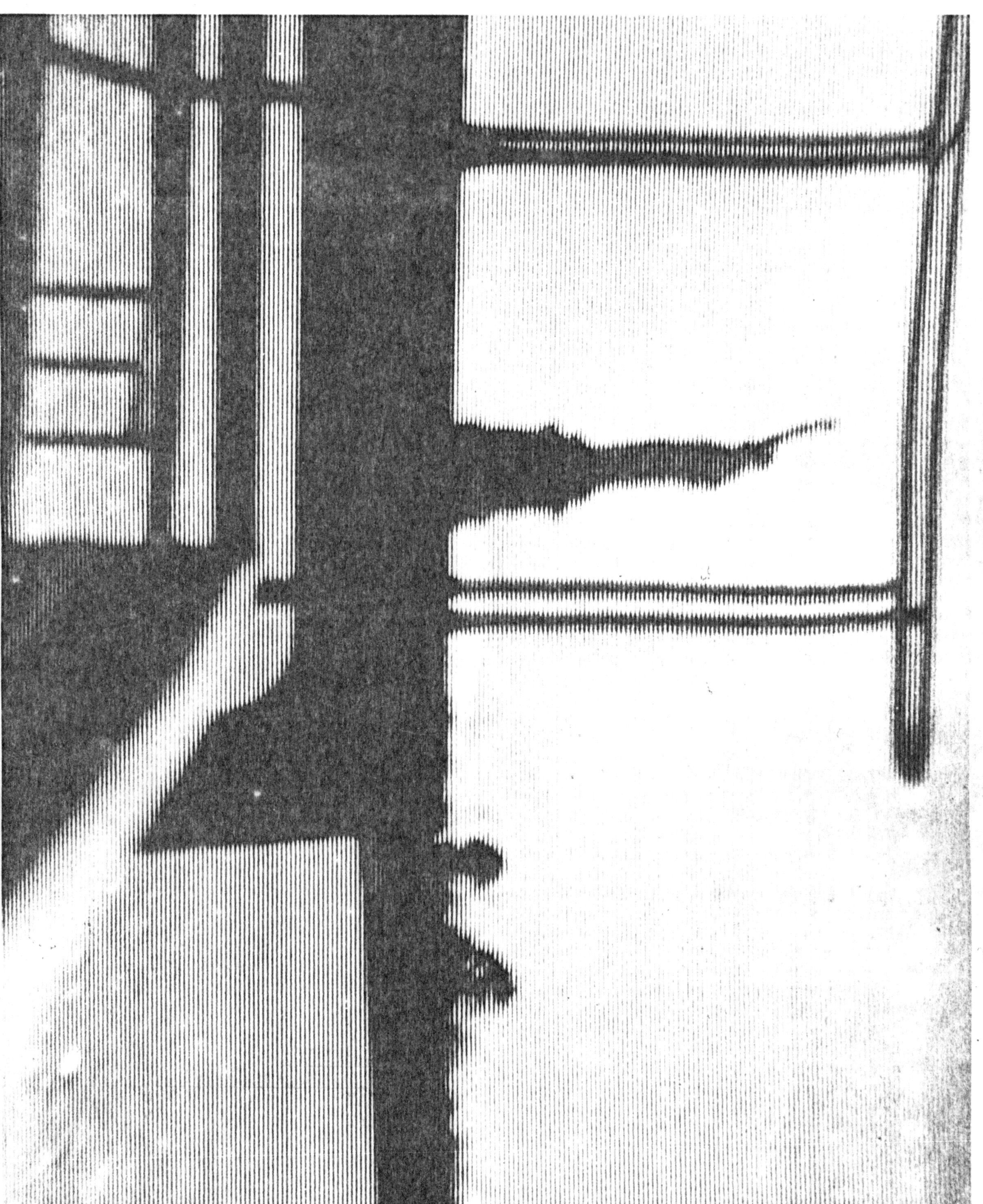

LIBERTY:

A DOZEN OR SO VIEWS

MAY 1976

NYC NY

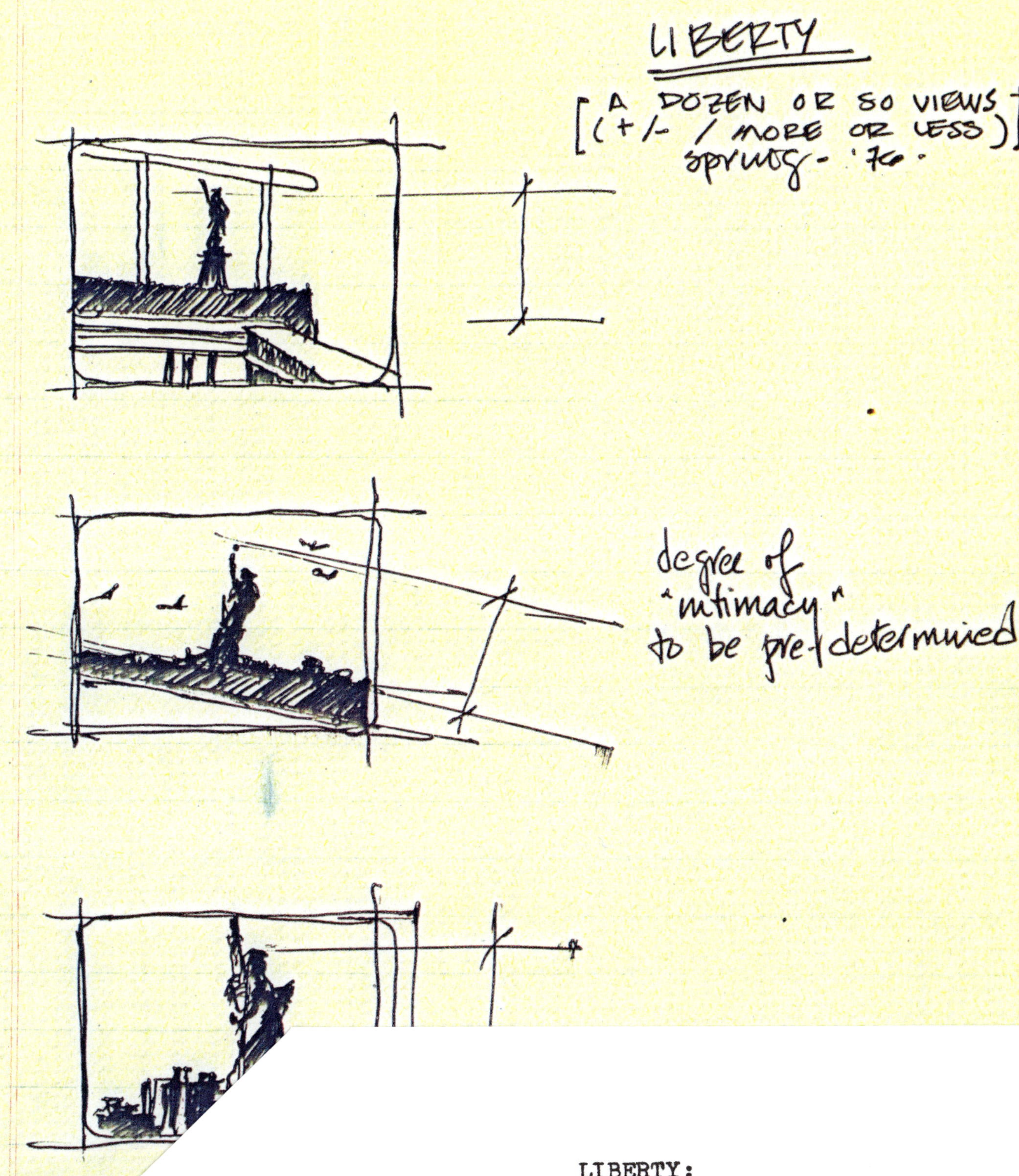

LIBERTY:
A DOZEN OR SO VIEWS
MAY 1976
NYC NY

A DOZEN OR SO VIEWS OF LIBERTY

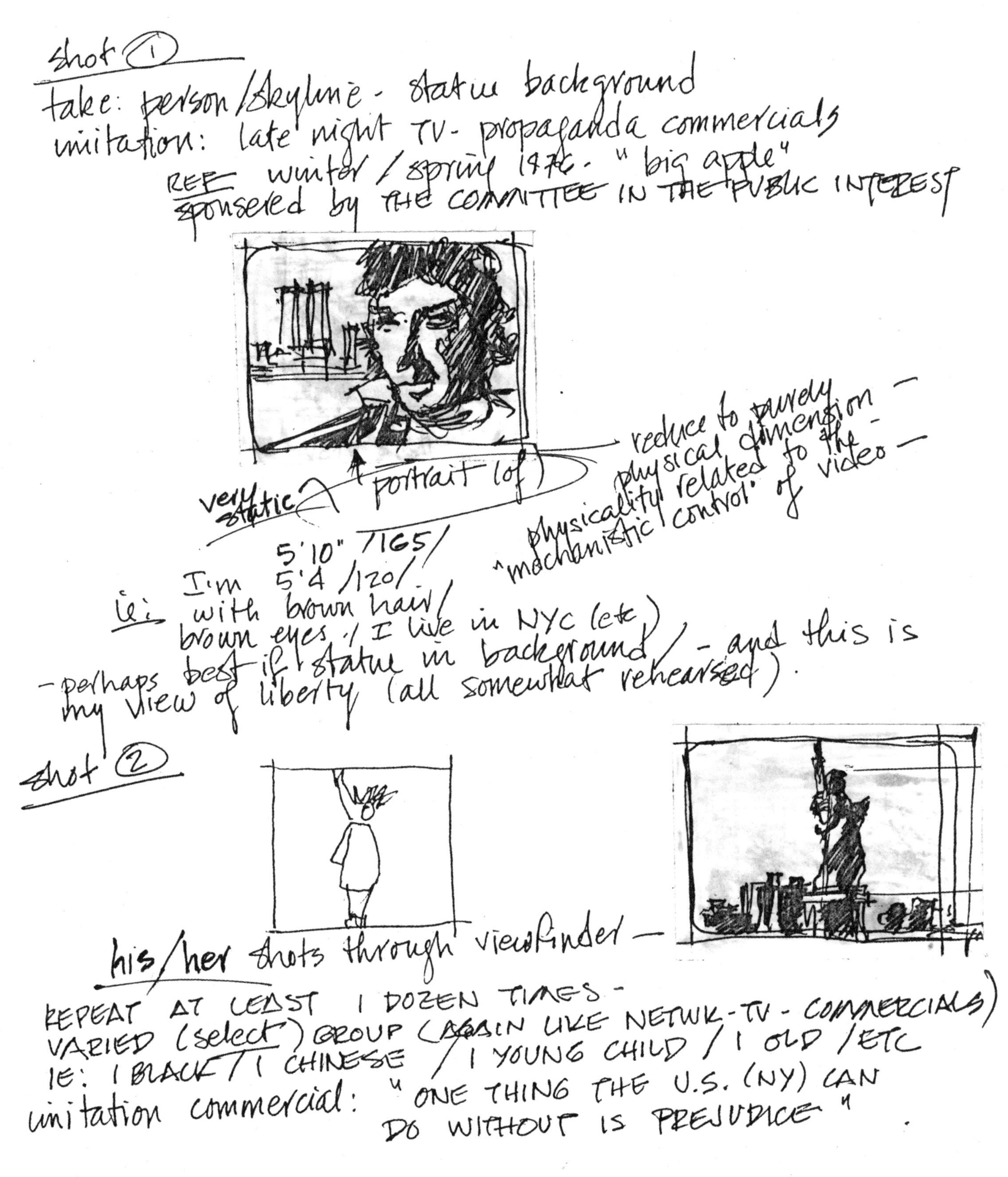

shots

2 nuns (1 in habit - upper deck
1 just self-declared sister) lower deck

2 children — 1 blond girl
1 chinese boy) very young U.D.

1 old man (70's ++) U.D.

1 late 30's balding man U.D.

1 heavier blond girl) U.D.
1 (her lover - thin - high cheeked)) young 20's U.D
1 jewish tall full guy
1 (his lover - dark haired)) young - late teen's (20's) U.D.
1 girl below deck - rear - hair pulled back - 20's L.D
1 black musician L.D.
1 French woman U.D.
1 puerto rican man (father in 20's +) U.D.

1. 20's. white / glasses hair tied back scarf
2. black musician
3. nun out of habit
4. young blond girl
5. handsome Jewish guy
6. his girlfriend
7. thin face, young 20's M.W.
8. nun in habit
9. Puerto Rican young father
10. Italian-Amer. M.W.

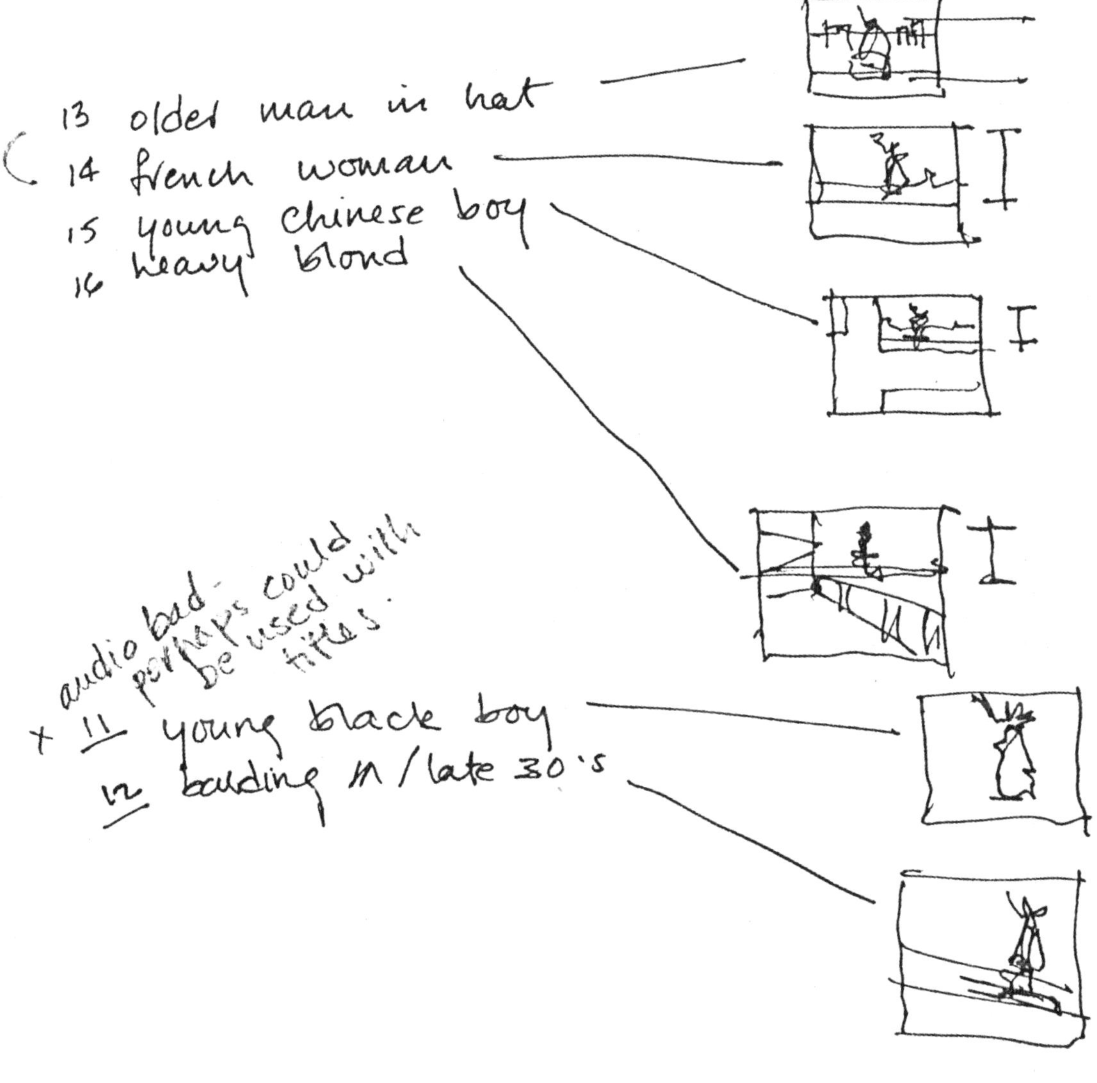

Se bra och se bra ut i höstens glasögon

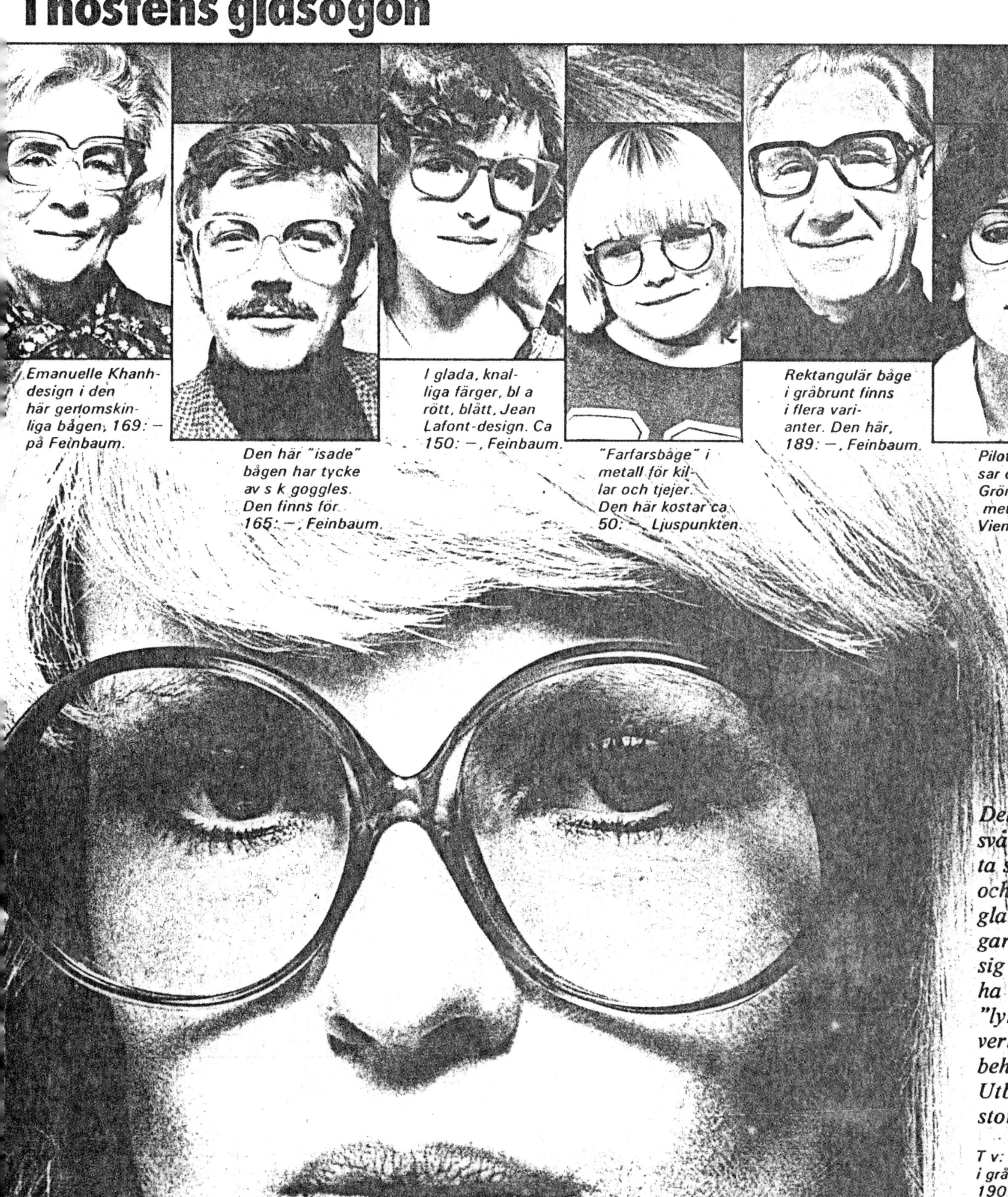

Emanuelle Khanh-design i den här genomskinliga bågen, 169:– på Feinbaum.

Den här "isade" bågen har tycke av s k goggles. Den finns för 165:–, Feinbaum.

I glada, knalliga färger, bl a rött, blått, Jean Lafont-design. Ca 150:–, Feinbaum.

"Farfarsbåge" i metall för killar och tjejer. Den här kostar ca 50:–, Ljuspunkten.

Rektangulär båge i gråbrunt finns i flera varianter. Den här, 189:–, Feinbaum.

Pilotbåg… sar de fl… Grön elle… metall, … Viennali…

Det är … svårt a… ta snyg… och pe… glasög… gar – … sig ma… ha den … "lyst" … verklig… behöve… Utbud… stort.

T v: solg… i grågrön… 190:–, … line, äver… slipade …

GERMAN ADVERTISING
TYPECAST / COMMERCIAL ADS
SET-UP FOR <u>LIBERTY:</u>

A DOZEN OR SO VIEWS

MAY 1976
NYC NY

LIBERTY PIECE

Order of Appearance - Specifications (general characteristics)

(1) SEX F
HT 5'2"
WT 115 lbs.
HAIR BR.
EYES BR.
AGE 23 YRS.
RACE WHITE

(MIKE ANGEL)
(2) SEX M
HT 6'-0"
WT.
HAIR BLACK
EYES BROWN
AGE 26 YRS
RACE BLACK

(SISTER - MARY ANNE (?) BRENNAN, SISTER OF CHARITY)
(3) SEX F
HT 5'-5½"
WT 145 lbs.
HAIR RED
EYES HAZEL
AGE 48
RACE WHITE

(4) COLEEN
SEX F
HT ?
WT. 50 lbs.
HAIR: BROWN
EYES: HAZEL
AGE —
RACE - IRISH, ITALIAN - IRISH

(5) SEX M
HT 5'-8"
WT —
HAIR: BLACK
EYES: BROWN
AGE: 21 YRS.
RACE: JEWISH

(6) SEX F
HT 5'-2"
WT. 120 lbs.
HAIR: BROWN
EYES: BLUE
AGE: 18 YRS.
RACE: GERMAN/IRISH

(7) SEX M
HT. 5'-9"
WT: 155 lbs.
HAIR: BROWN
EYES: GREEN
AGE: 21 YRS.
RACE: CAUCASIAN

~~(8)~~ (9) SEX M
HT. 5'-5"
WT. 130 lbs.
HAIR:
EYES:
AGE:
RACE: PUERTO RICAN

(8) SEX F
HT: 5'-4"
WT:
HAIR: DARK
EYES: BLUE
AGE: 35
RACE: CAUCASIAN

(10) SEX M
HT. 5'-8"
WT: 160
HAIR: GRAY
EYES: HAZEL
AGE 55 YRS
RACE: AMERICAN-ITALIAN/AMERICAN

(11) SEX M
HT: 6' MINUS 2
WT: 150 + x lbs.
HAIR: LIGHT HAZEL
EYES: BABY BLUE
AGE: 37
RACE: WHITE
(WHITE YES, WHITE)

(12) SEX F
HT 1 METER 65
WT 68 KILOGRAMS
HAIR: CURLY (TODAY)
EYES: GREEN RUSTED
AGE:
RACE: FRENCH, EUROPEAN (IS THAT A RACE?)

(13) SEX M
HT 5'10"
WT: 180 lbs
HAIR: GONE (BUT NOT FORGOTTEN)
EYES: BLUISH-GREEN
AGE: 66 YRS.
RACE: IRISH DESCENT, BORN IN BROOKLYN

(14) ROGER LEE
SEX M
HT: ? (I DON'T KNOW HOW TALL I AM)
WT: 56 lbs.
HAIR: DARK BROWN
EYES:
AGE: 9 YRS.
RACE: CHINESE

(15) SEX F
HT: 5'-8"
WT: TOO HEAVY
HAIR: RED
EYES: BLUE
AGE: 23 YRS.
RACE: CAUCASIAN

REVISE.

LIBERTY:

1 - water
2 - z.i. close up / INC. → flow (speeded)
3 - views of statue -
(maybe just 6-8 now - take ea. view that will be shown again in piece) | voice over dubbed title
4 - fade out (dissolve on last) | title repeats on fade.

5 - Ⓐ don't go back to water / directly into first statue pan cut to 10-15 sec. ± (on all)
6 - interview
7, next pan of statue Ⓐ (movement) / Ⓑ still.

5 - Ⓑ freeze frame of statue 'view'
6 - direct cut into interview

cut down to 8 or so views (make sure to include)
1 - first girl (glasses) ok
2 - chinese boy (roger)
3 - girl (coleen)
4 - balding guy
5 - 1 nun ?
6 - old (66) guy. ?
7 - black musician ?
8 - puerto rican father ?

not in this order

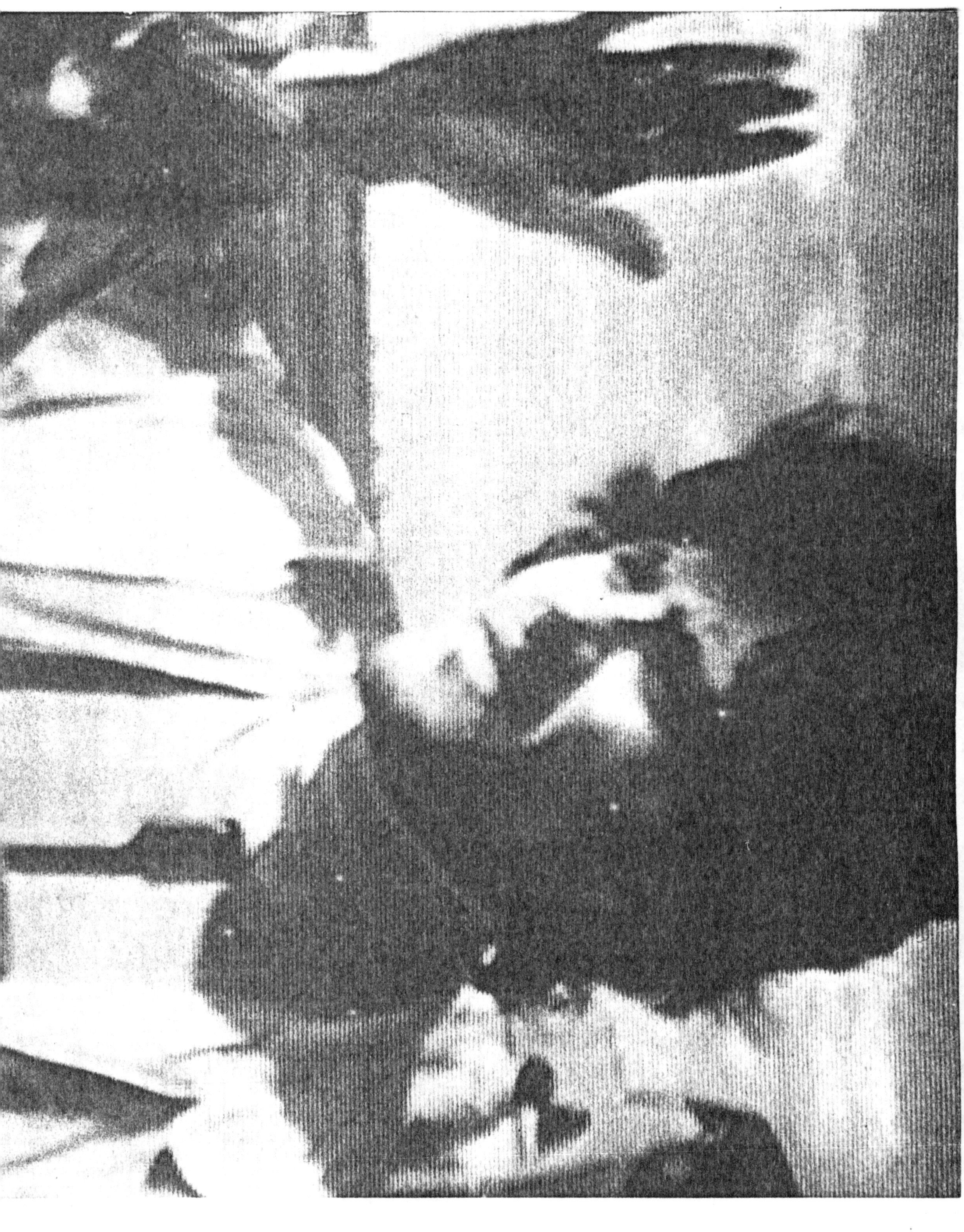

<u>LIBERTY:</u>
<u>A DOZEN OR SO VIEWS</u>

MAY 1976

NYC NY

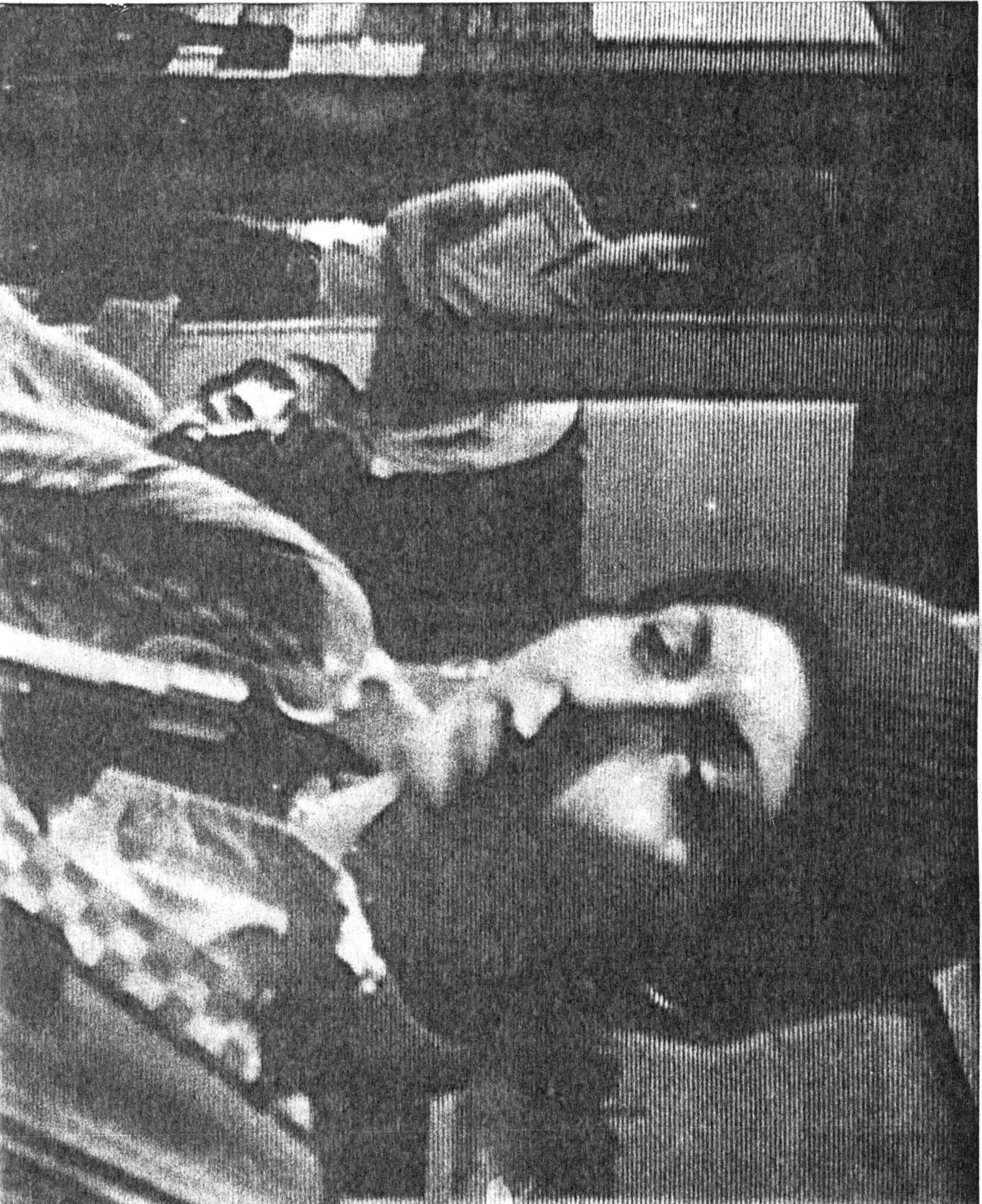

LIBERTY:
A DOZEN OR SO VIEWS
MAY 1976
NYC NY

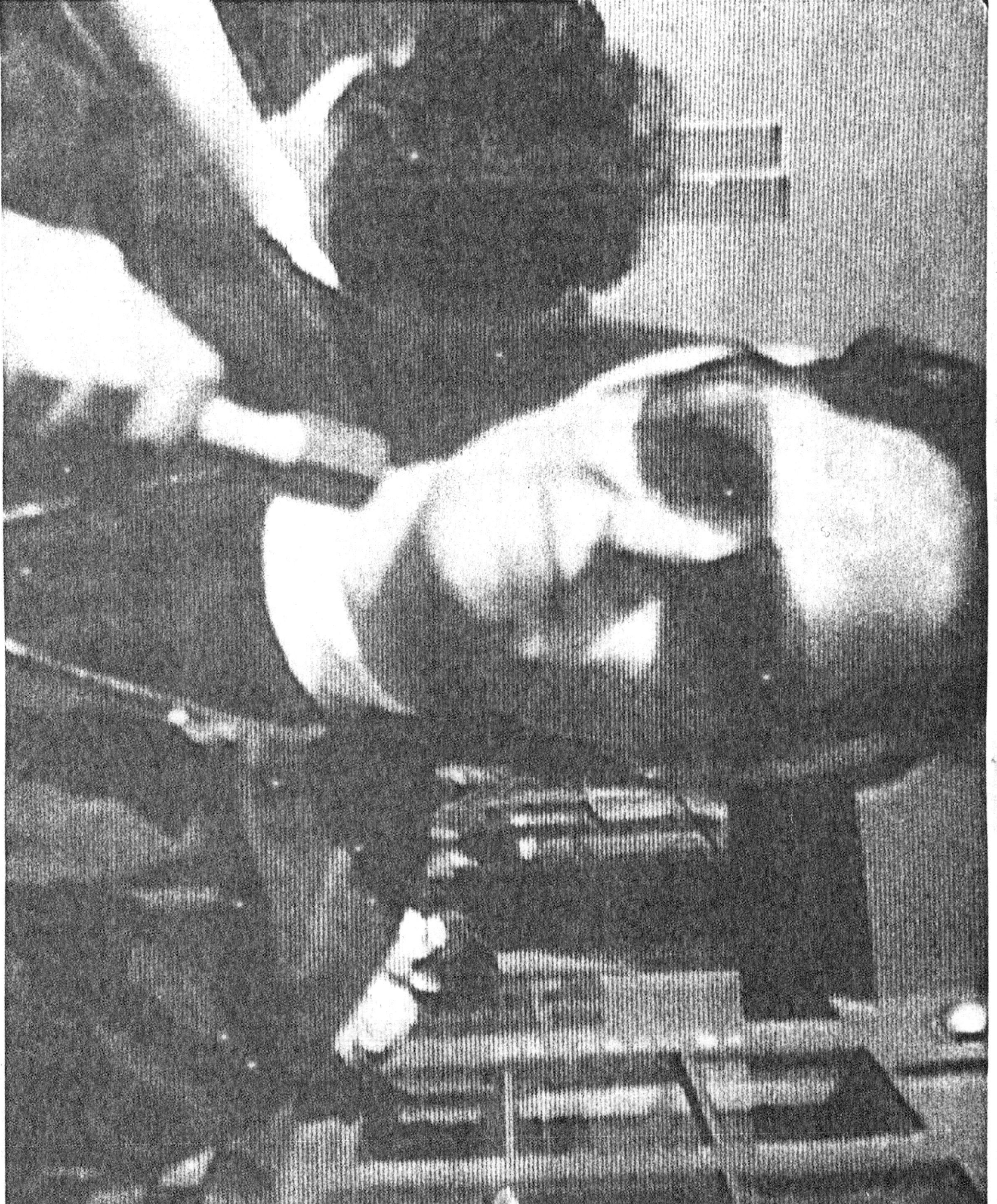

LIBERTY:
A DOZEN OR SO VIEWS

MAY 1976

NYC NY

CONCERNS (THAT TAKE ON / DEAL WITH) VIDEO FORMAT

<u>RE</u>: <u>LIBERTY: A DOZEN OR SO VIEWS</u>
<u>IE</u>: <u>CATALOGUING</u>

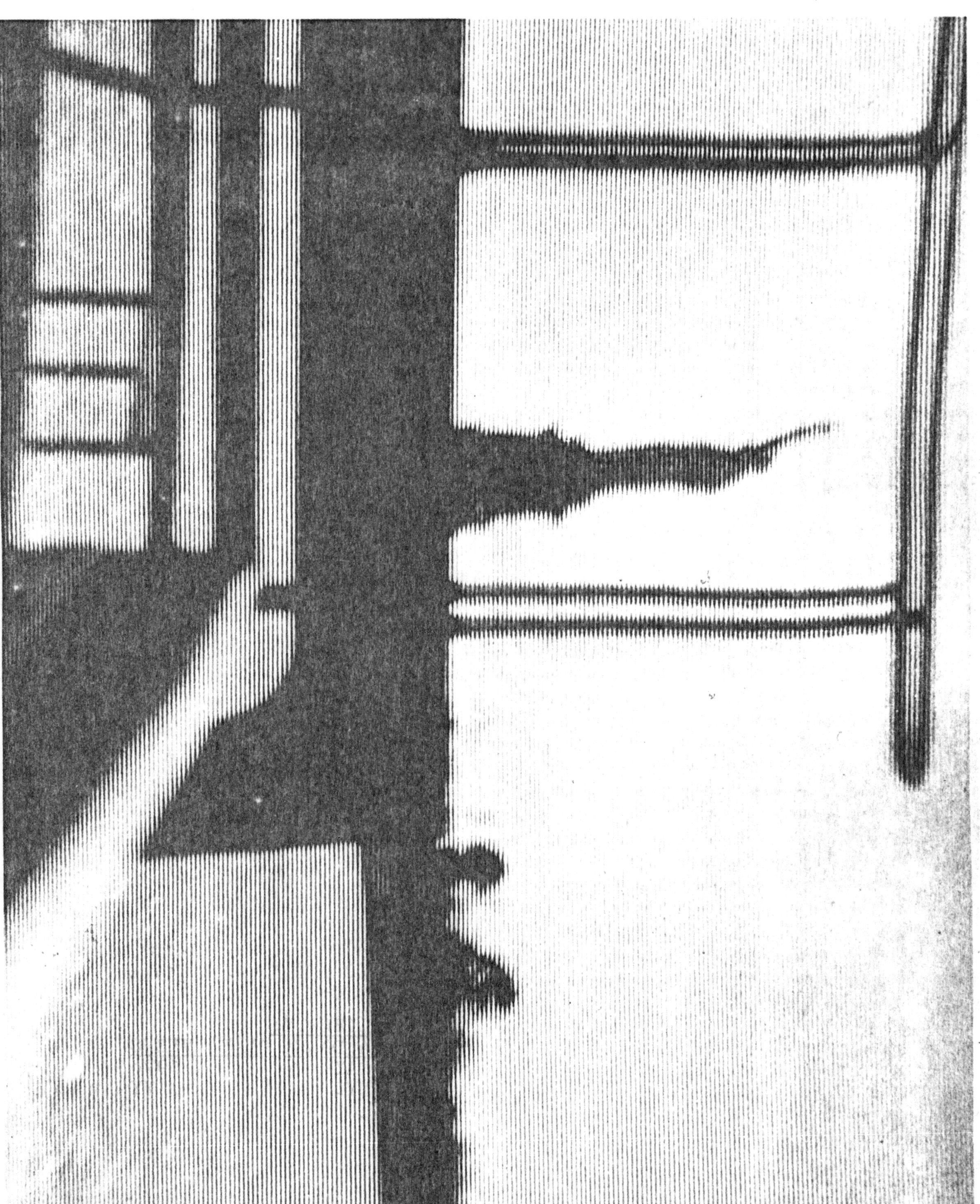

LIBERTY:
A DOZEN OR SO VIEWS
MAY 1976
NYC NY

203 cut /
readjustment

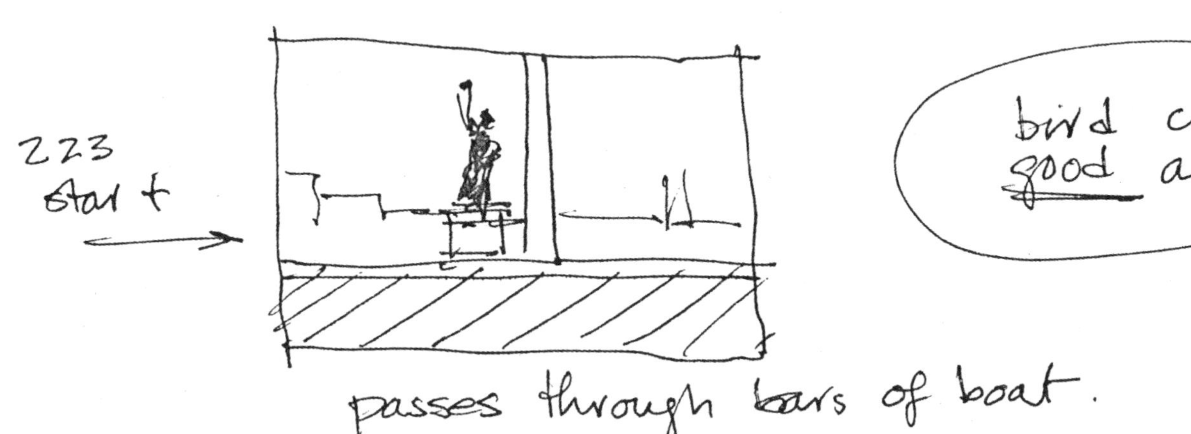

bird cries -
good audio

passes through bars of boat.

237 - excellent - pass'g through - pan bars as well

244 - world trade center

254 - excellent cut (sea gulls come into picture)

257 - bar fills in space in - between - towers
excellent

269 - tape crease - bad visual

276 - cut

281 - readj. -

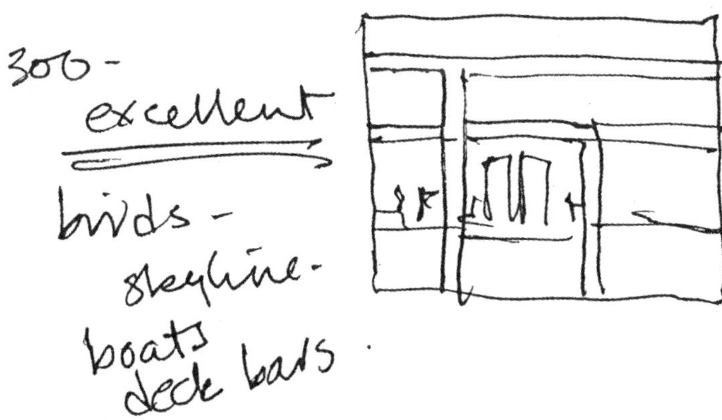

audio - not
as good -
just wind.
no bird
cries.

311- interior
backgr. noise.

mike test

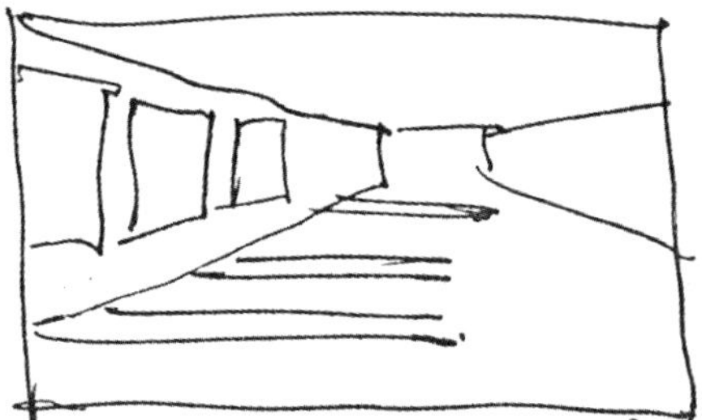

panning inside of ferry.

329. focus on couple outside
kissing - zoom in

335 - hugging - (through window) tight shot

340 - zoom out - inter. ferry -
window still visible + couple - long shot

345. dan - mike test -
↳ bad visually

352. 1st pan statue - ~~set up~~ no -
long shot
is first pan
by participant

~~37~~
361 -
ends.

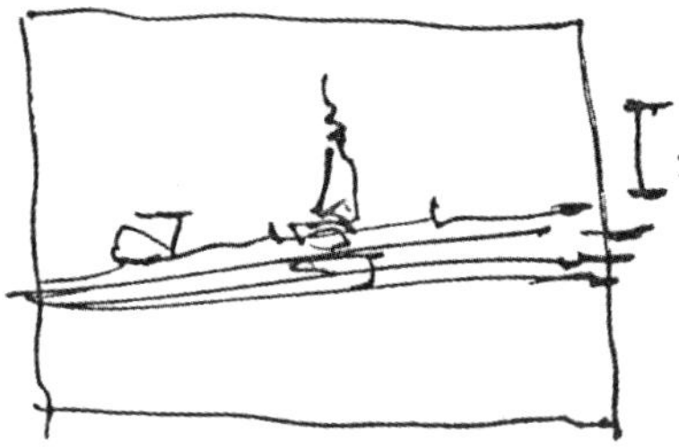

section filled

370. 1st portrait -
siloquetted. not good visual
audio flact obscured by wind.

370

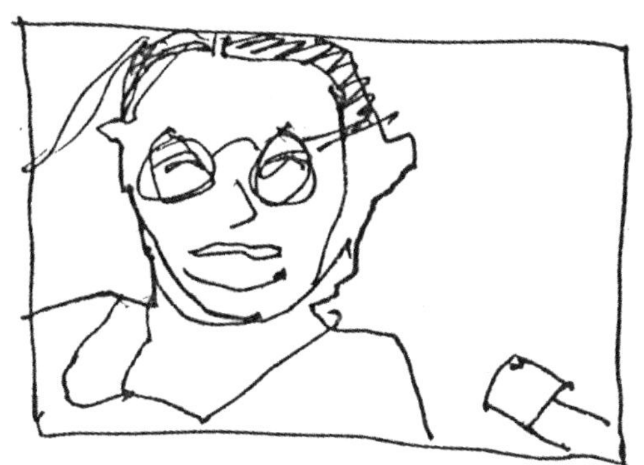

woman.
20's.
plaid shirt / glasses.

378. ends

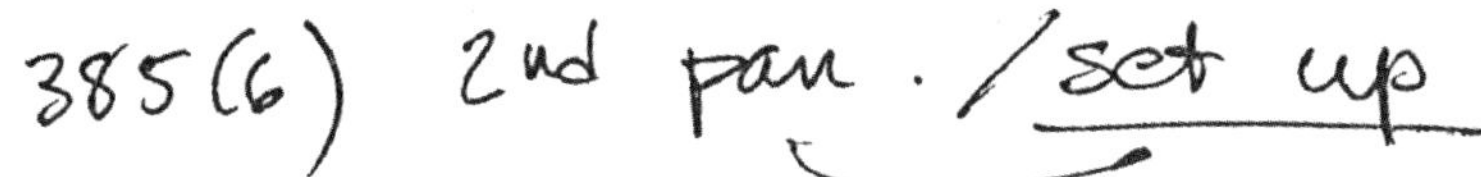

385(6) 2nd pan. / set up

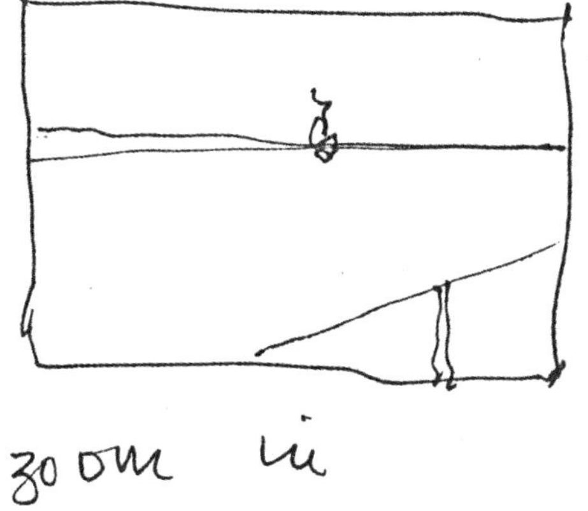

long shot

zoom in

395. 2nd pan begins.

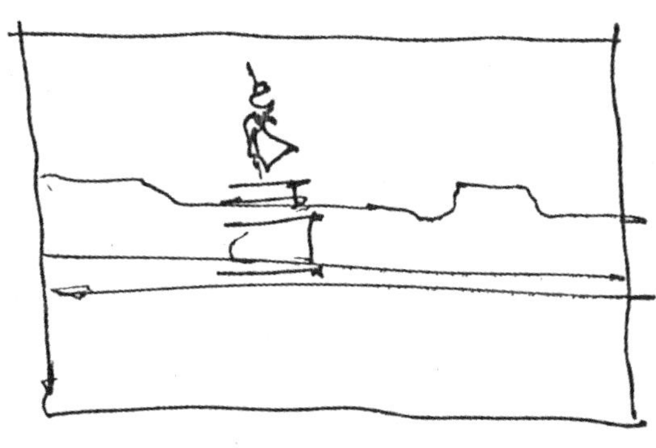

long/med shot

audio wind

participant somewhat shakey-

406 ends

406- 2nd interview

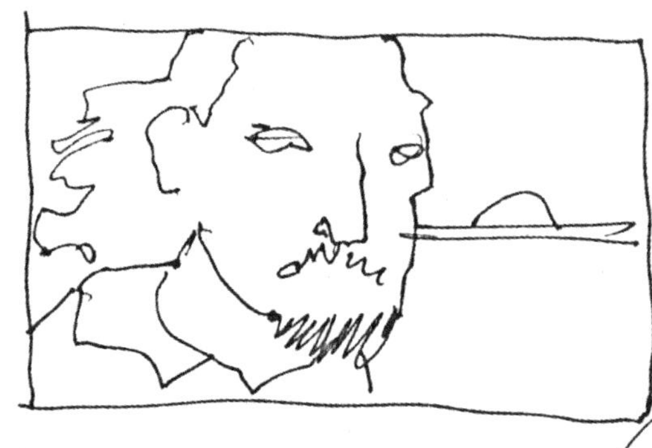

guy - young
20's -
plaid shirt -

audio not much
better - still
siloquette visual -

415 - ends -

ready - instructions

432 - starts shoot. (child)

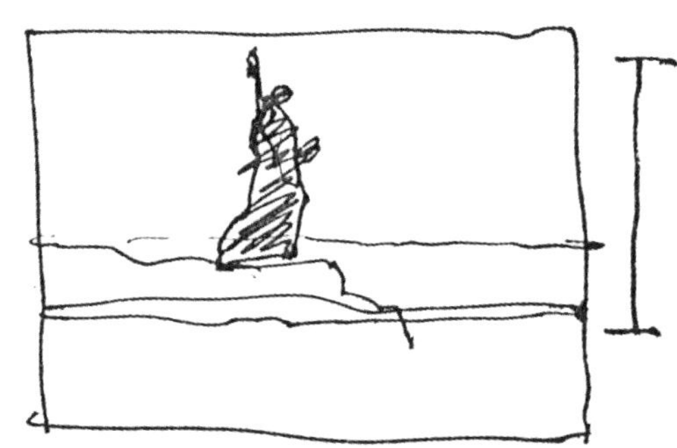

frame filled -

audio - wind

good - stable - medium shoot -

441 - ends -
- readjustment

444 - portrait

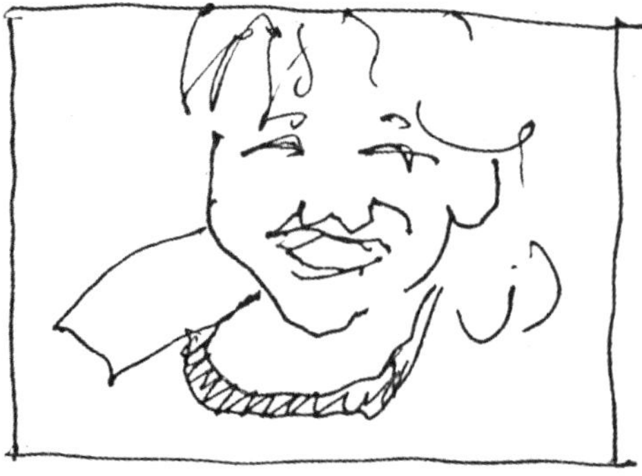

small
dark boy -

audio - still
bad -

just focusing in

453 - starts

audio better - starts interview

wind bad.

460 (1) - stops

461 - start pan.

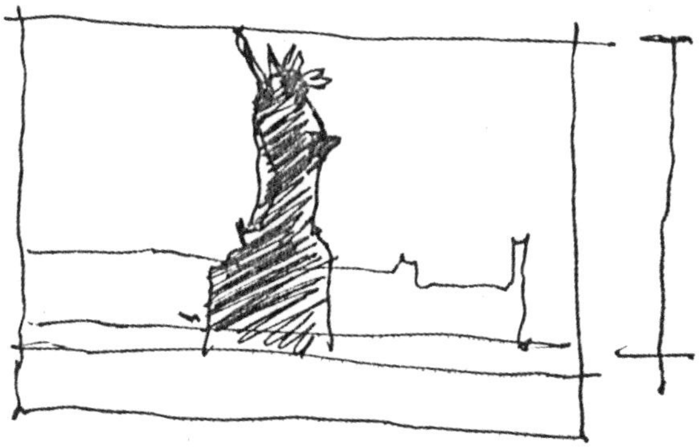

frame filled.

statue somewhat modeled on left.

work somewhat shakey
loses it @ times -
backgr. voices (good) - indistinguishable -
473 - out of frame -
back - out again -
some very tight shots @ end -

475½ over.

478 - portrait starts.

487 - really starts

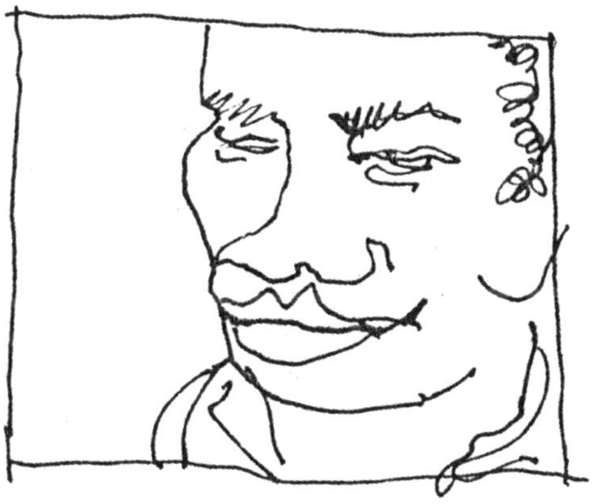

black young boy -

audio -
wind problem
speaks up
alittle ½ way
through.

499. pan starts

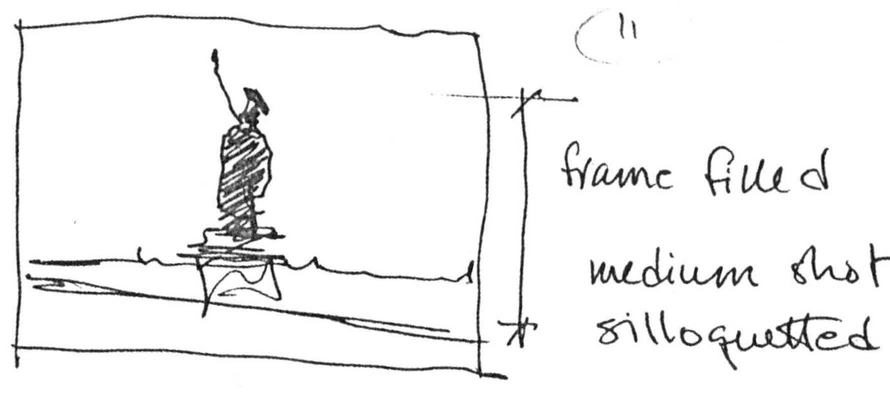

frame filled

medium shot
silloquetted

birds-
> 503
tilted

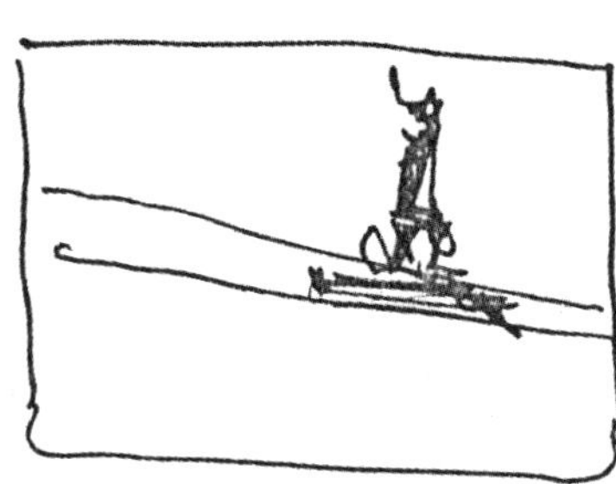

excellent
visual

audio- (should
not use talk-
dub over - say
with bird cries, etc.)

511 1/2 ends

515 + int. starts

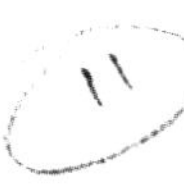

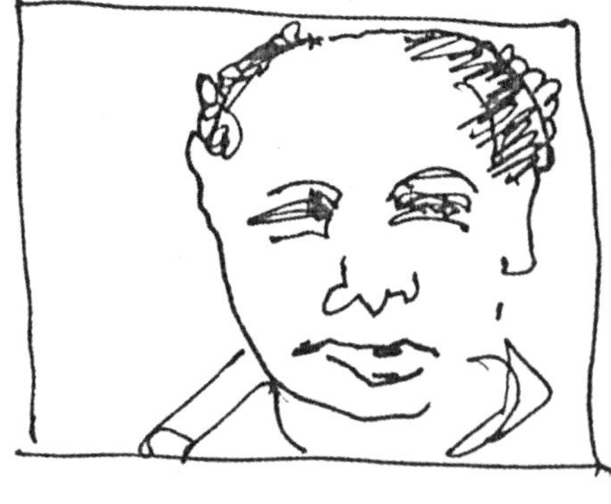

37 -
white
balding

audio
good-
but rambles talk
but audible.

> 525 - exact figures
very good

USE

533 ends

water close up begins
skyline -
z.i. on towers

539- towers as sculpture / close up

551 - settles on water -

535- z.i. to rapid speed -
slows again as pull away -
pull back further -

563- settle on skyline -
BEAUTIFUL

USE

566 pan begins -

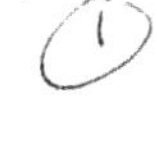

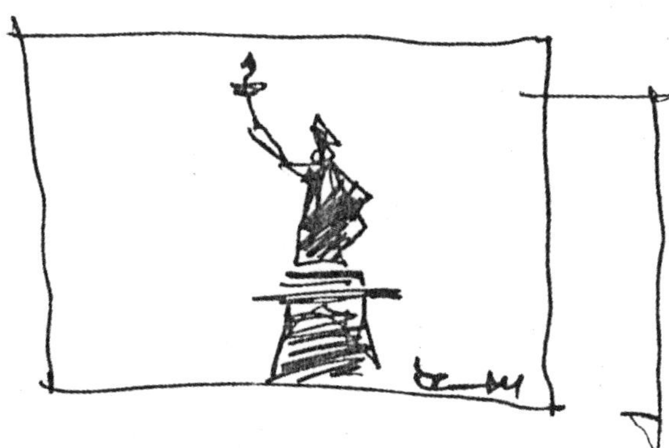

fills frame

beautiful siloquette.

607½ int. starts

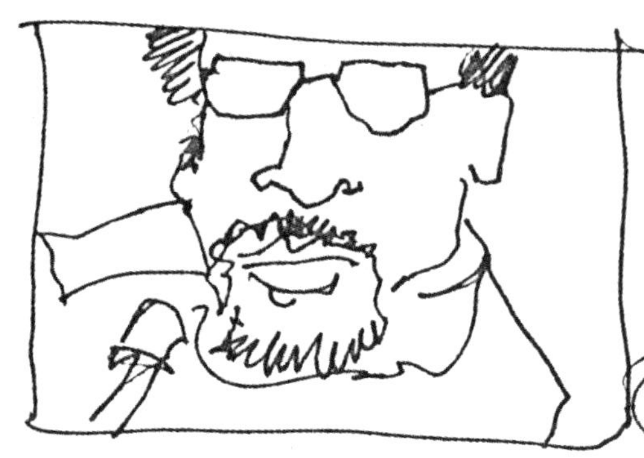

2

black musician

excellent audio + visual

USE

615 ends

start pan

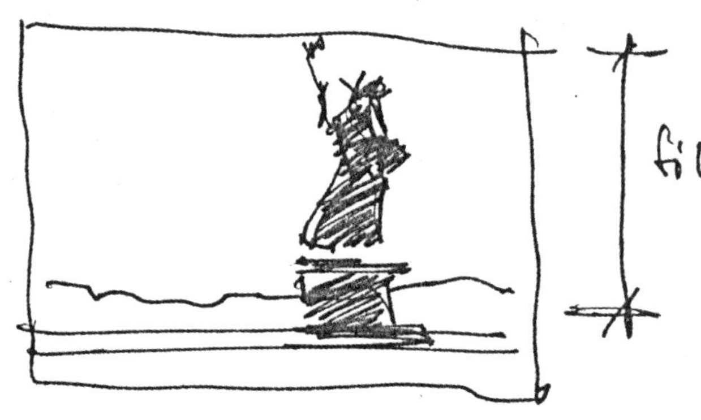

3

fills frame

statue lighter more modeled

excellent

(will have to erase video track possibly or leave in - it is dan's explanation of my piece).

627 ends

638. int. starts

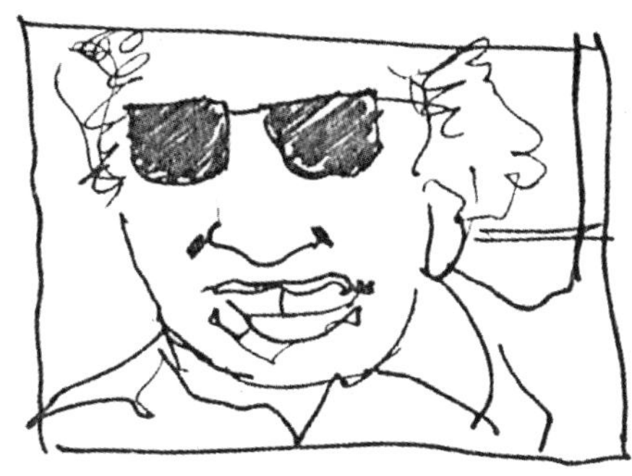

sister of charity-

good audio
visual low contrast
but could be used.

649. ends on "I'm white" — (smile)

END TAPE I .

TAPE II - LIBERTY PIECE

start with few loops. portrait of me by dan
> (really nice - maybe close on this for credit -
BEAUTIFUL SHOT)

6 - 003.

creased tape

012 stabilized

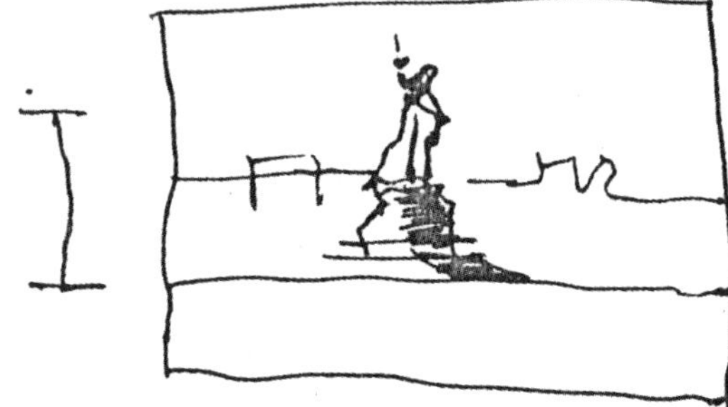

white
modeled
shadow
on right

audio -
might
habe to
dub over -
some irrelevant
talk on
professionalism
of portapak.

030 ends

047 ½ int. starts

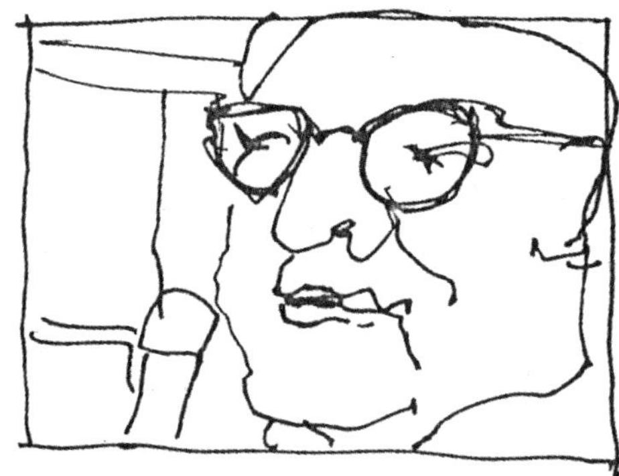

older man
in hat

excellent
audio + visual

USE

065 ends.

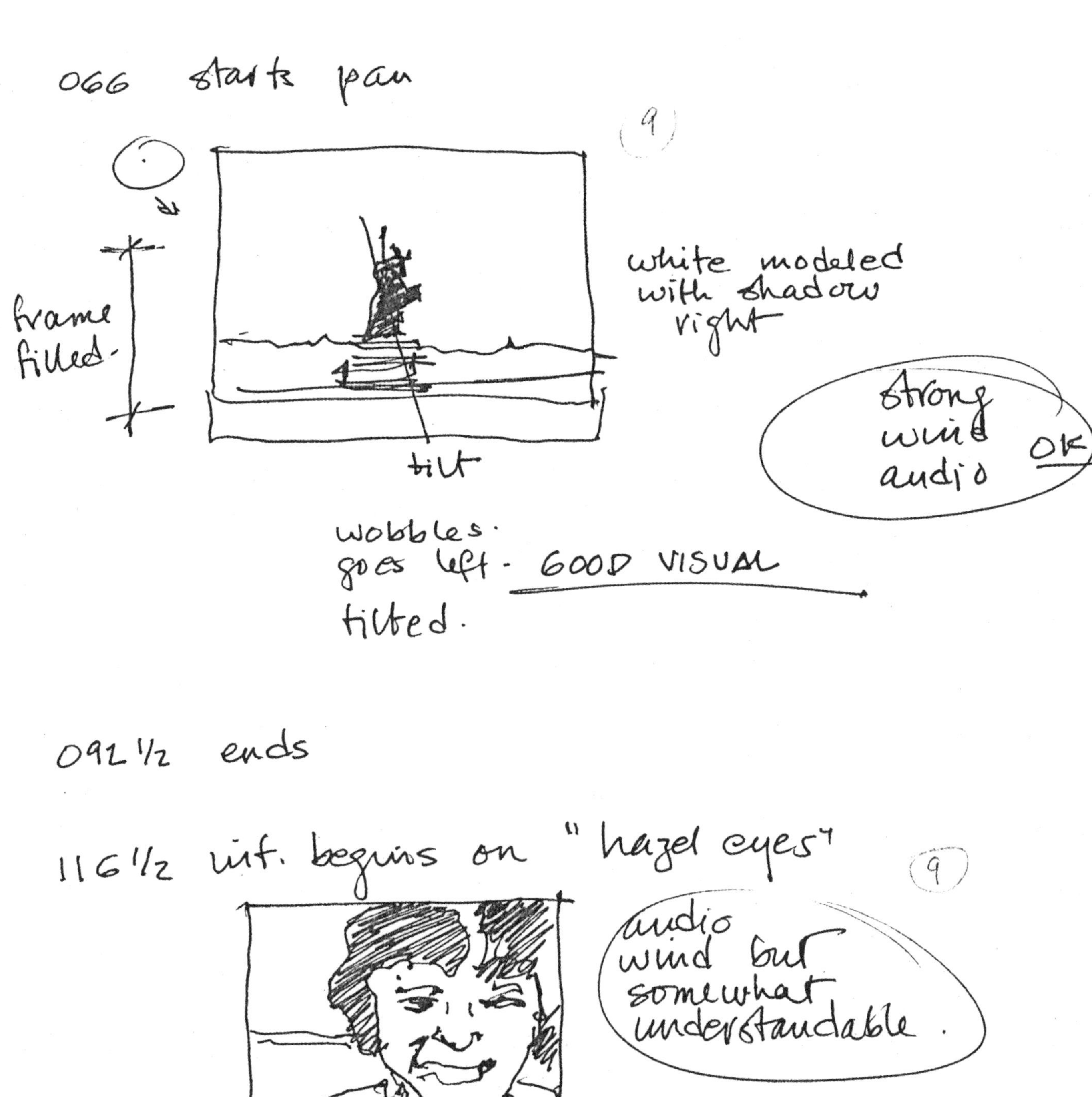

young (20's - father)
Puerto Rican -
very light / white coloring

132½ ends

218. pan starts -

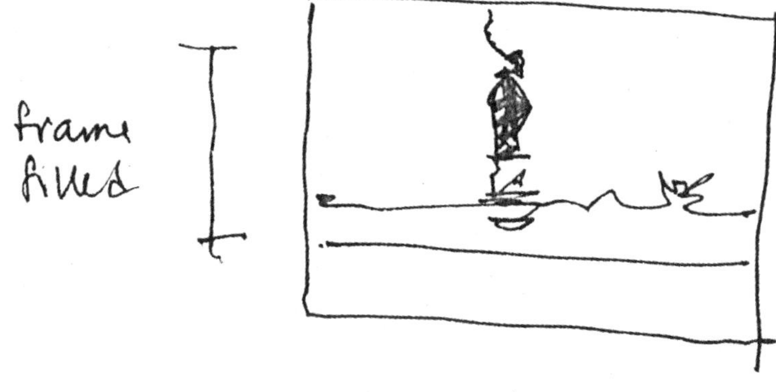

audio
wind.
usable.

siloquette.
good visual

232. EXCELLENT USE -

boat makes turn
frames statue
bird cries

EXCELLENT
audio

really beautiful

249. end

258 - inter. begins

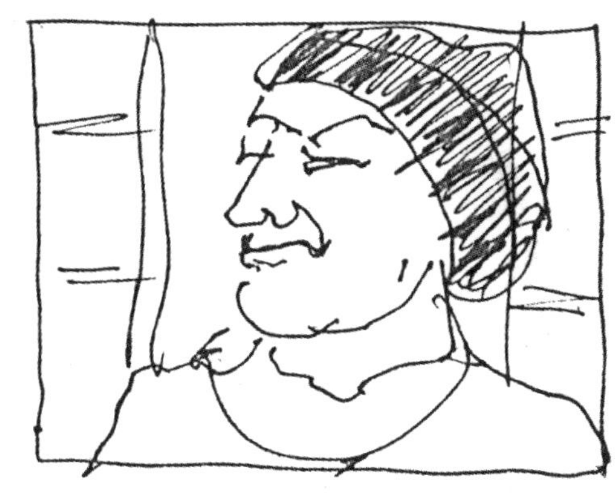

French 22 yr. old
woman - in hat
very nice.

good audio

USE

end approx
277 - "European - is that a race?"

284 - general pan to statue -
291 - zoom out - mostly water - *
(seems good end -
all siloquetted)
300 - ends
readjustment

313 on statue (audio talk w. dan - erase)
318 - huge jump due to wind -
326 - water - jumpy - quiet waves -
nice - wind really pushing it.
335 - ferry
zoom out quickly.
339 - ferry - skyline - people in ferry
`thg - nice visual

349. z.i. to towers + bldg's
skyline

pan left-
focus-
panning out to edge + water
crease in tape

<u>not really good</u>

363 - battery pk / water's edge -

367 - z. out to city - nice

(167)
<u>369½</u> pan start

frame filled

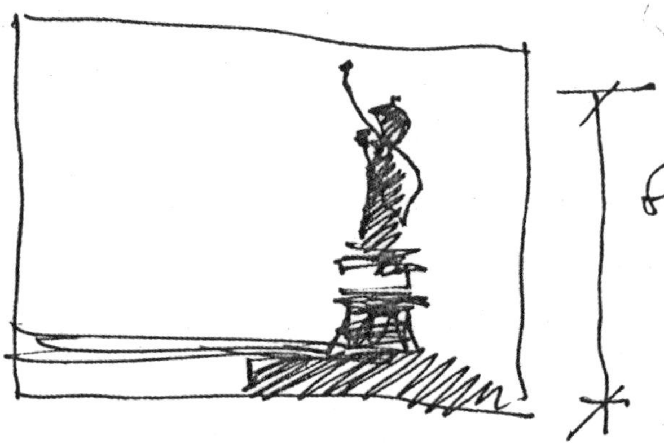

audio
wind -
good

<u>nice siloquette.</u>

jumping from wind
but very good

clouds - beautiful
(later in day)

391 - audio "it's getting closer + closer"
(include?)

393 - ends

400 int. starts

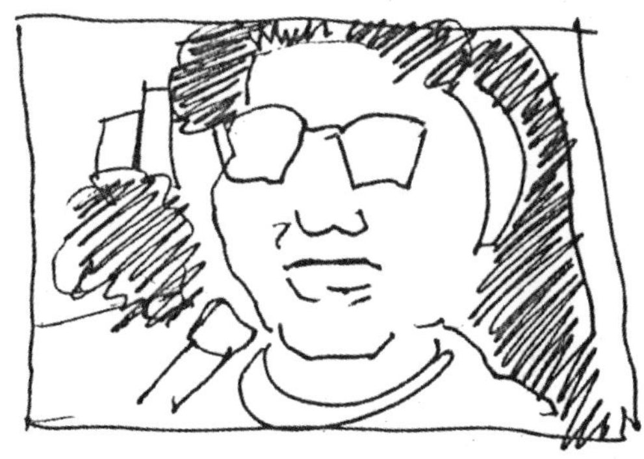

8

nun
35 mi habit
very good

USE

403 ends

404 pan starts

5

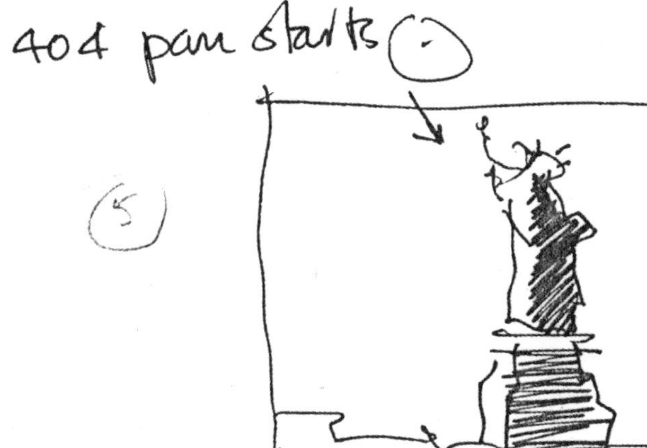

full frame

EXCELLENT
visual

close-
somewhat
modeled

jump'g abit

backgr.
noises
but
OK.
maybe

424- end

→ maybe
better to
dub over-
w. bird + wind
noise.

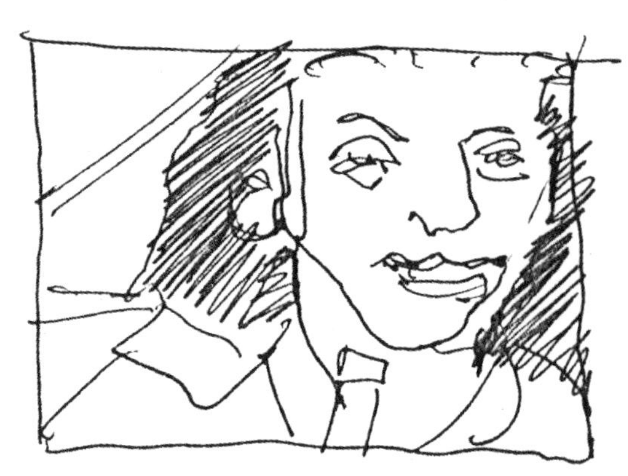

6

18 -
brown hair
girlfriend -

ends "german - irish - that's my race?"

464½ . ends .

mt. w. guy again (but use 1st one - its better) — audio better on 1st .

464½ -
470

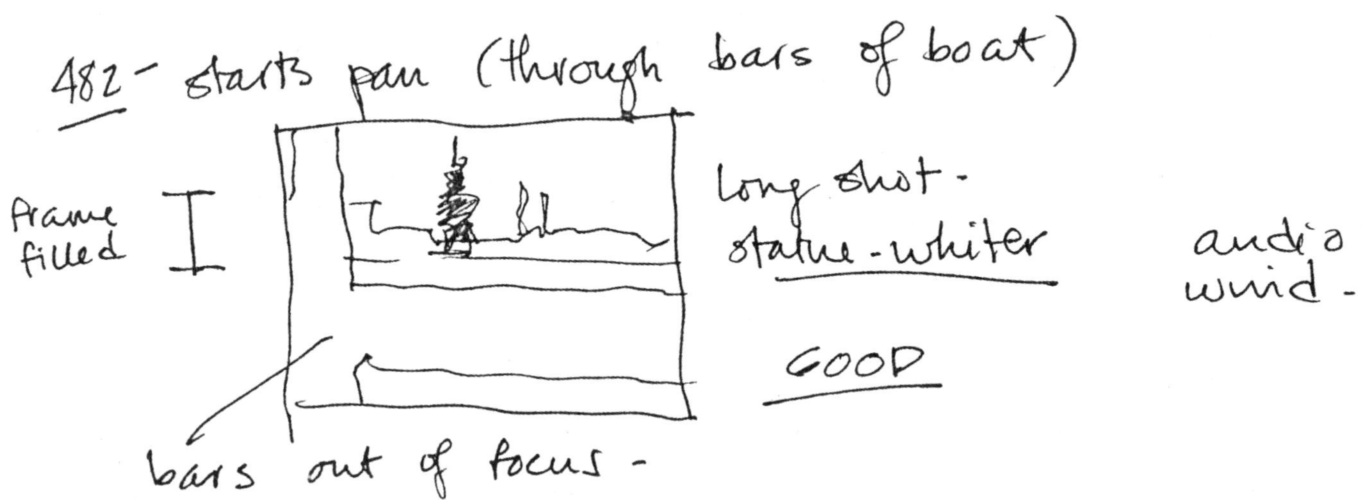

491 - erase audio -
his "beautiful
day"

495 . ends .

506. int. starts

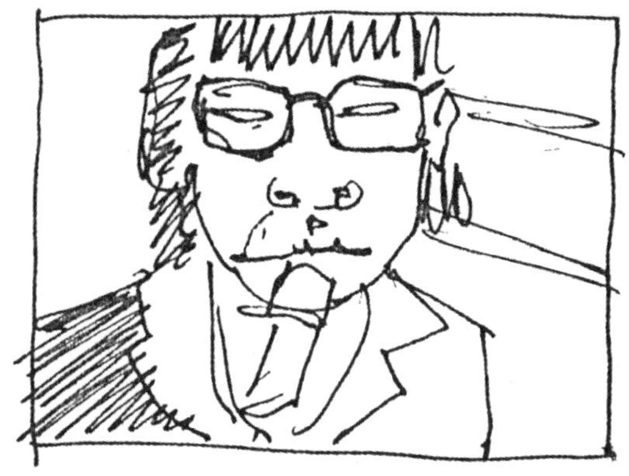

9 yr. old
chinese boy.

517 1/2 ends.
but perhaps end it
on I'm chinese. . . .
cut out likes models etc.
(513+)

518- pan starts.

(10)

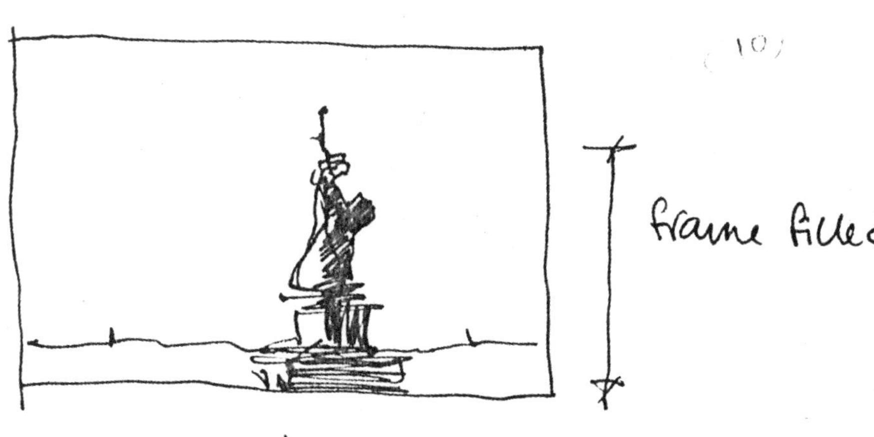

frame filled

audio
wind.

good visually
modeled.
light
windy- jumpy but holding
rapid jump back + frow
hold'g.

532 - ends

535 - int. begins

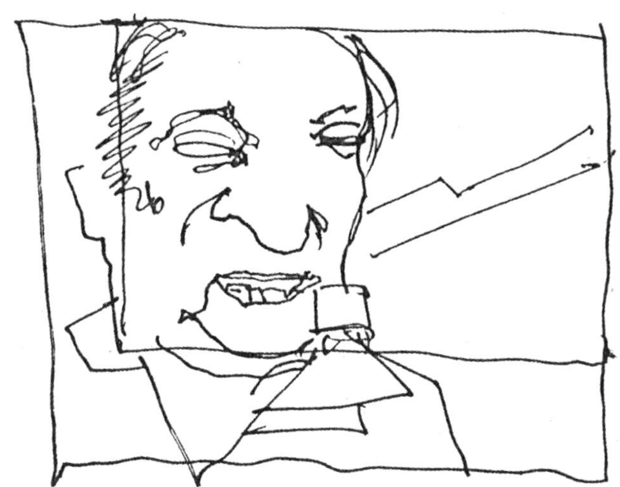

10

older man -
Italian -
Amer.

audio -
windy -
hard to
hear at @ times
but usable -

Italian - American

543 - end on "before 2 What's the object?"

GOOD all around USE.

(45½ +)
547 - pan begins

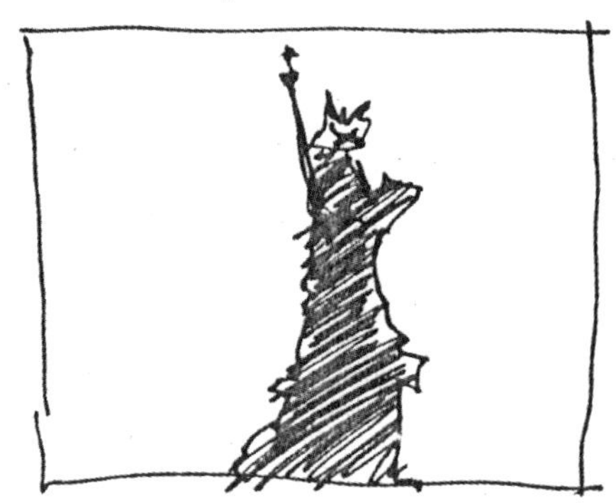

(7)

BEAUTIFUL

tight siloquette

audio
wind

EXCELLENT

loses - up again -
loses - up again -
good - windy
to + fro - but good

568 - ends

573½

begins w. "I'm 5'9- "

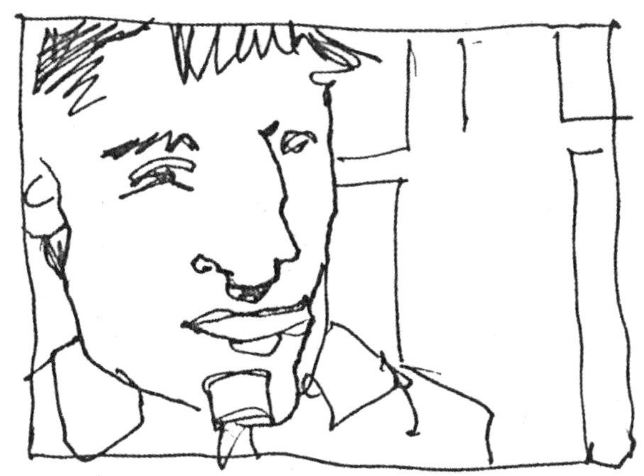

21 young guy- thin face-

audio windy but OK

GOOD use

578 ends

586½ pan begins

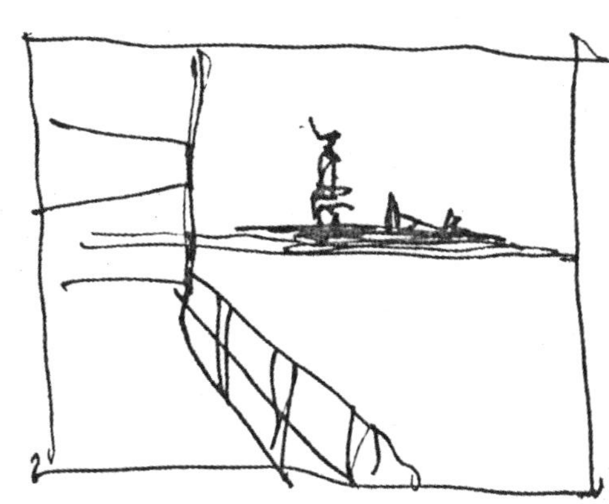

long shot very nice-

audio wind- good

some boat visible-

birds come in-

609 behind boat - not visible

613 comes up again framed by boat - good (use all)

615 ends.

620+ int. begins

"OK. I'm 23

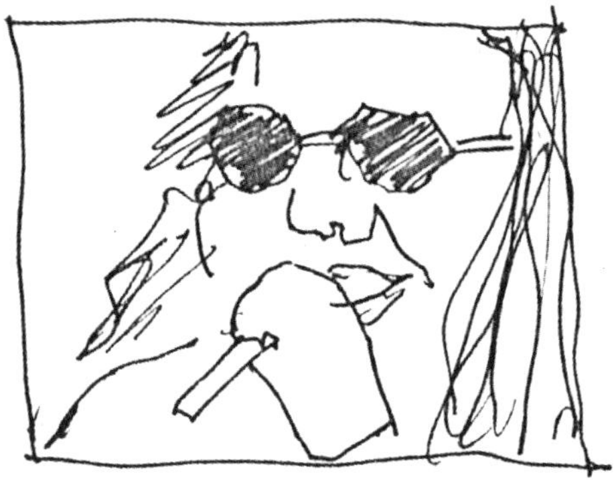

heavier
blond - 23

good
audio

GOOD use

624 - ends

pan begins

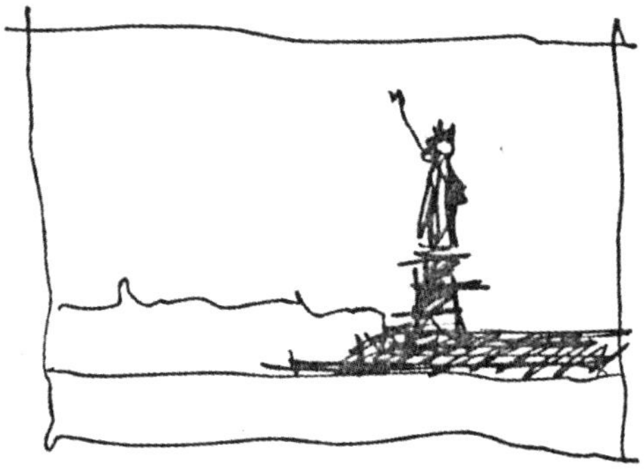

siloquetted

627. zoom out -

630 - z.o. way out.
just line on horizon -

634 - z.i.s in on statue
focus -
jumpy - not as good as other
midway through.

641 - ends

END OF REEL II.

CONCERNS (THAT TAKE ON / DEAL WITH) VIDEO FORMAT

: ADDENDUM
RE: SCRIPTING

AS IN:

NOTES: FOR A VIDEO SHOOT
: (CABLE COLLABORATION)

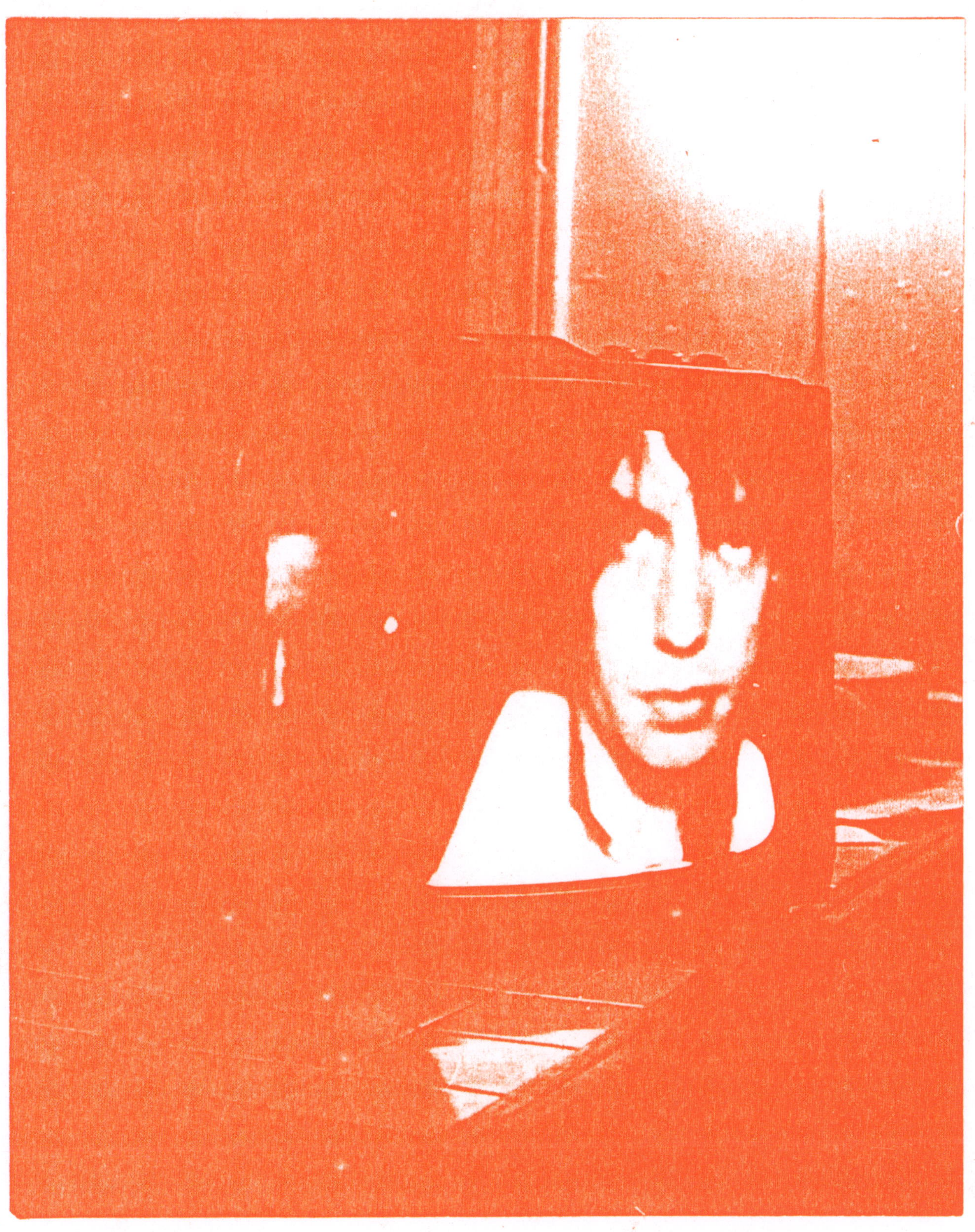

NOTES: FOR A VIDEO SHOOT
(CABLE COLLABORATION)
WITH PETER ZUMO / STEPHANIE WOODARD

NOTE: GO WITH 3400 SONY CAMERAS - PORTAPAK
WILL TRY RUN THROUGH "HAND HELD" WIRED INTO STUDIO SYSTEM. CONSOLE
BRACE FOR STATIONARY SHOTS

(A)

1. trombone in tight / kept close to body
face - hand movement — direct cut from black into ECU / → ZO loose CU

subtle sound variations (with plunger) — mike up close - on boom to catch subtleties.
2½ min

2. motion expansion
2½ min

⇨ need also establishing shot related to "stage" motion setting - z.o. to cover - but kept framing tight - side shots front shots

// CUT

3. start up with paddle
tight movements (as in 1.)
kept close to body → z.in start CU on paddle (define "new instrument")

3b. expansion of movements
(paralleling 2.)

⇨ zoom out to cover as needed

hand movements become less inter-
related - more for the sake
of motion

ROTATE about him
side shots

zi on ECU
then breathe

end up on ECU - mouth of trombone / paddle. HOLD /CUT.

// CUT //

// BLACK - //

segment with Stephanie in frame -
but kept upstage

⇨ DIRECT CUT into a medium-long shot.

her movements are relatively slow
Peter continues playing downstage

o - Stephanie
both in frame
x - peter
→ 2 pools of light to accent

ADDITIONS

(B)

> start very tight (ECU)
trombone front / plunger only.

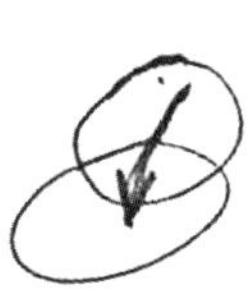

pull back as
motion starts
out from front

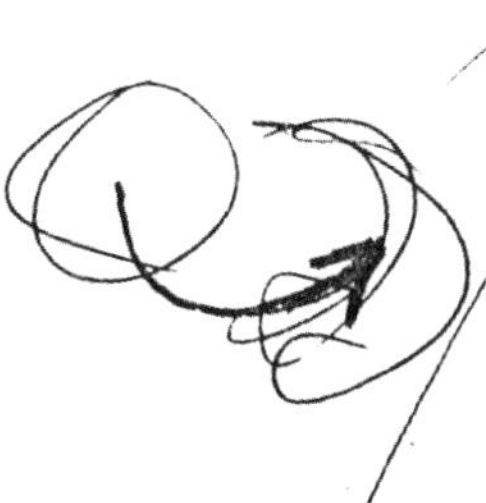

NOTE:
will
require
some hi-gain
microphone
work

motion will expand out / out

|| CUT

> open on paddle — further out than opening segment

> after motion increase -
paddle will take on all axis - 3.0. be PREPARED
to cover - can come in
tight occassionally
for the CU.

in 3.D.

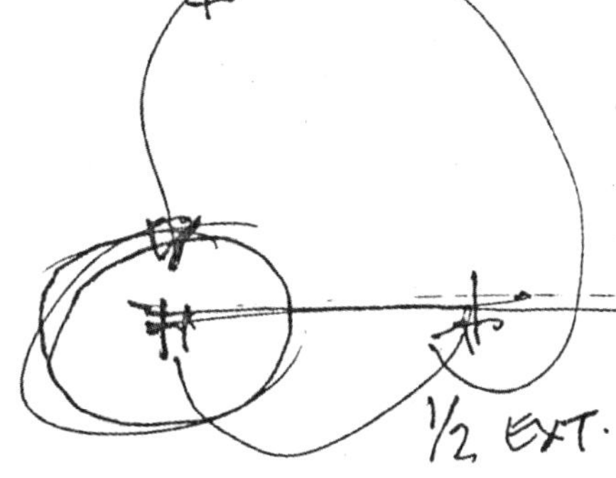

total arm
extension

2 1/2 min
(maybe 1st
take will be
longer)

NOTE:
paddle - in tight
reveals good reflection
on trombone - dot pattern
go in on it

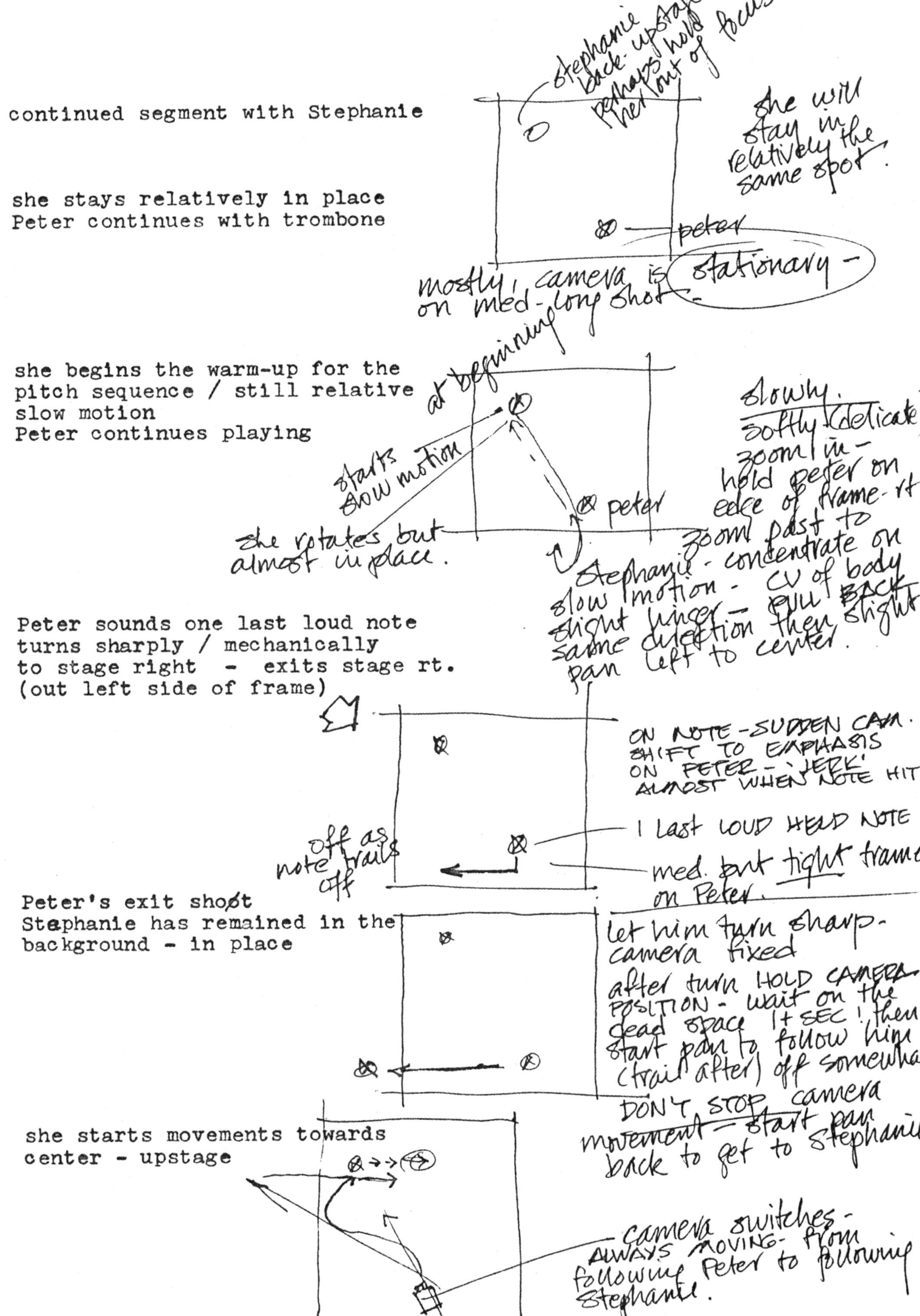

continued segment with Stephanie

she stays relatively in place
Peter continues with trombone

she begins the warm-up for the
pitch sequence / still relative
slow motion
Peter continues playing

Peter sounds one last loud note
turns sharply / mechanically
to stage right - exits stage rt.
(out left side of frame)

Peter's exit shoot
Stephanie has remained in the
background - in place

she starts movements towards
center - upstage

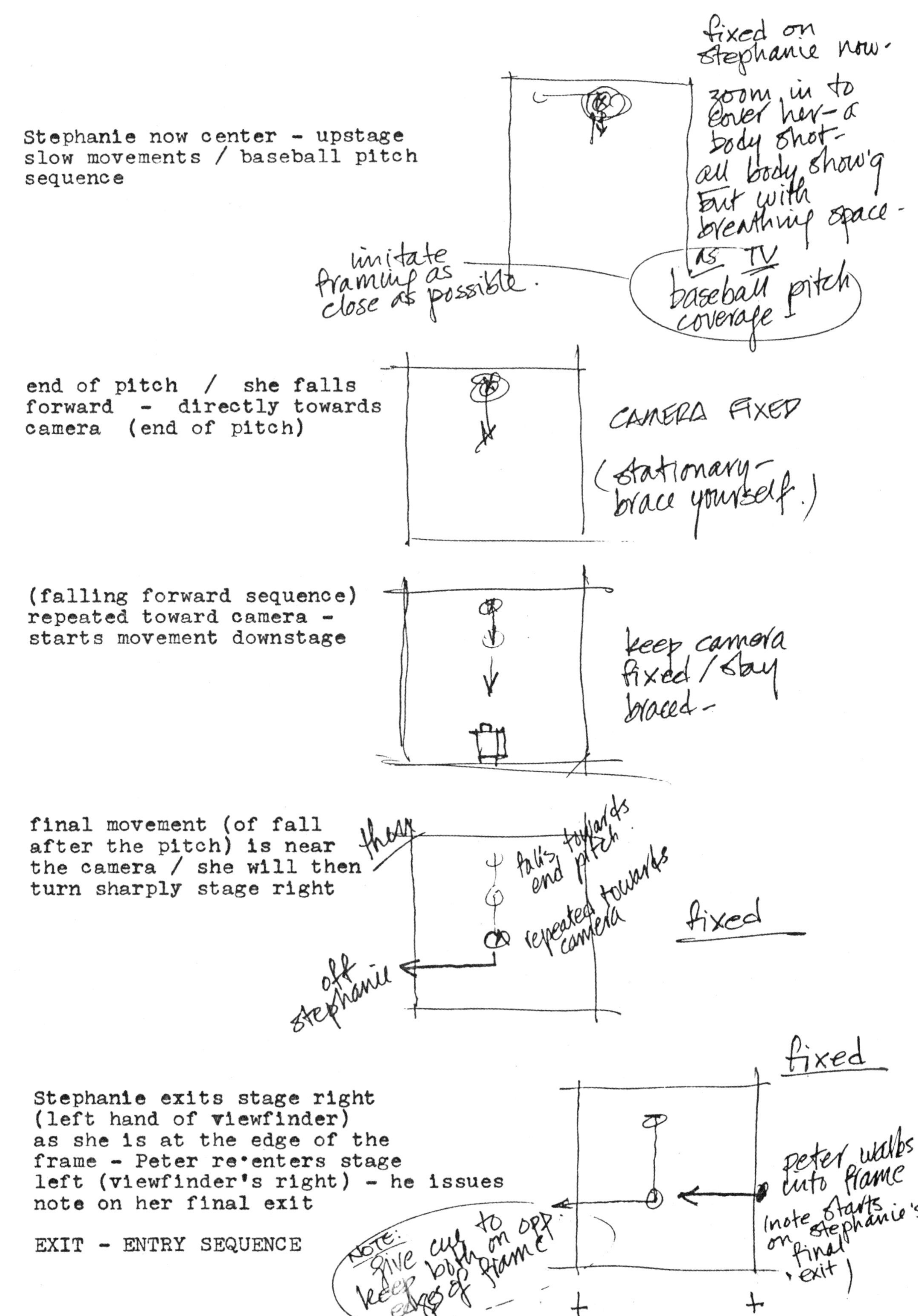

Stephanie now center - upstage
slow movements / baseball pitch
sequence

end of pitch / she falls
forward - directly towards
camera (end of pitch)

(falling forward sequence)
repeated toward camera -
starts movement downstage

final movement (of fall
after the pitch) is near
the camera / she will then
turn sharply stage right

Stephanie exits stage right
(left hand of viewfinder)
as she is at the edge of the
frame - Peter re-enters stage
left (viewfinder's right) - he issues
note on her final exit

EXIT - ENTRY SEQUENCE

STATIONARY

Peter's first note (edge of frame / right) is his ANNOUNCEMENT NOTE ....

sharp pivot 90° stage rt.
walks to center of the stage (set)

faces front (towards camera) directionality

walks into center on second note

announcem't — announcement notes

front directional

PIVOTS

HOLD FIXED CAMERA

(cue him) frame so just 1/2 trombone showing.

movement towards camera on notes / then backwards - then forward into camera again repeated (2 phrases after coming into frame)

back & forth

2 phrases after coming full into frame

NOTE:

(1) camera pulls back - fast - move camera as far downstage as possible in set give him plenty of breathing rm. for movements.

(2) camera will subtlely movements - but opposed ↑↑

ie — move with camera forward towards him as he moves to camera - CREATING ↑↑ APPROACH SHOT - @ these points, subtle Z.I. tight.

AS HE PULLS BACK - CAMERA PHYSICALLY BACK AND Z.O. SLIGHTLY. REPEAT.

final forward - trombone in tight
ends up on high sea-gull like note

end up on high sea-gull note

ON SEA-GULL NOTE
SHARP (QUICK) SUDDEN Z.I. TIGHT on trombone - come in from under - distort perspective - look'g up @ trombone - some face showing - EXAGGERATED - completely takes over frame / make it POWERFUL shot to match note. HOLD / linger - 1++ SEC. after note starts fade, in camera dissolve when tight

fade out

CUT TO BLACK / in camera dissolve - then run black trailer -

RE: CONCERNS (THAT TAKE ON / DEAL WITH)
INTER•PROCESS(ES)
INTER'PLAY(S)

IE: RELATIONSHIP PERSPECTIVES :
PERSPECTIVE RELATIONSHIPS

AMERICA: LAND OF CONTRASTS
(A DAY OF AWAKENING)
(A SHOT IN THE DARK)

LESSON PLANS TO KEEP THE REVOLUTION ALIVE
NEW INFORMATION NEEDS NEW STRUCTURE

(3) THREE WORKS IN PROGRESS

IE: WORK(ING) NOTES

RELATIONSHIP PERSPECTIVES : PERSPECTIVE RELATIONSHIPS
AND
AMERICA: LAND OF CONTRASTS
(A DAY OF AWAKENING)
(A SHOT IN THE DARK)

(2) TWO CONCURRENT WORKS IN PROGRESS

1976-1977

RELATIONSHIP PERSPECTIVES : PERSPECTIVE RELATIONSHIPS

Relationship
Perspectives

PERSPECTIVE
RELATIONSHIPS

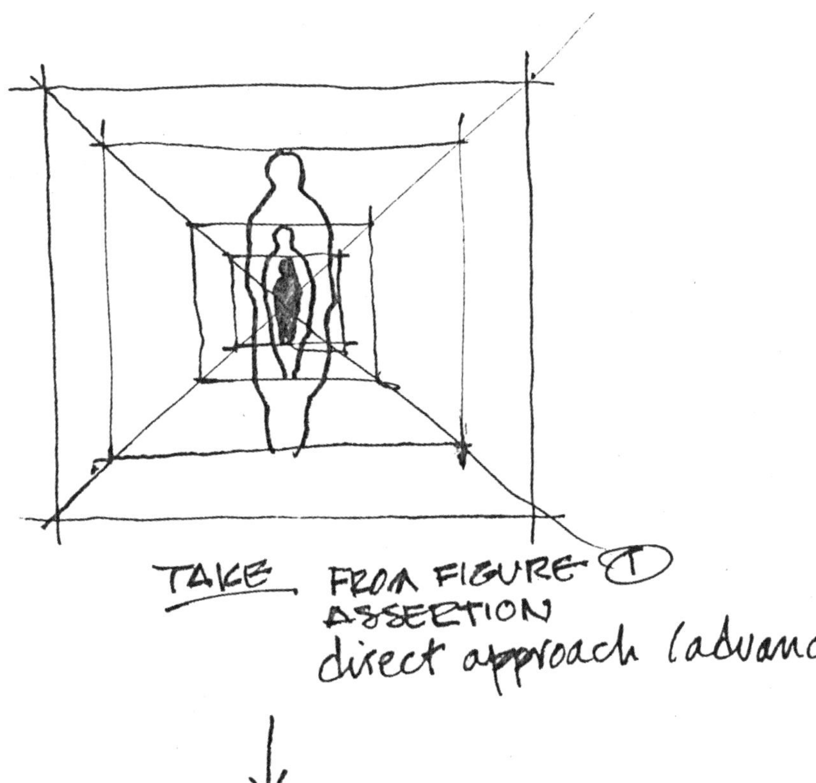

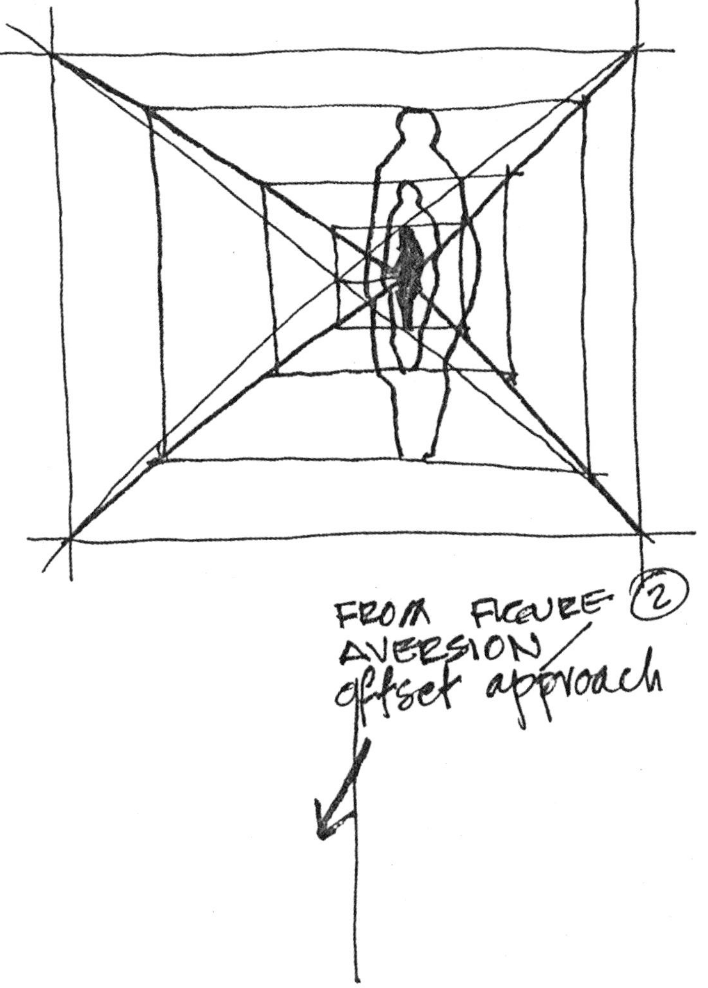
FROM FIGURE ②
AVERSION / offset approach

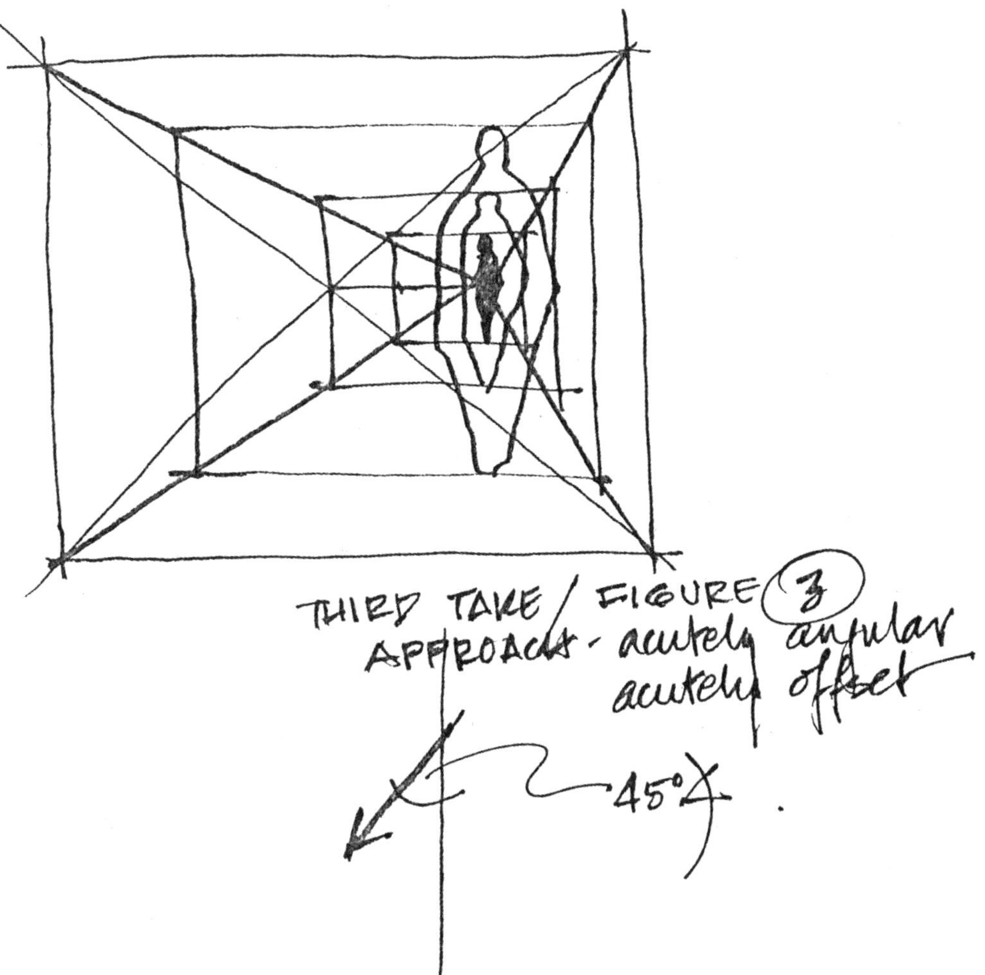
THIRD TAKE / FIGURE 3
APPROACH - acutely angular
acutely offset
45°

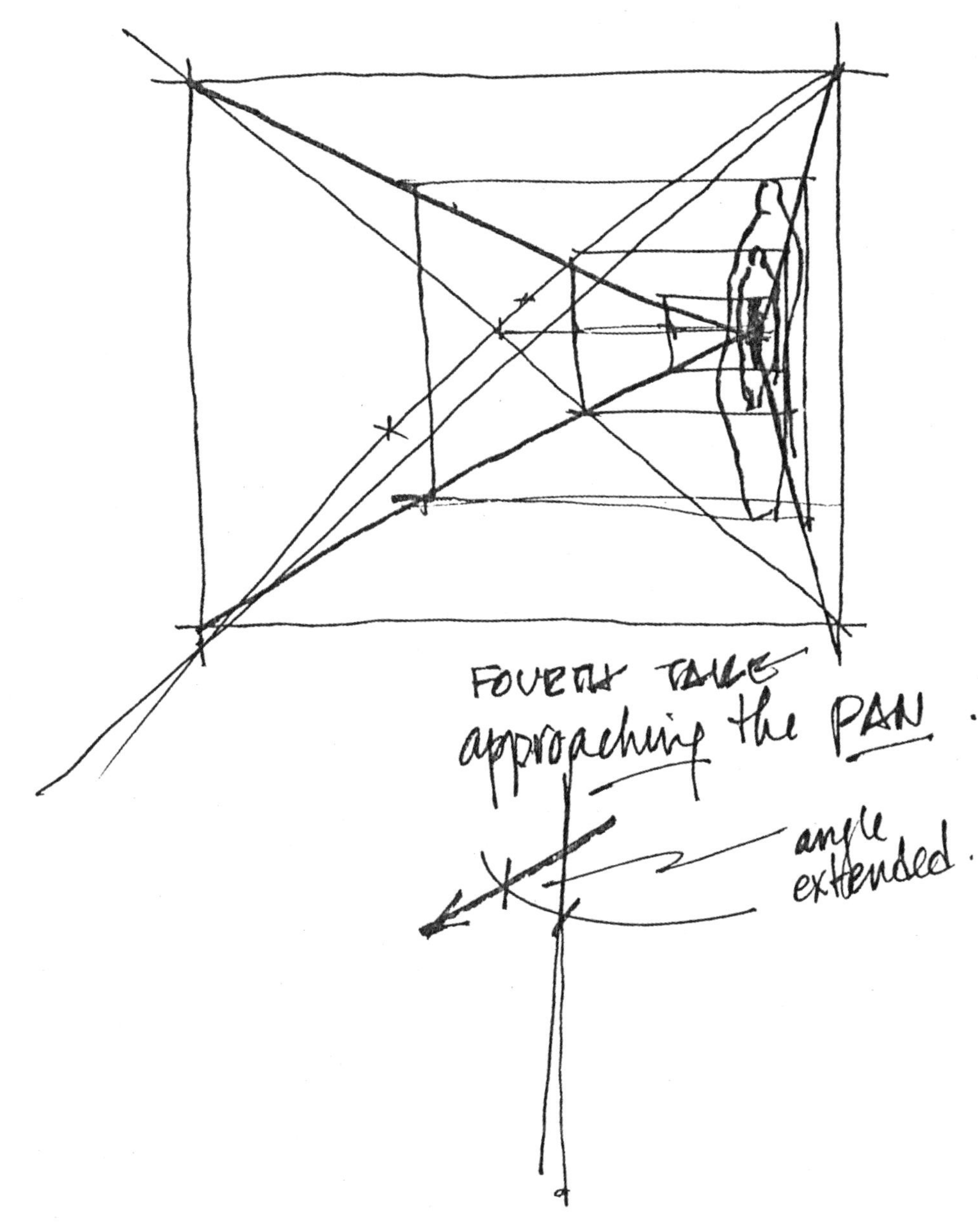
FOURTH TAKE
approaching the PAN.
angle extended.

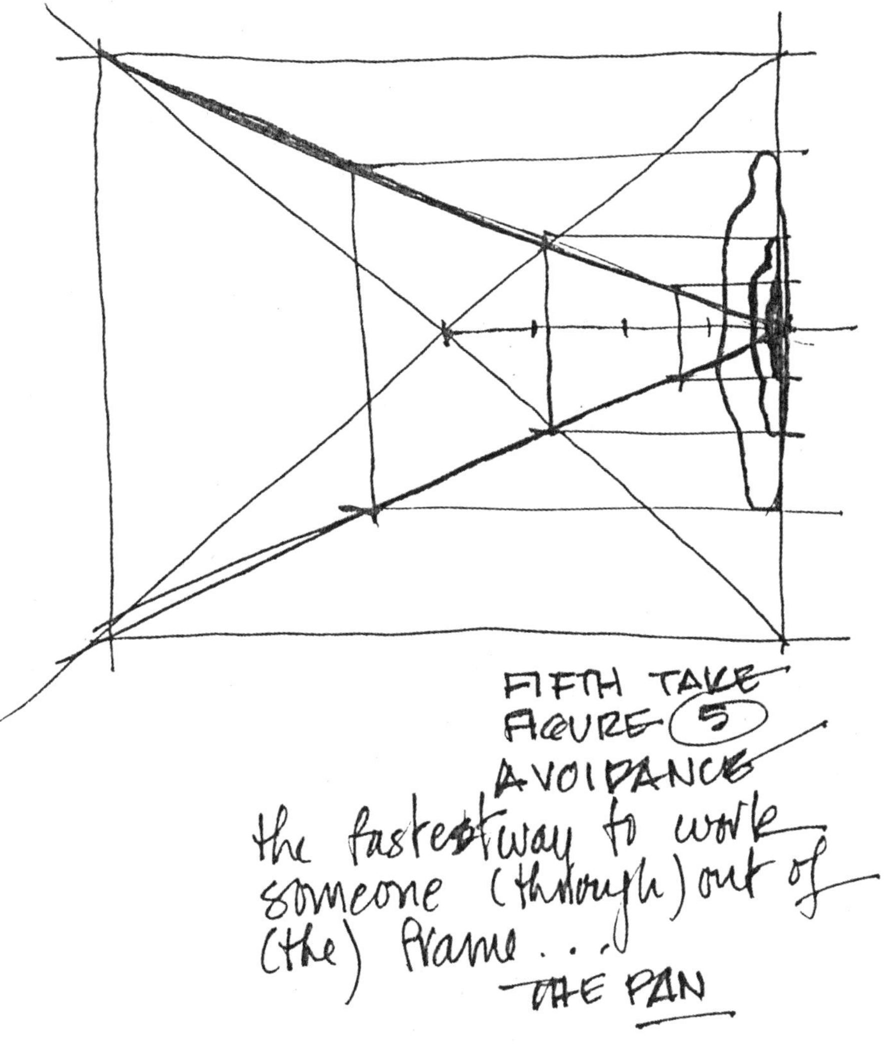
FIFTH TAKE
FIGURE 5
AVOIDANCE
the fastest way to work
someone (through) out of
(the) frame . . .
THE PAN

pan

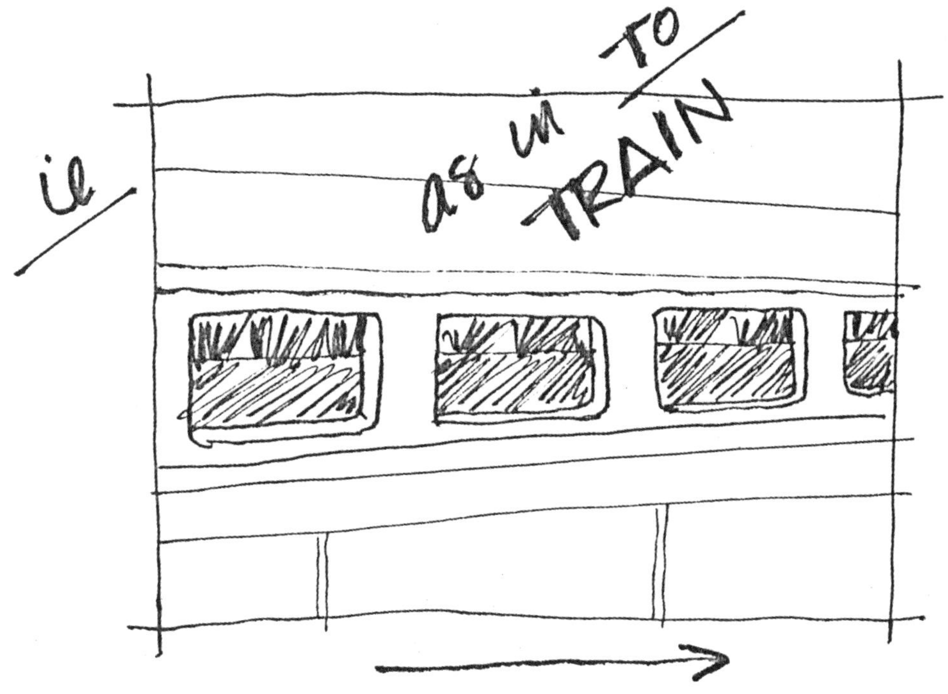
ie
as in
TO
TRAIN

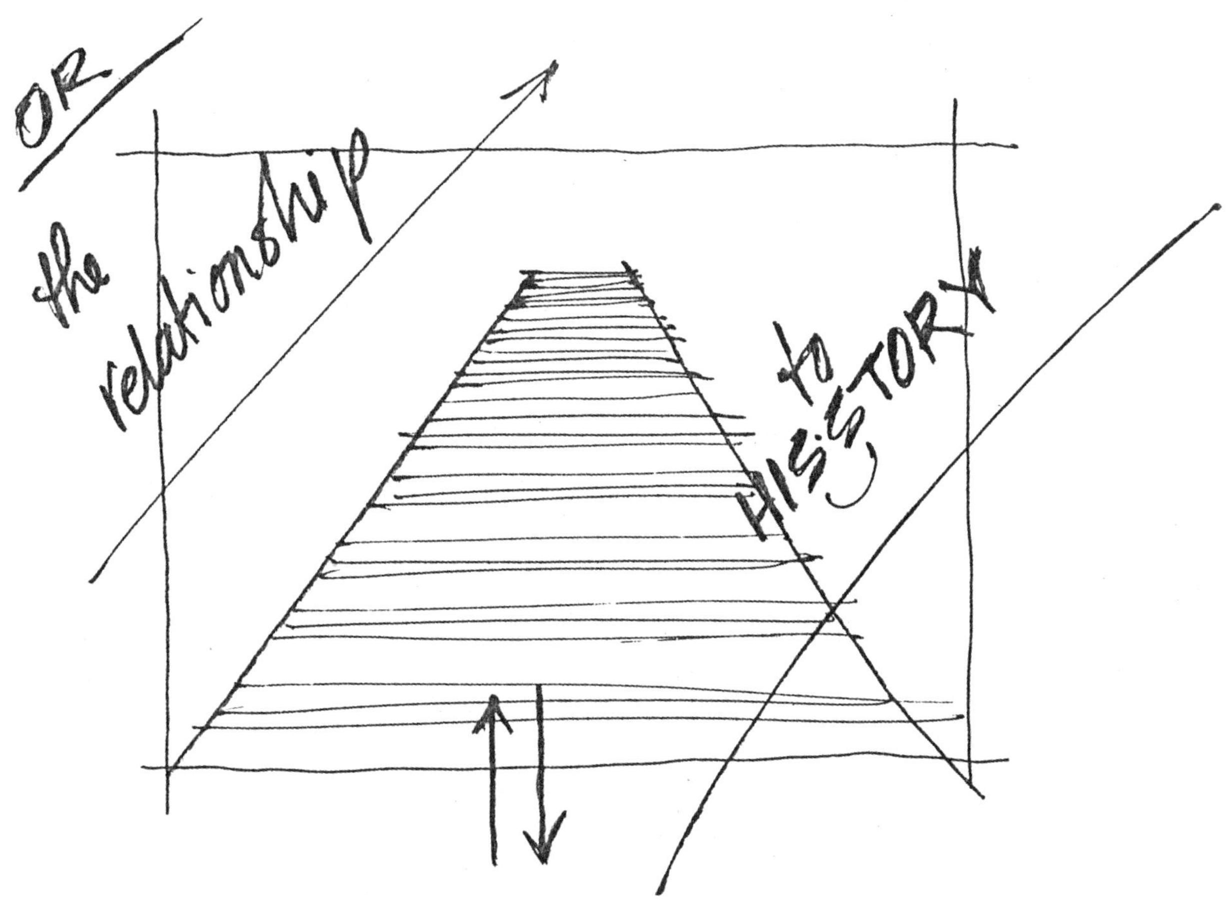
OR
the relationship
to HISSTORY

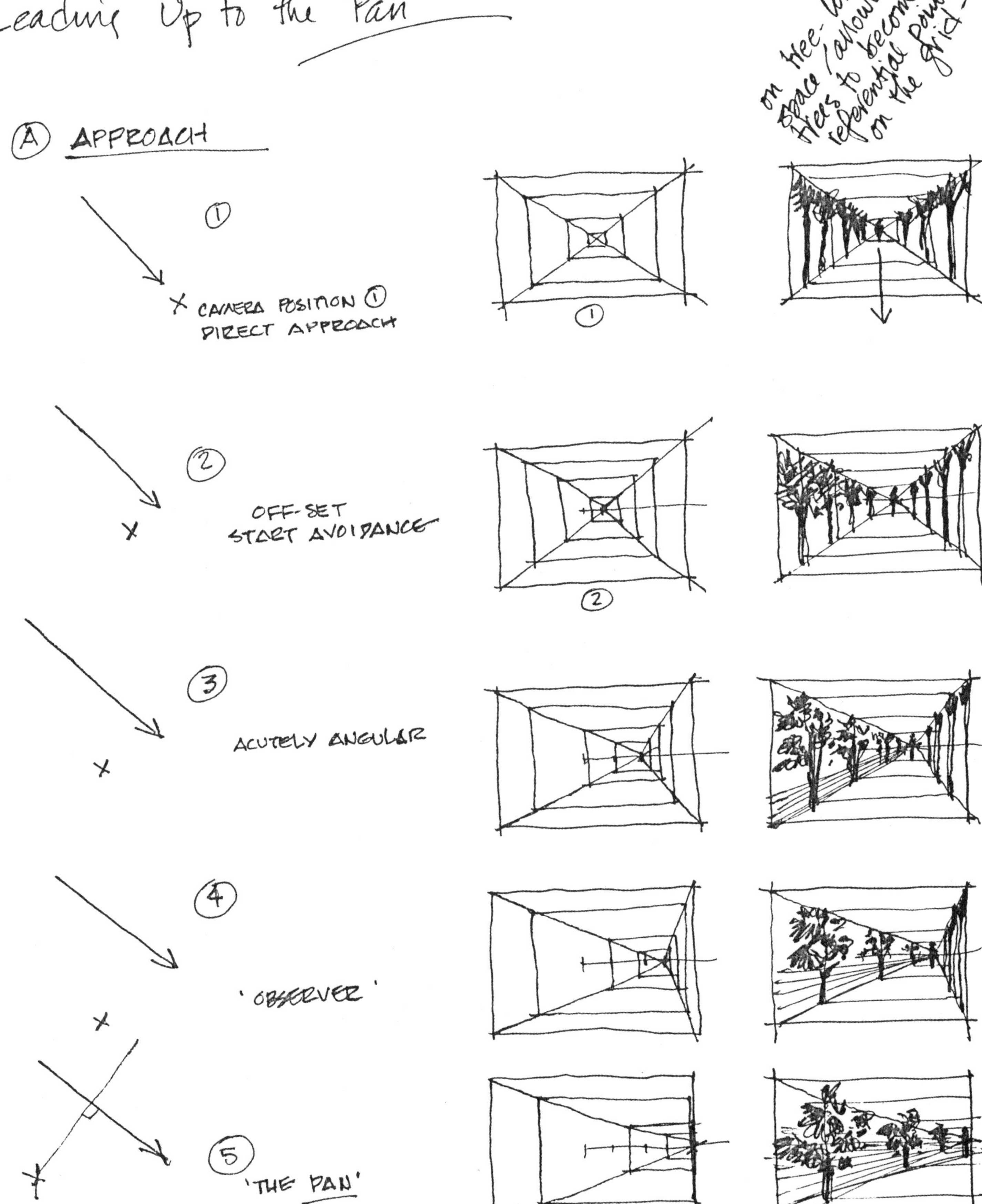

Leading Up to the Pan
A APPROACH
on tree-lined space / allowing trees to become referential points on the grid
1
CAMERA POSITION 1
DIRECT APPROACH
1
2
OFF-SET
START AVOIDANCE
2
3
ACUTELY ANGULAR
4
'OBSERVER'
5
'THE PAN'

Relationship Perspectives: Perspective Relationships

leading out of
the 2D into 3D -
(two dimensionality
into "realized" state).

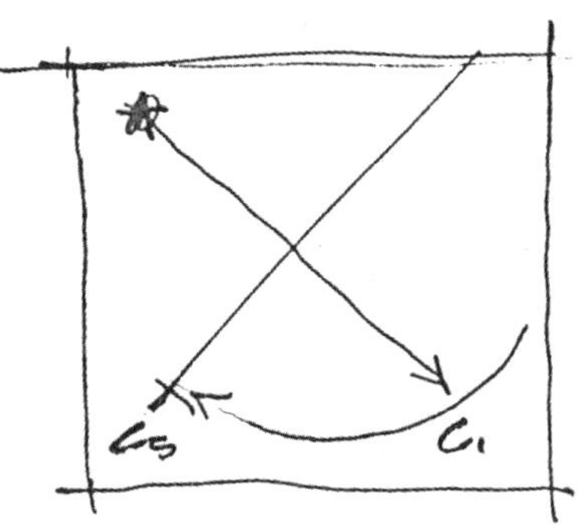

series:
leading up to the
full - pan.

starting with
ICONIC FIGURE
(figure ground) -
push into a
three-dimensionality.

(what theater/stage
accomplishes - a 3 dimensionality
"framed" - we are still the
"voyeurs" / lead up to
life description)

we go from 'ROBBE-GRILLET'
film / to stage film ie
STREETCAR NAMED DESIRE or
DEYER

think about

moving in (ie: as on a situation relationship) → loosing perspective
loosing ground.

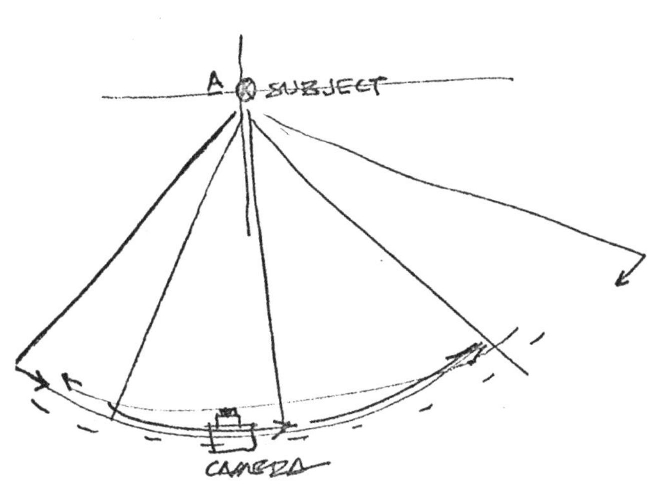

S

esp. true when subject is reduced to flat screen (as in film)

subject becomes 2-D (mass media attempt reduces subject to image to flat screen).

the perspective of (on that person) changes - it is reduced further - the distortion becomes greater - so, esp. close-up we can relate to less + less of an area - (must remain 1st within 180° to relate to flatness + then to a further reduction to keep distortion within range of allowing subject to keep a 'reality base'.)

a girl moves toward the camera -
her walk / head down / a support UNICEF motif
her movements are slow, dejected, but firm -

'til she notices the camera /
raises her head / faces it directly +
abruptly stops

this movement will repeat / being reinserted /
its perspective changing / until it becomes a 'cut' -

it cuts our plane of vision / across our field of vision -
instead of moving towards (to join) / it starts moving
'out of frame' / detaches itself / starts a movement away -

the dialogue will be attempting at a intimacy to
the relationship. the greater the attempt - the more
the viewing ∡ becomes rejecting. the closer the 'psychology'
attempts to come / the more the physical ∡ is cut -

at the beginning

the movement is slower
moving into the camera

towards a closure

the movement is hastened
(this will happen automatically -
even if the movement itself is
kept constant - due to a "panning"
effect of the camera).

there is a change of perspective (renaissance) to

(1 pt. - a horizon line
flattened, the loss of a perspective)

this should ↑↑ a change
of perspective in (towards)
the dialogue (relationship) developing -
the dialetic.

opening up
coming in on / to

multi-directional
(asymmetrical)

closing off
a wipe /

ea pt. →
a new perspective

a flattening out
limited perspect
becomes
symmetrical
there is a
repetition of
info. started –
the 'yield'
becomes halved
yield → 1/2'd.

mirror-image starts
(closing out of 'other' /
begins reflectiveness of 'self')

size change
in movement
towards
speed so slowed → 'constant'

size remains constant
movement is relatively hastened
but still 'k' (constant) = fast relative
to perspective slow.

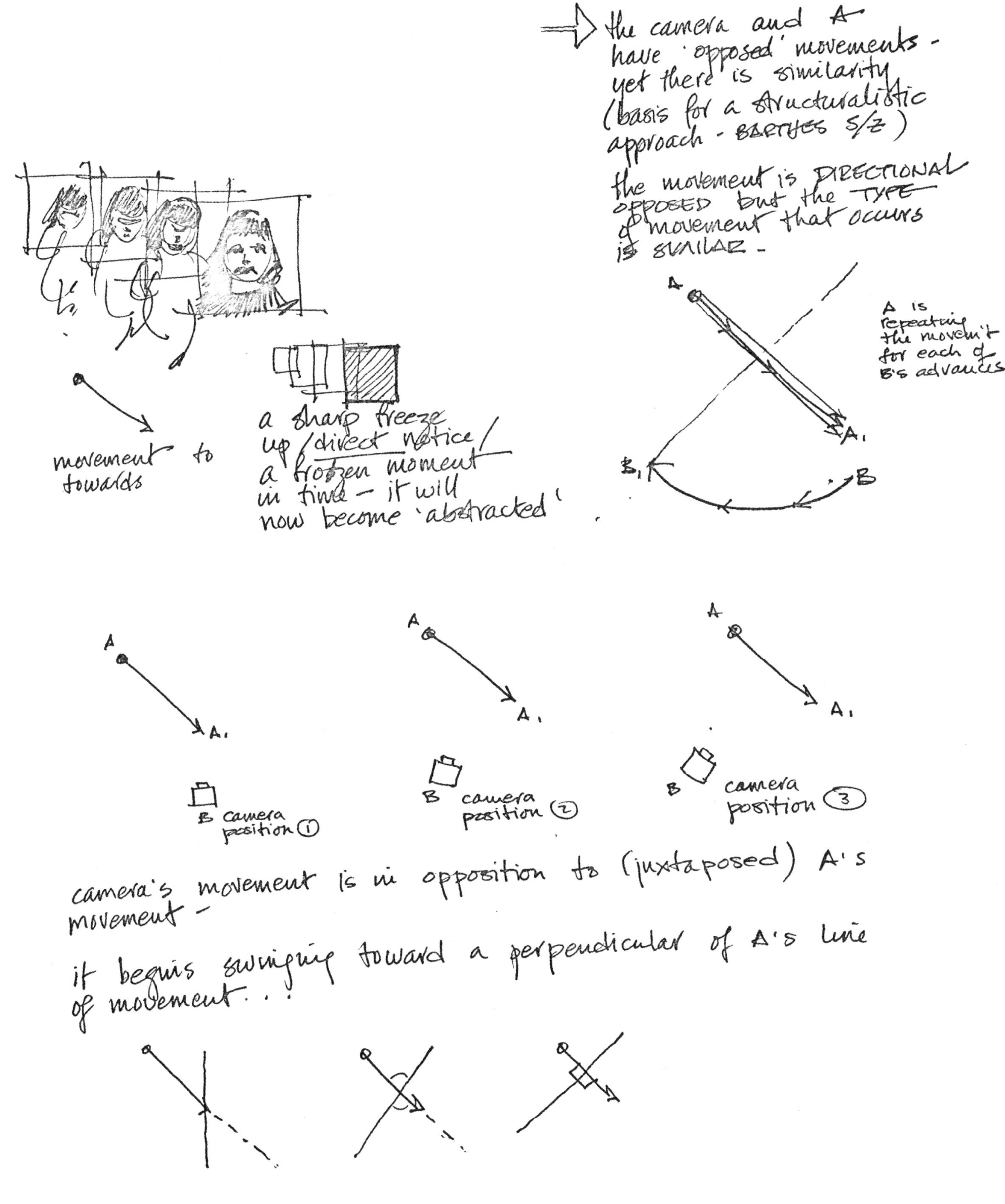

the camera and A have 'opposed' movements - yet there is similarity (basis for a structuralistic approach - BARTHES S/Z)
the movement is DIRECTIONAL OPPOSED but the TYPE of movement that occurs is SIMILAR -
A is repeating the movem't for each of B's advances
A
A₁
B₁
B
movement to towards
a sharp freeze up / direct notice / a frozen moment in time - it will now become 'abstracted'.
A
A₁
B camera position ①
A
A₁
B camera position ②
A
A₁
B camera position ③
camera's movement is in opposition to (juxtaposed) A's movement -
it begins swinging toward a perpendicular of A's line of movement . . .

→ we can take this relation of A to B
and extend it to the positioning of 2 personages –
ie bill to me
the movement into the relationship
the movement leading out
through a time duration (that is 7 yrs) that becomes one
of B's arc of travel . . .

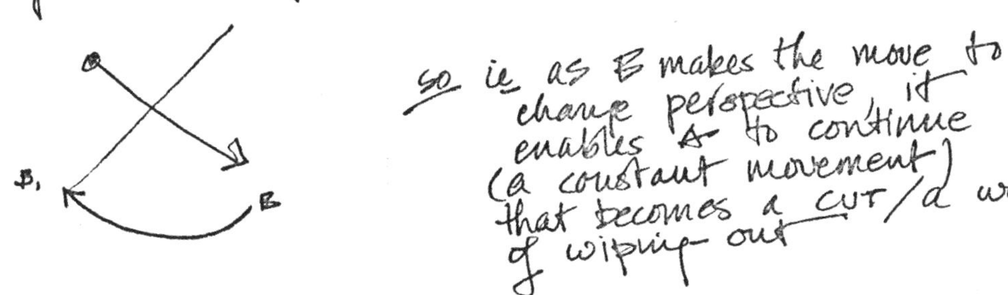

so ie as B makes the move to
change perspective, it
enables A to continue
(a constant movement)
that becomes a CUT/a way
of wiping out

(NOTE: THIS COULD ALSO BE EXPLORED AS A 'REVERSE' SITUATION/OF B TO A)

in relation we could talk about the relation of part to whole –
where in the first situation A is always IN RELATION to B
in the second situation A becomes a RELATION OF/TO B .

whereas in the 1st, A's movement is registered by B
is paralleled by B
is opposed by B
is recorded by B

in the 1st, a type of competitiveness may be encountered –
one can gain control OVER the other
(manipulate a field of vision/view/speed/etc)

in the 2nd instance, ONE MUST BE SEEN AS AN INTERGRAL
PART OF THE OTHER .

there is a sense of 'belonging' to the other
A IS A RELATION OF B
and it is interchangeable
B IS A RELATION OF A .
the situation cannot exist without the sense of whole .

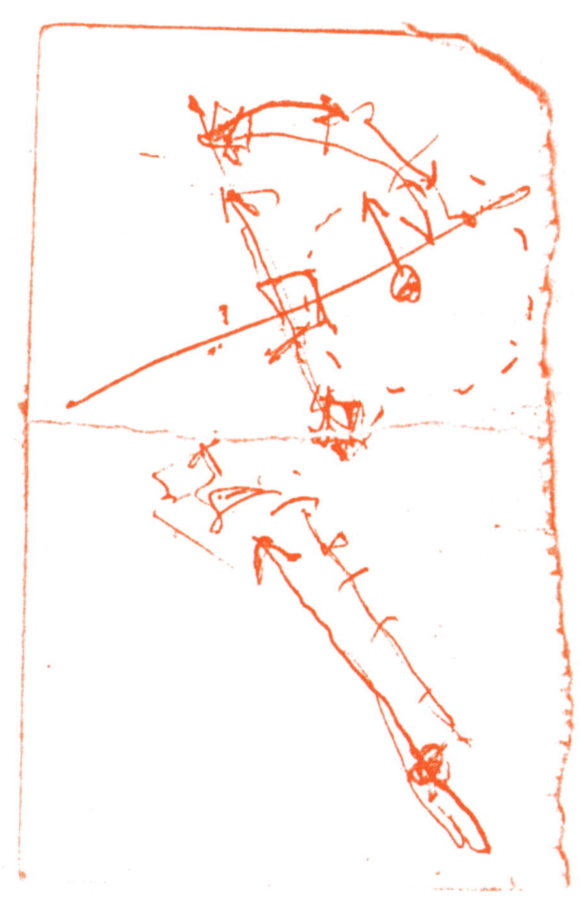

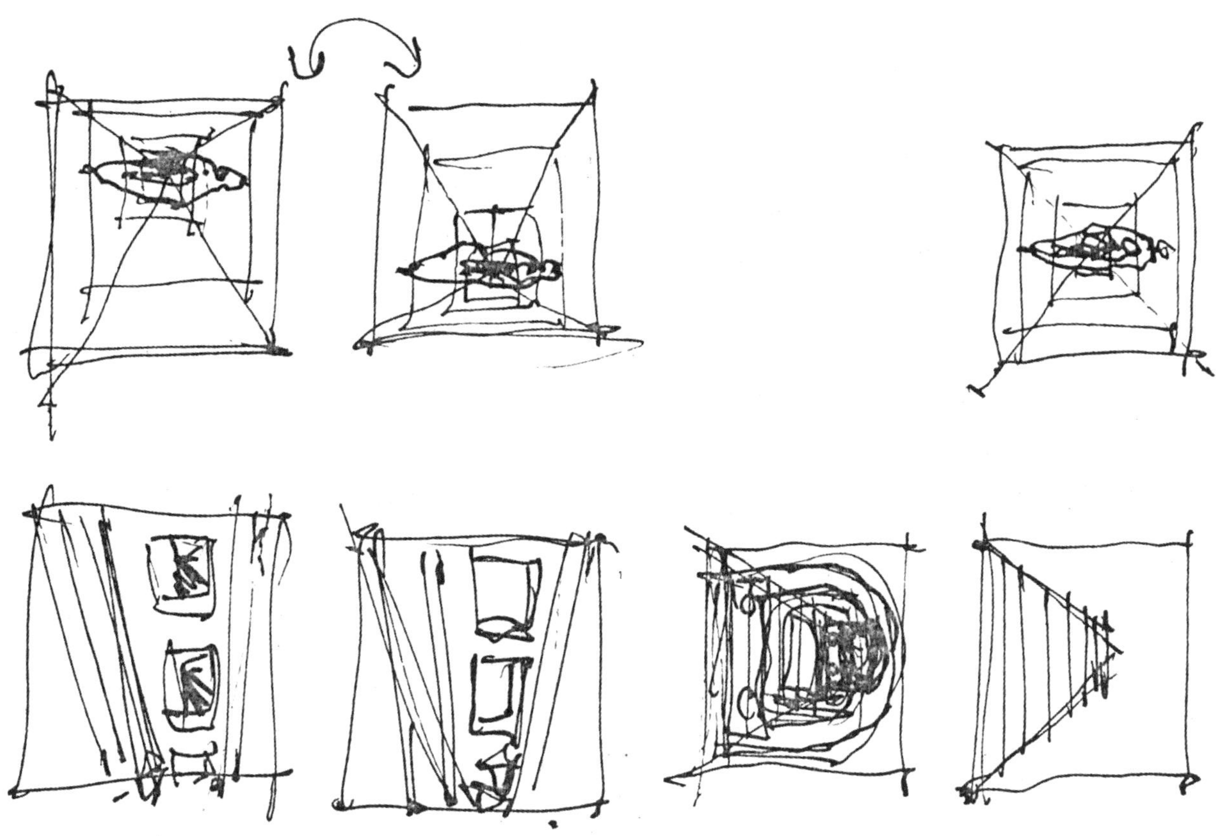

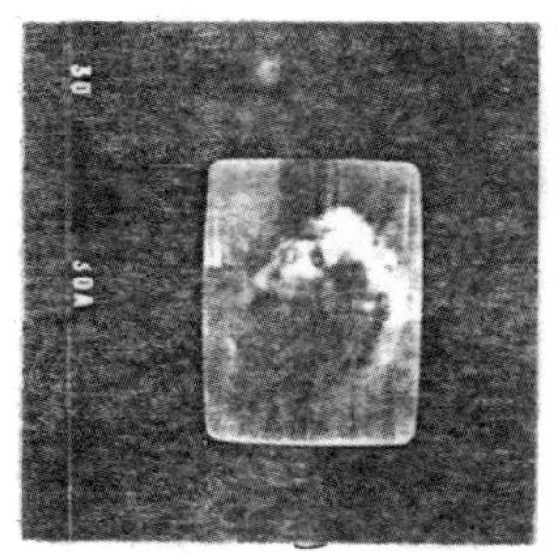

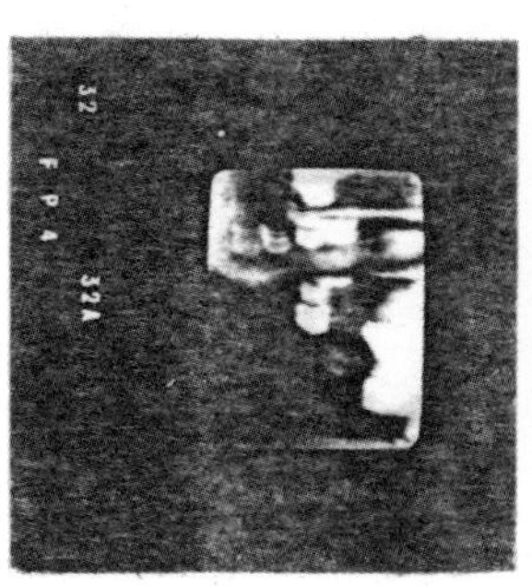

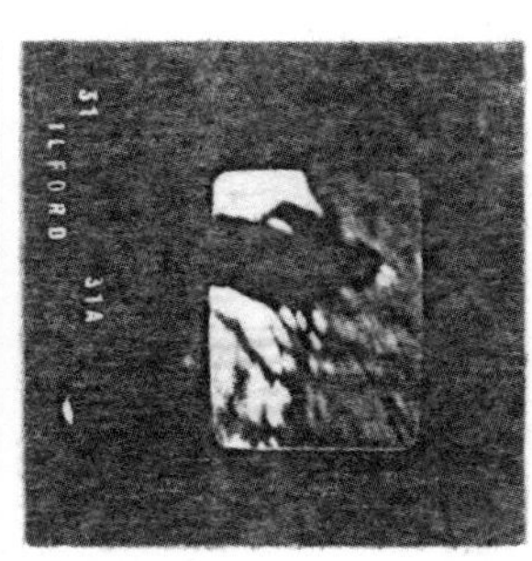

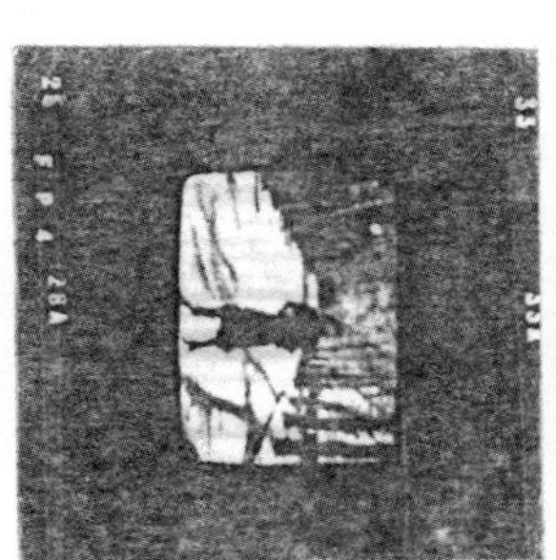

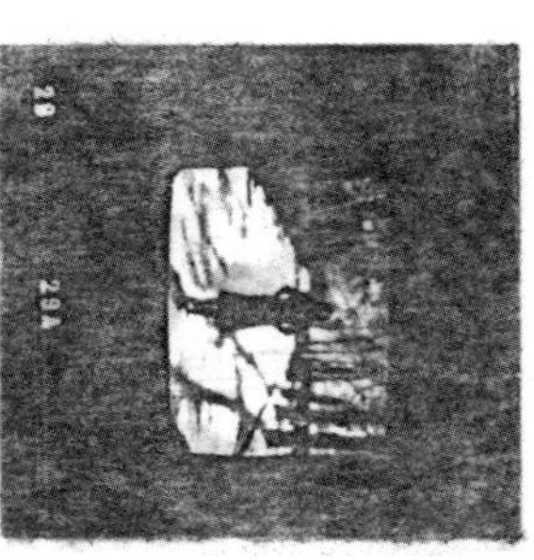

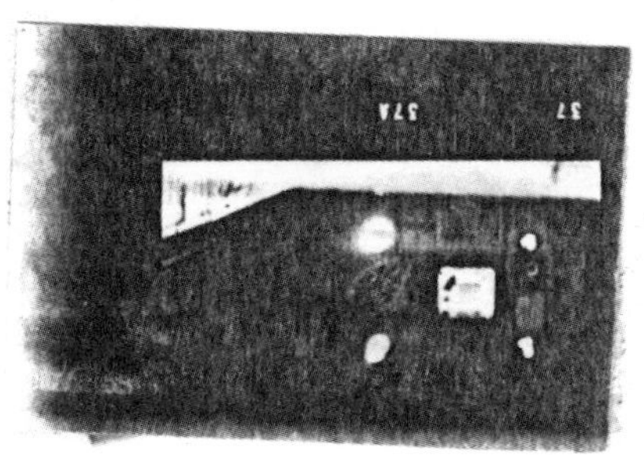

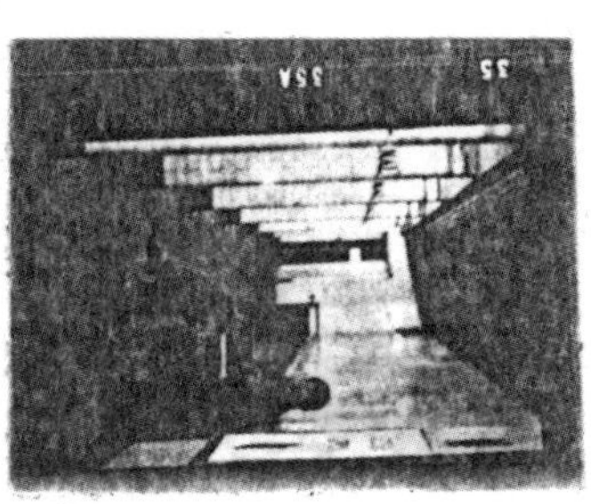

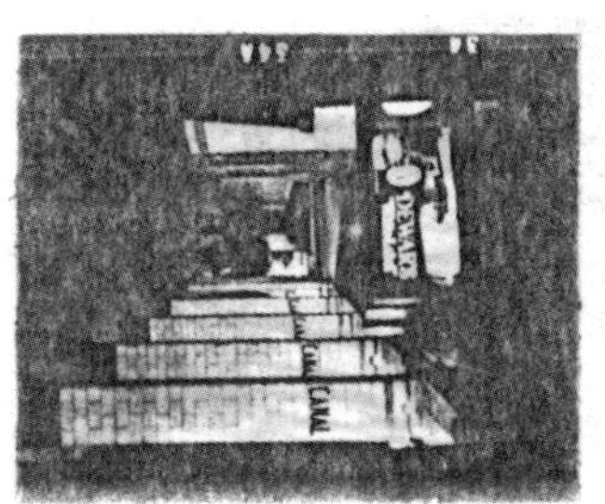

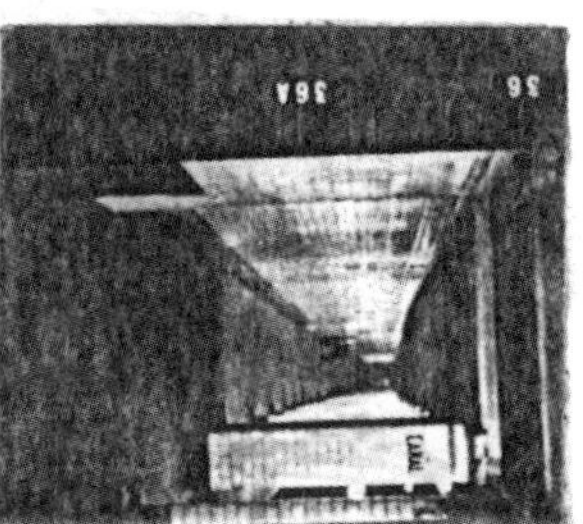

RELATIONSHIP PERSPECTIVES :
PERSPECTIVE RELATIONSHIPS
NYC 1976-1977

APPROACH - TO COME NEARER (OR NEAR) IN SPACE, TIME, OR MAGNITUDE
- TO COME NEAR OR NEARER TO
- TO CAUSE TO COME CLOSER
- TO COME CLOSE TO IN APPEARANCE, QUALITY, CONDITION OR OTHER CHARACTERISTICS; TO APPROXIMATE
- TO MAKE A PROPOSAL TO; MAKE OVERATURES TO
- TO BEGIN TO DEAL WITH OR WORK ON
-

- THE ACT OF COMING OR DRAWING NEAR
* - A FAIRLY CLOSE RESEMBLANCE; AN APPROXIMATION
* - A WAY OR MEANS OF REACHING SOMEONE OR A DESTINATION(ACCESS)
* - THE METHOD USED IN DEALING WITH OR ACCOMPLISHING SOMETHING
* - AN ADVANCE OR OVERTURE MADE BY ONE PERSON TO ANOTHER
* - GOLF - STROKE FOLLOWING THE DRIVE FROM THE TEE WITH WHICH THE PLAYER TRIES TO GET THE BALL ONTO THE PLAYING GREEN
- MILITARY WORKS SUCH AS TRENCHES OR BULWARKS FOR THE PROTECTION OF TROOPS BESIEGING A FORTIFIED POSITION

APPROACHABLE - CAPABLE OF BEING APPROACHED OR REACHED; ACCESSIBLE
- EASILY APPROACHED; RECEPTIVE TO OVERTURE; FRIENDLY

PERSPECTIVE - (REPRESENTATIONAL TECHNIQUES)
- (ANY PICTURE IN PERSPECTIVE)
- A VIEW OR VISTA
- APPEARANCE OF OBJECTS IN DEPTH (BINOCULAR VISION)
* - THE RELATIONSHIPS OF ASPECTS OF A SUBJECT TO EACH OTHER AND TO A WHOLE: A PERSPECTIVE OF HISTORY
* - SUBJECTIVE EVALUATION OF RELATIVE SIGNIFICANCE; A POINT OF VIEW

- TO SEE THROUGH OR INTO INSPECT

PERSPICACIOUS - ACUTELY DISCERNING, PERCEPTIVE, OR UNDERSTANDING
PERSPICACITY
PERSPICUITY

PERSUADE
PERSUASIBLE
PERSUASION
PERSUASIVE

PERTAIN
PERTINACIOUS
PERTINACITY
PERTINENT

PERTURB

DIRECT
APPROACH
PERSPECTIVE (ONE POINT)

DIRECT - TO CONDUCT THE AFFARIS OF; MANAGE; REGULATE
- TAKE CHARGE OF; CONTROL
- CONDUCT (MUSIC)
- TO MOVE (SOMEONE OR SOMETHING) TOWARD A GOAL; AIM; POINT
- GIVE INSTRUCTIONS FOR FINDING A PLACE
- ADDRESS TO A DESTINATION
- TO ADDRESSTO A PERSON (AUDIENCE)
- GUIDANCE / INSTRUCTION TO ACTORS IN REHEARSAL PERF OF PLAY OR FILMING OF A MOTION PICTURE
- PROCEEDING OR LYING IN A STRAIGHT COURSE / NOT DEVIATING
- STRAIGHT FORWARD / CANDIDE / FRANK
- WITHOUT INTERVENING PERSONS (CONDITIONS) IMMEDIATE
- BY ACTION OF THE VOTERS RATHER THAN THROUGH ELECTED REPS
- OF UNBROKEN DESCENT (LINEAL)
- THE EXACT WORD OF A WRITER OR SPEAKER
- ABSOLUTE; TOTAL (DIRECT OPPOSITES)
- MATH VARYING IN THE SAME MANNER (OPP INVERSE)
- ASTRONOMY DESIGNATING A WEST TO EAST MOTION OF A PLANET IN THE SAME DIRECTION AS THE SUN'S MOVEMENT AMONG THE STARS

IN A DIRECT MANNER; STRAIGHT

<u>DIRECT ACTION</u> - THE USE OF STRIKES, DIMONSTRATIONS, AND SABOTAGE TO ACHIEVE AN END (<u>DIRECT ACTIONIST</u>)

<u>DIRECT ACTION</u> - OPERATING WITHOUT INTERMEDIATE INGREDIENTS, COMPONENTS, STAGES OR PROCESSES

DIRECT CURRENT - CURRENT FLOWING IN ONE DIRECTION

<u>DIRECTED ANGLE</u> - AN ANGLE HAVING AN INDICATED POSITIVE SENSE

<u>DIRECTED DISTANCE</u> - A SEGMENT OF A LINE HAVING AN INDICATED POSITIVE SENSE

DIRECTION - ACT OR FUNCTION OF DIRECTING
- MANAGEMENT (SUPERVISION / GUIDANCE)
- MUSICAL / THEATRICAL (ART OR ACT OF)
- A WORD OR PHRASE IN A MUSICAL SCORE (INDICATING HOW A PARTICULAR PASSAGE IS TO BE SUNG OR PLAYED)
- SERIES OF INSTRUCTIONS FOR DOING SOMETHING
- ORDER OR COMMAND - AUTHORITATIVE
- DIST- INDEPENDENT RELATIONSHIP BETWEEN TWO POINTS SPECIFIES THE ANGULAR POSITION OF WITHER WITH RESPECT TO EACH OTHER
- A POSITION TO WHICH MOTION OR ANOTHER POSITION IS REFERRED
- LINE LEADING TO A PLACE OR POINT

DIRECTION - LINE OR COURSE ALONG WHICH A PERSON OR A THING MOVES
- COMPASS DIRECTION
- A COURSE OR AREA OF DEVELOPMENT; TENDENCE TOWARD A PARTICULAR END OR GOAL

<u>DIRECTIONAL</u> - OF OR PERTAINING TO SPACIAL DIRECTION, ESP A SINGLE SPECIFIED DIRECTION

DIRECTIONAL ANTENNA - ADAPTED FOR RECEIVING SIGNALS FROM OR SENDING SIGNALS IN A PARTICULAR DIRECTION

DIRECTIONAL SIGNAL (AUTO)

DIRECTION FINDER (DETERMINING THE SOURCE OF A TRANSMITTED SIGNAL

*<u>DIRECTIONAL INDICATOR</u> (COMPASS AIRPLANE NAVIGATION) TO COMPARE AN INTENDED HEADING TO THE ACTUAL HEADING

<u>DIRECTIVE</u> - ORDE OR INSTRUCTION - ESP ONE ISSUED BY A GOVERNMENT OR MILITARY UNIT (SERVING TO DIRECT, INDICATE, POINT OUT

<u>DIRECTLY</u> * IN A DIRECT LINE OR MANNER
- WITHOUT ANYONE OR ANYTHING INTERVENING; IMMEDIATE
- EXACTLY; TOTALLY; ABSOLUTELY
- AT ONCE; INSTANTLY

*<u>DIRECT OBJECT</u> - IN ENGLISH AND SOME OTHER LANGUAGES, THE WORD OR WORDS OF THE SENTENCE DESIGNATING THE PERSON OR THING RECEIVING THE ACTION OF A TRANSITIVE VERB.

DIRECTOR

DIRECTORATE

DIRECTORIAL (SERVING TO DIRECT; DIRECTIVE)

<u>DIRECT PRIMARY</u> - A PRELIMINARY ELECTION IN WHICH A PARTY'S CANDIDATE FOR PUBLIC OFFICE ARE NOMINATED BY POPULAR VOTE

DIRECTRESS (FEMALE DIRECTOR) RE: <u>A DIRECTRESS IN DISTRESS</u>
TITLE

A FLATBED
A SIDEBOARD

A FLATBED (PRESS)

FLAT
FLATBOAT - A BOAT WITH A SQ BOTTOM AND SQ ENDS - USED FOR TRANSPORTING FREIGHT ON INLAND WATERWAYS; A BARGE. ALSO CALLED FLATBOTTOM

SIDEBOARD - A PIECE OF DINING RM FURNIATURE FOR HOLDING DISHES OF FOOD AND USUALLY HAVING DRAWERS AND SHELVES FOR LINENS AND TABLEWARE

SIDECAR - ATTACHED TO A MOTORCYCLE
- A COCKTAIL

SIDEEFFECT (SIDE EFFECT) SECONDARY

*SIDELIGHT - LIGHT (COMING FROM THE SIDES)
- NAUTICAL
- INCIDENTAL INFO

*SIDELINE (SIDE LINE)- A LINE
- THE PT OF VIEW OF THOSE WHO OBSERVE RATHER THAN PARTICIPATE IN SOME ACTIVITY
- SUBSIDIARY LINE OF MECHANDISE
- AN ACTIVITY IN ADDITION TO

*SIDELINED - TO REMOVE OR TO KEEP FROM ACTIVE PARTICIPATION AS IN ATHLETIC CONTESTS

SIDELING - DIRECTED TO ONE SIDE; OBLIQUE
- SLOPING; INCLINED

SIDELONG - DIRECTED TO ONE SIDE; SIDEWAYS;. A SIDELONG GLANCE

SIDEMAN - AN INSTRUMENTALIST IN A JAZZ BAND

*SIDESHOW - A SMALL SHOW OFFERED IN ADDITION TO THE MAIN SPECT ATTRACTION, AS AT A CIRCUS
- A DIVERTING INCIDENT OR SPAECTACLE

(SIDESADDLE)

SIDESLIP - TO SLIP OR SKID TO ONE SIDE
- SIDEWAYS SKID (AUTO)
- AVIATION FLYING SIDEWAYS AND DOWNWARD ALONG THE LATERAL AXIS TO REDUCE ALTITUDE WITHOUT GAINING SPEED OR AS THE RESULT OF BANKING TOO DEEPLY

SIDESPIN - IE: A BALL

SIDE SPLITTING - AS IN LAUGHTER

*SIDE STEP - TO STEP ASIDE
- TO DODGE AN ISSUE OR RESPONSIBILITY
- TO STEP OUT OF THE WAY OF
- TO EVADE; SKIRT

*SIDE STEP - TO STEP ASIDE
A STEP ON THE SIDE OF SOMETHING

(SIDESTROKE)

SIDESWIPE - TO STRIKE ALONG THE SIDE IN PASSING
- A GLANCING BLOW ON OR ALONG THE SIDE

*SIDETRACK - TO SWITCH FROM THE MAIN TRACK TO A SIDING
- TO DIVERT FROM THE MAIN ISSUE OR COURSE
- TO DIVERT (A PERSON) TO A LESSER POSITION

- TO RUN INTO A SIDING
- TO DEVIATE FROM THE MAIN SUBJECT OR COURSE
- A RAILROAD SIDING

SIDEWALK - A WALK OR RAISED PATH ALONG THE SIDE OF A ROAD FOR PEDESTRIANS
(SIDEWALK SUPERINTENDANT) A PEDESTRIAN WHO STOPS TO WATCH CONSTRUCTION OR DEMOLITION WORK

SIDE WALL (SIDE SURFACE OF AUTO TIRE)

SIDEWARD - MOVING OR DIRECTED TO ONE SIDE
SIDEWAYS - FROM ONE SIDE
- TOWARD ONE SIDE; IN A SIDE WARD DIRECTION
- PRESENTING THE SIDE INSTEAD OF THE FRONT OR THE BACK
- TOWARD OR FROM ONE SIDE

SIDE WHEEL

SIDEWINDER - SMALL RATTLESNAKE - MOVES BY DISTINCTIVE LATERAL LOOPING MOTION OF ITS BODY
- A POWERFUL DELIVERED BY THE FIST FROM THE SIDE
-MILITARY (SHORT RANGE AIR TO AIR MISSILE)

SIDING - RR SHORT SECTION OF TRACK CONNECTED TO THE MAIN BY SWITCHES
- MATERIAL (BLDG)

*SIDLE - MOVE SIDEWAYS; EDGE ALONG FURTIVELY OR INDIRECTLY
MAKE ADVANCES IN A FAWNING MANNER
SIDELONG STEP OR MEOVEMENT

SIDEARM - WEAPON / BASEBALL
SIDEBAND - BAND OF FREQUENCY (EITHER OF THE TWO BANDS OF FREQ ONE JUST ABOVE AND ONE JUST BELOW A CARRIER FREQ THAT RESULT FROM MODULATION OF THE CARRIER WAVE

SIDED - HAVING SIDE USUALLY OF A SPECIFIC NUMBER (SPECIFIED NO OR KIND. USED IN COMBIN..

AMERICA: LAND OF CONTRASTS
(A DAY OF AWAKENING)
(A SHOT IN THE DARK)

REBIRTH OF AMERICA - LAND OF CONTRASTS

A SHOW COMPRISED OF 2
2 OPPOSITES
2 EXTREMES
- AS AMERICA IS EXTREME -

"A SHOT IN THE DARK"

"A DAY OF AWAKENING"

1. "A DAY OF AWAKENING" "SHOW" IN DAYLIGHT
WE TALK ONLY ABOUT THE THINGS THAT WE HAVE "BROUGHT TO LIGHT" HERE ... (AS WATERGATE PHENOMENON BROUGHT TO LIGHT IN 70'S)

WHAT HAS COME TO PASS
WHAT HAS ALREADY BEEN PROVEN

2. "A SHOT IN THE DARK" "SHOW" IN THE DARK
WHAT WE ARE STILL HIDING
WHAT WE ARE STILL HIDING FROM
A "GUESS" AT WHAT MAY COME TO PASS BECAUSE OF IT
("TAKE A SHOT AT IT")

LAND OF CONTRASTS
LAND OF EXTREMES
AS IN
DAY vs NIGHT
WRONG vs RIGHT ETC

OR: STATEMENT / ANSWER "YES" OR
"NO"
BECOMES: STATEMENT / ANSWER "WRONG" OR
"RIGHT"
ANSWERS: TAKE ON MORAL REFERENCES

FURTHER, LET EACH STATEMENT HOLD TO ITS OWN INHERENT LOGIC:
IE: A "CARTER" TYPE PHILOSOPHY

POLITICAL ADVERTISEMENT:
"THERE IS A SIMPLE AND EFFECTIVE WAY FOR PUBLIC OFFICIALS TO REGAIN PUBLIC TRUST - BE TRUSTWORTHY."

ANSWER (COMMAND) RIGHT OR WRONG ON THIS STATEMENT
YES OR NO ON THIS STATEMENT
LEAD TO IMPLICATIONS ... YOU ARE WRONG

LET'S STOP TALKING ABOUT RELATIONSHIPS FOR AWHILE
AND START TALKING ABOUT WINNING

ON A GRANDIOSE SCALE

WINNER TAKE ALL
LOSER TO TAKE NONE

"WINNER TAKE ALL"
"THE LOSER IS EMPTY HANDED"

WINNING AMERICAN STYLE
VS
LOSING (LO(O)SING) AMERICAN STYLE

WHICH IS ALL THE WAY

"THAT'S THE WAY IT'S BEEN"
"THAT'S THE WAY IT WILL ALWAYS BE"
"THERE'S NO CHANGING THAT"
"THERE'S NO GETTING AROUND IT"
"YOU CAN'T FOOL ME"

"IT'S ONE FOR ALL AND
ALL FOR ONE"

"IT'S PLAIN AS BLACK AND WHITE"
"IT'S WRONG OR RIGHT"

AND THERE'S NO GETTING AROUND IT   ANY MORE

YOU'LL HAVE TO FACE IT   EVENTUALLY

THIS IS THE LAND OF OPPOSITE(S)
THIS IS AMERICA: LAND OF CONTRASTS
THERE ARE NO SECTIONS OF GRAY
THERE ARE NO INBETWEENS
THERE ARE ONLY THE EXTREMES

"RIGHT OR WRONG"
"WRONG OR RIGHT"
"DAY OR NIGHT"

A DAY OF AWAKENING
A SHOT IN THE DARK

WHAT'S WRONG IS WRONG
WHAT'S RIGHT IS RIGHT

SO IT GETS DOWN TO THIS   IT COMES DOWN TO THIS
YOU EITHER DO IT OR YOU DON'T
YOU EITHER GET ANGRY ABOUT IT   "LAID BACK"
WHICH WILL IT BE?
WINNING
OR
LO(O)SING
THE AMERICAN WAY   IN AMERICA

TRY THIS ONE ON FOR SIZE

WINNER TAKE ALL
THE LOSER ALWAYS ENDS UP EMPTY HANDED
LET ME SAY IT IN A WAY YOU'LL UNDERSTAND IT
THAT'S THE WAY ITS BEEN
THAT'S THE WAY IT WILL ALWAYS BE
THERE'S NO CHANGING THAT
AND YOU CAN'T GET AROUND IT (EITHER)

IT'S AS PLAIN AS BLACK AND WHITE
IT'S WRONG OR RIGHT

AND THERE'S NO GETTING AROUND THAT EITHER

YOU'LL HAVE TO FACE IT (EVENTUALLY)

THERE ARE ONLY THE EXTREMES
THERE ARE NO IN-BETWEENS
RIGHT OR WRONG
WRONG OR RIGHT

IF YOU DON'T LIKE IT YOU CAN LUMP IT
YOU CAN ALWAYS LEAVE
YOU DON'T HAVE TO STAY HERE

DAY OR NIGHT
IT'S AS PLAIN AS THE NOSE ON YOUR FACE, BUDDY

SO IT COMES DOWN TO THIS
HEAR ME NOW
MIND ME WELL

YOU EITHER DO IT OR YOU DON'T
YOU EITHER SHIT OR YOU GET OFF THE POT
YOU EITHER GET ANGRY
OR YOU STAY "LAID BACK"

(CONDESCEND OR COMPREHEND
WHICH WILL IT BE?)

WINNING OR LOSING
WHERE DID ALL THAT GOOD OLD AMERICAN SPIRIT (ANGER) GO TO?

IF YOU DON'T DO IT FOR ME
DO IT FOR OLD GLORY
IT'S THE AMERICAN WAY
IT'S THE ONLY DECENT THING TO DO (UNDER THE CIRCUMSTANCES)

(IT'S EITHER THAT OR DEVELOPING A SENSE OF HUMOR)

perspective relationships
relationship perspective

AMERICA: LAND OF CONTRAST (S)

1 SCREEN / 2 IMAGES

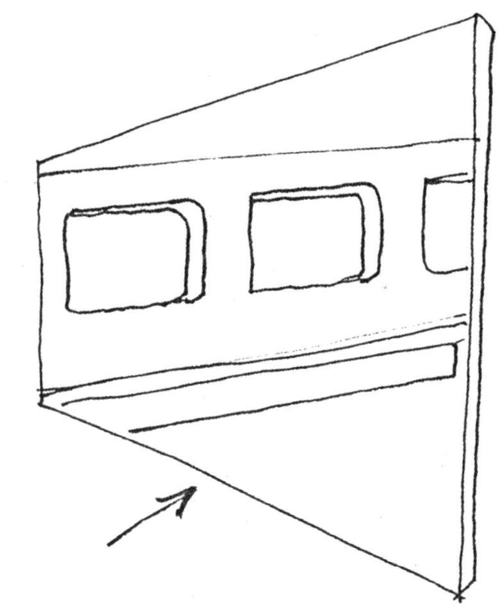

we set the scene (an attempt @ alternative resolutions)

- THERE IS A ONE DIMENSIONALITY TO THESE IMAGES
- they pass by us as a film
- we have no perspective to them

WE LIVE IN A 'ETERNAL PRESENT'

(all images are presented this way - FLAT - there is a perspective (as in perception) loss . . .

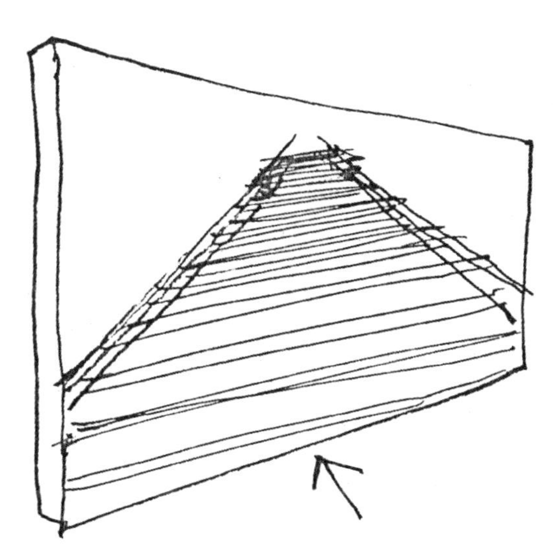

we make the resolution
we determine the DIRECTED PATH

(it approaches - we can sense it / we gain perspective - we become resolved to the task at hand)

DIRECT APPROACH
gaining perspective

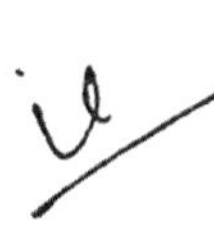

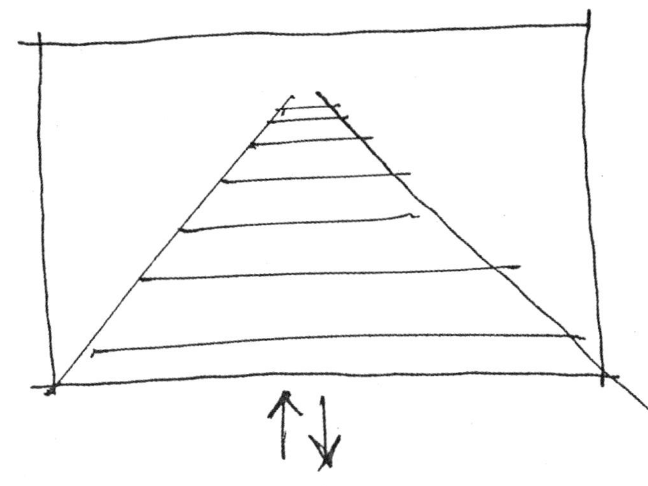

WE RIDE THE FRONT OF THE TRAIN.
WE SEE THE PATH TO COME
THE RAILS SET THE PERSPECTIVE BUT NEVER MEET.
WE ARE IN THE CONDUCTOR'S SEAT WE SENSE WHAT IS TO COME / THE PATH IS DIRECT / THE REVOLUTION IS (WAS) DETERMINED BY HISTORY.

PAN – cutting through the frame

ie

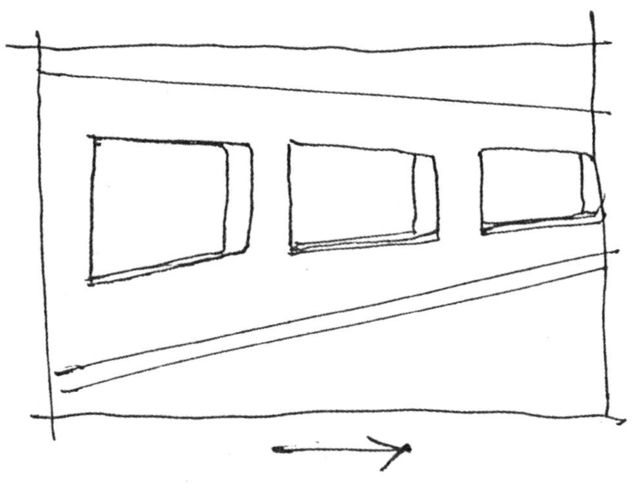

WE RIDE THE SIDE-CAR
WE ARE IN THE PASSENGER'S SEAT-
WE GLIMPSE THE 'PRESENT' AS IT GOES BY-
IT IS ETERNAL/CONTINUOUS
THERE IS NO HISTORY - ONLY NOW-
WE HAVE NO CHOICE - WE OBSERVE

TO CHANGE THE RELATIONSHIP -
from a perspective of (OUR) ~~[illegible]~~ SELFS -
to a perspective of HISTORY

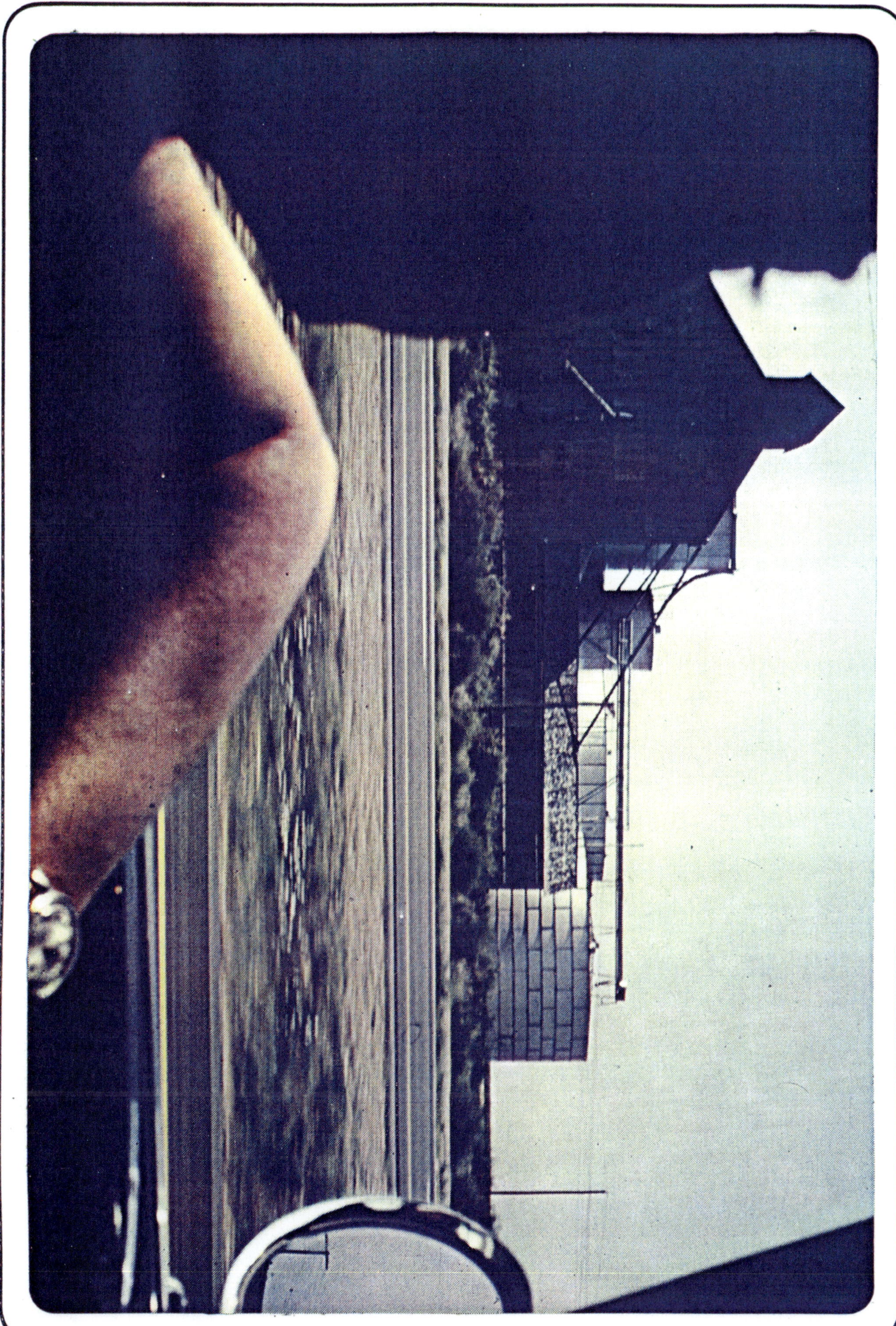

<u>AMERICA: LAND OF CONTRASTS</u>
<u>(A DAY OF AWAKENING)</u>
NYC (+)   1976-1977

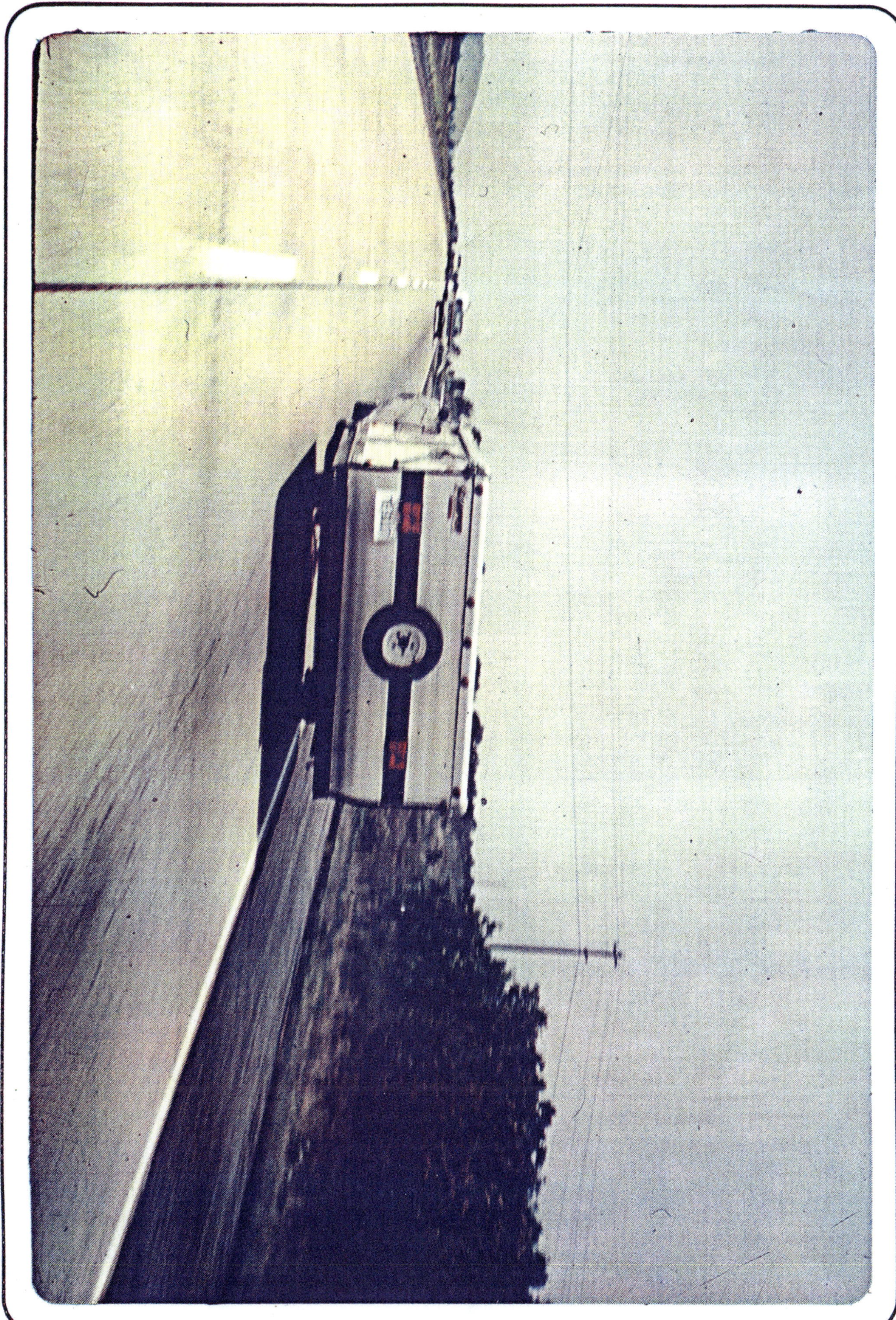

AMERICA: LAND OF CONTRASTS
(A DAY OF AWAKENING)
NYC (+) 1976-1977

THE SCENE IS:

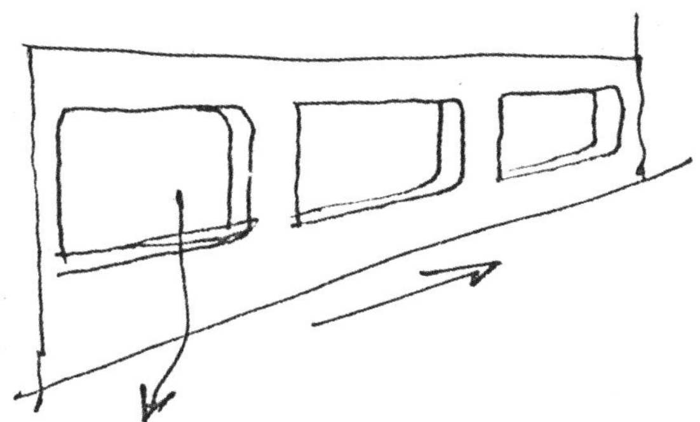

DESCRIPTION OF WHAT IS
YIELDS A CHOICE OF RESOLUTION(S) +
THAT WHICH CAN (STILL) BE +
(OR FROM) THAT WHICH HAS BEEN +

I CAN CHANGE THE PERSPECTIVE FOR YOU
I CAN MAKE YOU UNDERSTAND WHAT WILL COME
(FROM THE "IMMEDIATE" TO A "CONTROL OVER")
A PERSPECTIVE ON - THE FINAL RESOLUTION - THE ONE CORRECT PATH
(ADD REF. SEE DUNE / DUNE MESSIAH - FRANK HERBERT)

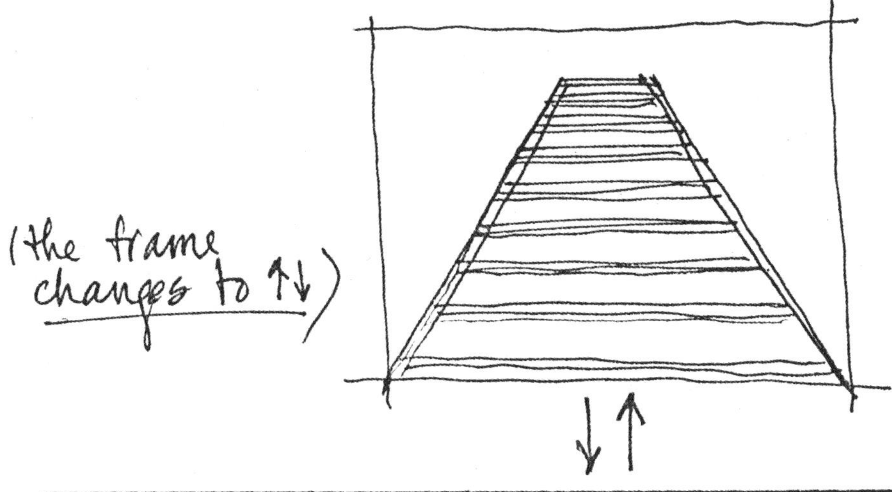

---

we can supply you with the scene (set)
the script (language)

it is *you* who must commit the act (action)

---

the storyline: opening shot -
(we open on a dream) first / take

---

and so as we passed
the countryside became scenes
and the windows, frames ...

and so as we passed through
the countryside became scenes
and the windows, frames ...

THE STORYLINE:
OPENING SHOT - FIRST TAKE
(WE OPEN ON A DREAM)
(THE DREAM COULD BE AMERICA / THE DREAM COULD BE FREEDOM)
(THE DREAM COULD RELATE THE TWO)

---

you can dismiss most of the evidence ...
but never all of it ...

I had come back from Europe almost two years ago
The train ride was long and seemingly endless
In the last moments I knew
that the place I had chosen was indeed the correct one
in which to make the next move
There, there would be no one road
The alternatives towards a chosen destination were great and many
the possible resolutions, even greater
The paths would revolve around those people
whom I had chosen to make contact with
and they would guide me
It was a fruitful time of great expectations

Until, one day
I looked out the window
and realized
that I had never really gotten off the train
That the others had merely joined me on it
That the trip was more unending than I had thought was possible
That all we had lived through in the past two years
Were single shot scenes made up for our amusement(s)
to pass the time
and that it was true that the element common
to each of these scenes
was that they lacked depth - were devoid of perspective
and though each was different and seemingly filled
they were simply single frames - incomplete parts of the same film
and that the film laid parallel to us and we were only being
exposed to a frame at a time
and this certainly did not seem correct (perhaps it seemed unfair)
For it was impossible to understand the film as a whole
In fact, upon questioning, none of us could interpret the story
line
we had missed the punchline
we had missed the dénoûment

And in fact, if we had proceeded into a state of resolution
none of us seemed aware of that fact either
So, you see that we all were quite lost
Though it is a fact known to all that we were still moving
and that the direction was obviously "ahead"
Though those scenes that intrigued us so
were always pulling our observations to the side
And though they amused us greatly
Even to the extent that at times we would all forget the trip
And that most of us had a destination they wished to reach in time
At times, some of us showed a strong desire to change position
To see what would happen to us if our angle of vision were changed
After all there seemed to be something wrong with the fact
that we all had the same type of seat; the same type of view;
obviously, it produced the same type of conclusion(s) and
this eventually lead to boredom

It was a worse type of boredom than any of us would like to
admit to at this time
At first it seemed reasonable to avoid the scenes
to turn inward - perhaps even a few of us started by
observing ourselves and then the others
But this had its own sense of futility -
for we knew each other too well
For the entire period of our trip together we had, after all
been observing the same facts, presented pretty much the same way
- and of course, there was again the case of always seeing
these things from the same angle - of perspective
Then, I realized (only through the course of time)
my original attempt - at leaving one place for another
of resettling in order to gain new (in)sights
I had lost sight of this when the others were on(board) with me
Perhaps we simply distracted each other
as so many scenes had distracted each of us in turn
for the past few years
It was obvious now that one had to change positions
once more
to get up front
to see where the tracks lead to ...

The inside compartments were endlessly long
It was a battle to reach the front
The side scenes move as frames would in an old time movie
It was as if I were turning the projector by hand
At first slowly and then faster until each no longer represented
a single vision but simply a piece of time
and then there was the sense of space again but
here it was directed by me
My speed through it gave it new substance
It was no longer a void that contained
It was a solid to move through and be supported by
At the front (as I suspected) was indeed the conductor
He was perhaps overly joyful at my presence saying that
It had indeed been a long trip - and he was glad to have
company again
He offered me his seat for awhile and with it came the most
spectacular view of tracks leading into the far distance
but never meeting
And all the scenes and their variations we had been observing
were there - but all at once along the sides
When you're up front there you simply aim directly outward(s)
There is no more interest in those side steps
That had absorbed each of us so fully (before)
And then he leaned over and said
If you want, there is one more thing that I can reveal to you
(here and now)
Fearing, I leaned forward only slightly but still close enough
to allow myself to hear
"We have already crossed the ocean, we're setting down
On dry land ... "

(note: this piece relates back, and again to,
<u>LO(O)SING IN AMERICA</u> 1975)

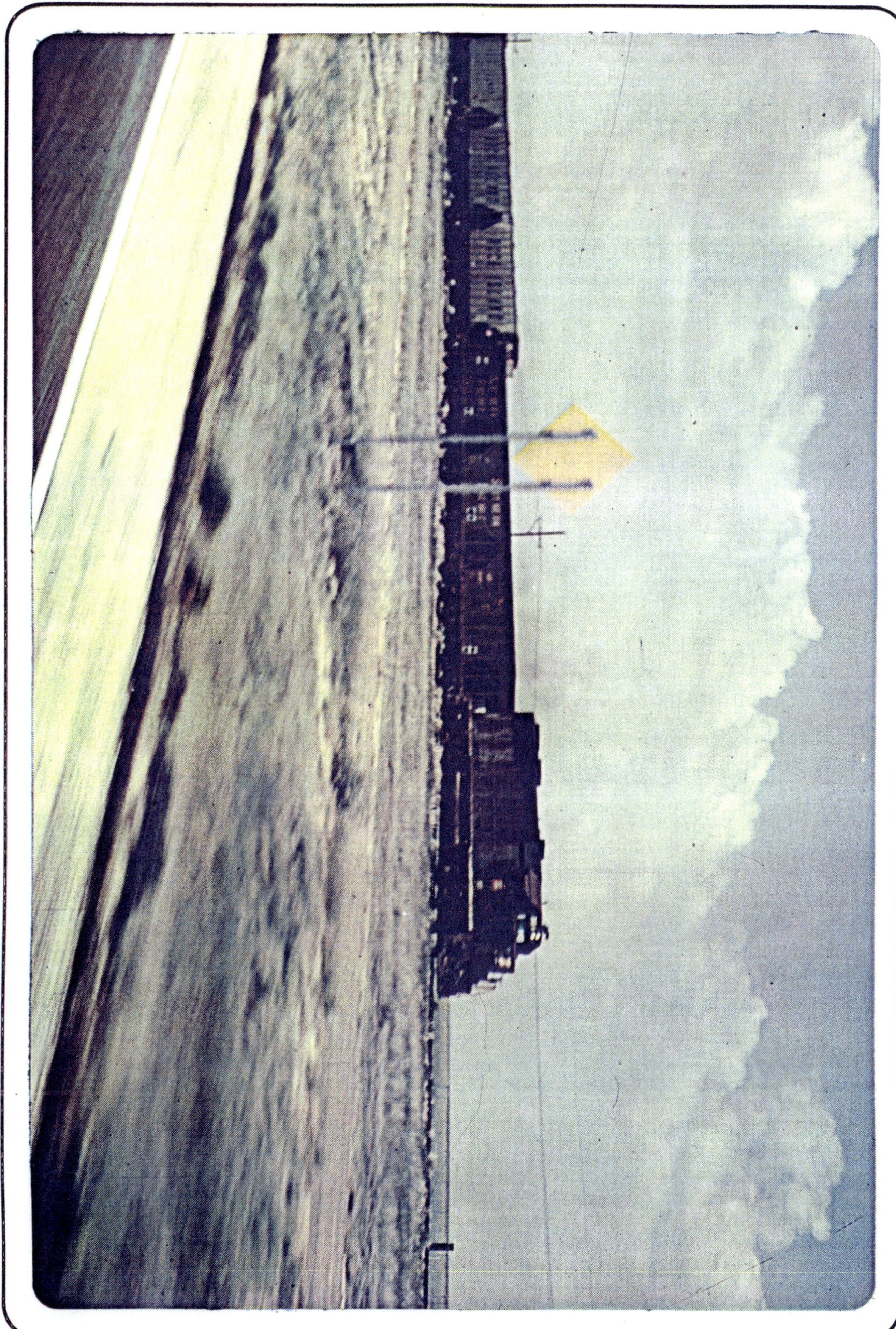

AMERICA: LAND OF CONTRASTS
(A DAY OF AWAKENING)
NYC (+) 1976-1977

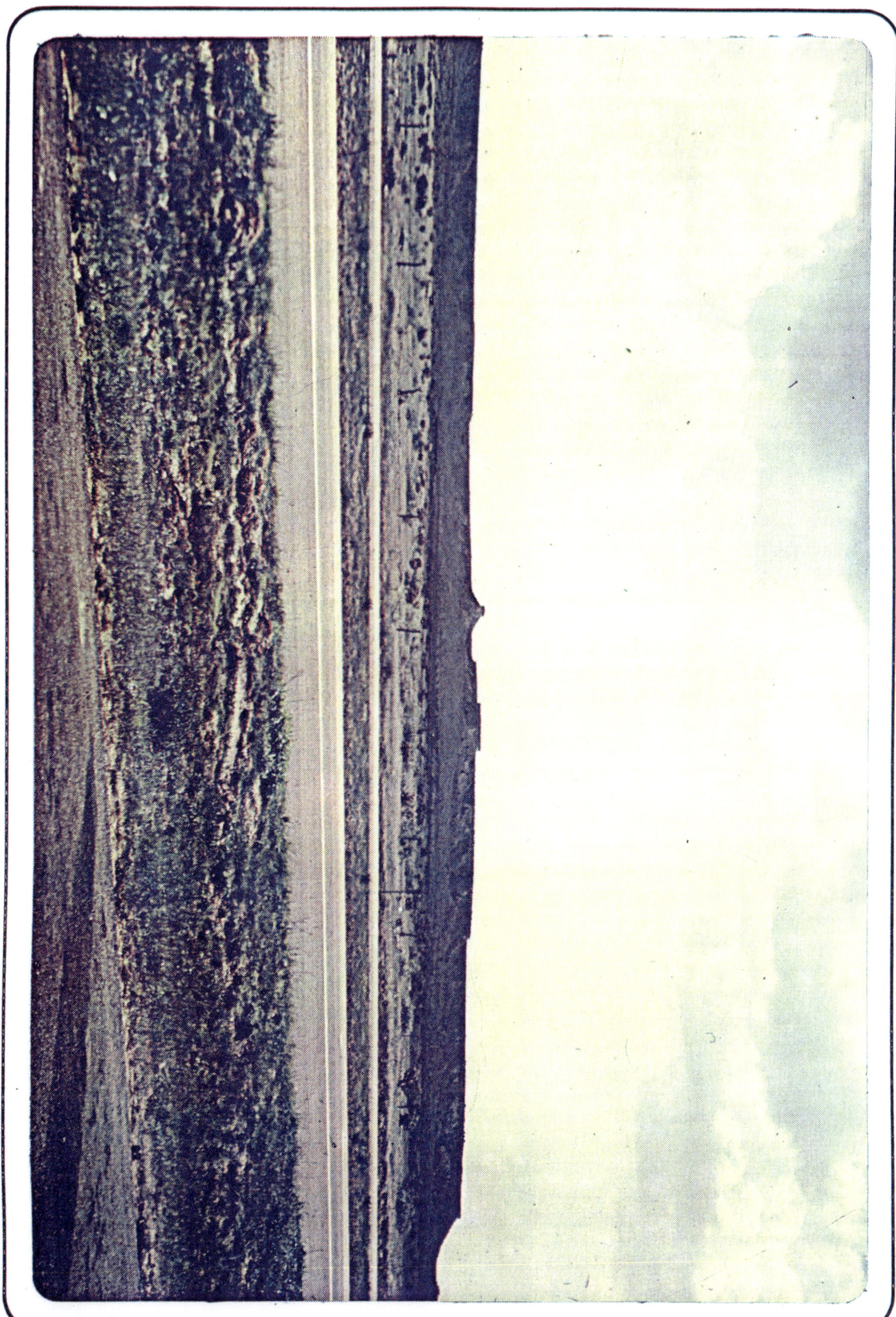

AMERICA: LAND OF CONTRASTS
(A DAY OF AWAKENING)
NYC (+) 1976-1977

here is the script:
it may have six resolutions (following a bicennential year giving it its due) no more no less

the first is to state the problem
we have reached a dead end(ing) the audiences are unsatisfied they have not received there (their) due they will walk out on us they will simply label a bad film from a still worse genre

the solutions could be simple

we could repersonalize things again go into ourselves consider the issue simply a projection of an internal statee of affairs the cure of each will be the cure of all

we could relate to each other in simple groupings one to one leading next to groups of three and then even fours
(we will form supportive communes)

we could externalize our problems when they are stated half of the problem will be over and likewise half of the solution reached - we will again allow for self-introspection

we will rela te only to those like (unto) ourselves we will become nationalistic

(we will understand that there are no more friends and that there is no correct place for this - there is only time now)

we will protect the underdog we will form minorities of which ~~wil~~- we all can and will be a part

we will form a self supportive internal network

we will develop a sense of conscience (science fiction)

we will develop a sense of time and space

we will use technology to further support our condition

we will divide the guilt between us

we will find a scape goat

we will blame it on the other - the audience is over critical of us - the audience is undercritical of us and has caused us to go slack

((we will set the scene - it is you who must committ the act))

she could now notice everything ... the beveled edge of the mirror

had destroyed the illusion ...

the quickest method for working someone out of frame would be a pan shot - pan straight across the body

he would be able to treat her to a beer of her chosing
but he would not be able to kiss her good-night

his ex-wife had been too much like me - we would have to start over again

I must be weak so that he may treat me well once again

I must stay at a distance so that my perspective will (can) vary

he did not know me well enough to know what I wanted for my birthday, so he sent me money and allowed me to make the selection for him

he has come back again ... but in two weeks he will be gone

why did you select to make that a jump cut?

is it because everything really just stays in place for you

a jump cut would ensure that it will be the same while being different
I would just have to give up very little of myself

it is not time yet for an extremem close-up
we know each other too well

balance it out
I've seen him do it - three girls (pick-ups) in the same night

balance it out
I've seen him do it - a transvestite disco with an after hours club as a chaser

balance it out
I've seen him do it - retreat to Europe where it didn't matter that he didn't write

balance it out
it's either too much money or too little

why do you want me - I've been so weak in front of you?
I've been so weak in front of you - that's why you want me ...

I can tell each phone call by its ring - by its own type of intrusion

reduce it - flatten it
minimize the depth of field - make it an idol

reduce me - flatten me
make me an icon

move in space - dramatize it - theatricize it for me - one more time she noticed everything now - five years ago the star of the film had black hair - this year it is red

she notices everything now - they reset the camera to a fixed point of focus - she will recede beyond that and it will seem that our vision of her becomes blurred

she notices everything now - she is younger than I am; healtier; and has done more

she notices eve ything now - she is older than I am; she has made (now) one too many mistakes - she will soon fail - there will be no return

playing with power

resist political ties - allegences

just once she allowed the mike to be seen in the final film - was this just an unrepeated mistake or a purposeful act?

British feminists retreat back to Freud

American feminists are soon to follow

what will become of Jung??

recycle

a story: they passed by the disco, Intermission (get the name right) they wanted to go in - procur a card - get the extra money - they didn't go - it will be forgotten

a story: they only meet a few times by accident

a story continued: she accepted his proposal - showed up at the opening wished him well -

a story continued: she wanted to meet him again by accident - two days later she did -

a story continued: it might never happen agian

a story continued: it might happen again

a story again: she may insure that it will never happen the same way but she may not insure the likelihood that it will happen the same way

if she would just stop talking she would realize that she really had nothing to say - all her recent lovers told her that

they wanted her to be good in bed - but not that good

they only had that one time - after he pursued her for over a year once she had outdone him he realized that this couldn't have been what

telling stories and having ourselves a time
when we should have been dancing

it was a trick shot

it was a cheap shot

it was (a) still

try to move in closer on him
(it will be hard to do with this lens - it doesn't allow for
much distance)

it will be hard to do with this lens - it doesn't allow for much
difference ....

dis-concert

take the edge off (it)

crop

one way or the other - does it really matter now?

there is no definite conclusion

drawing to an end - I wish, she had given up painting years ago for this

when
~~qhwn~~ it hits , it hurts

where it hits, it hurts

take time out - re-examine the question

do unto others

he only referred to her and she not you and me

what could I possibly mean to you

he had forgotten me years ago, before we meet

why don't you just try to tell stories in your own language
it seems to come so naturally to you
(and you're so good at it)

she had every excuse in the book
she had written them all

there is nothing that you are ready to give - even if you say
you'd give up everything

employ your political tendencies - don't just think about them

how can I loose weight at a time like this - I'll need everything
I have behind me (to fight this off ? / ward off the dangers)

TRAIN SHOTS -

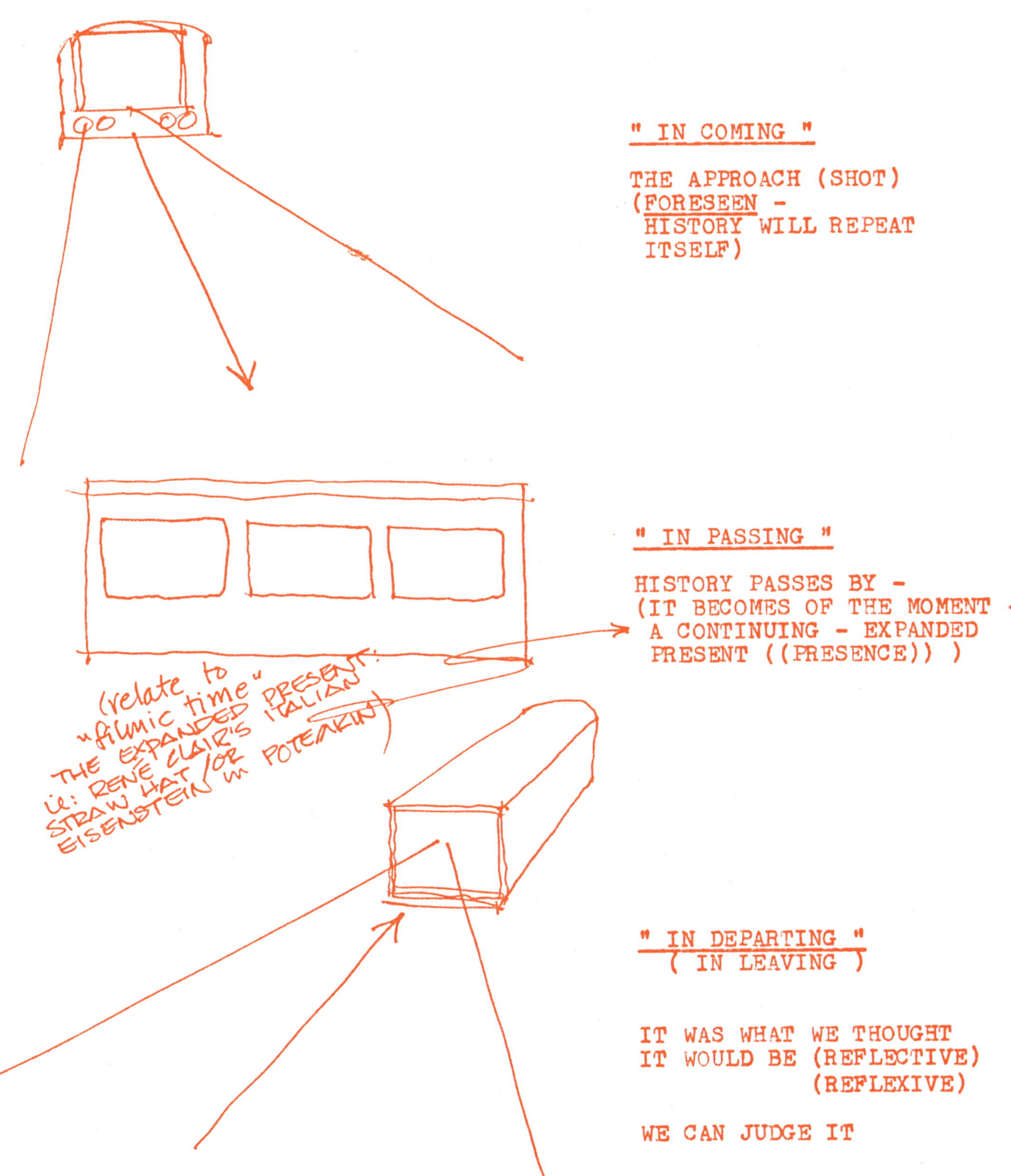

" IN COMING "
THE APPROACH (SHOT)
(FORESEEN -
HISTORY WILL REPEAT
ITSELF)
" IN PASSING "
HISTORY PASSES BY -
(IT BECOMES OF THE MOMENT -
A CONTINUING - EXPANDED
PRESENT ((PRESENCE)))
(relate to
"filmic time"
THE EXPANDED PRESENT:
ie: RENÉ CLAIR'S ITALIAN
STRAW HAT /OR
EISENSTEIN in POTEMKIN)
" IN DEPARTING "
(IN LEAVING)
IT WAS WHAT WE THOUGHT
IT WOULD BE (REFLECTIVE)
(REFLEXIVE)
WE CAN JUDGE IT

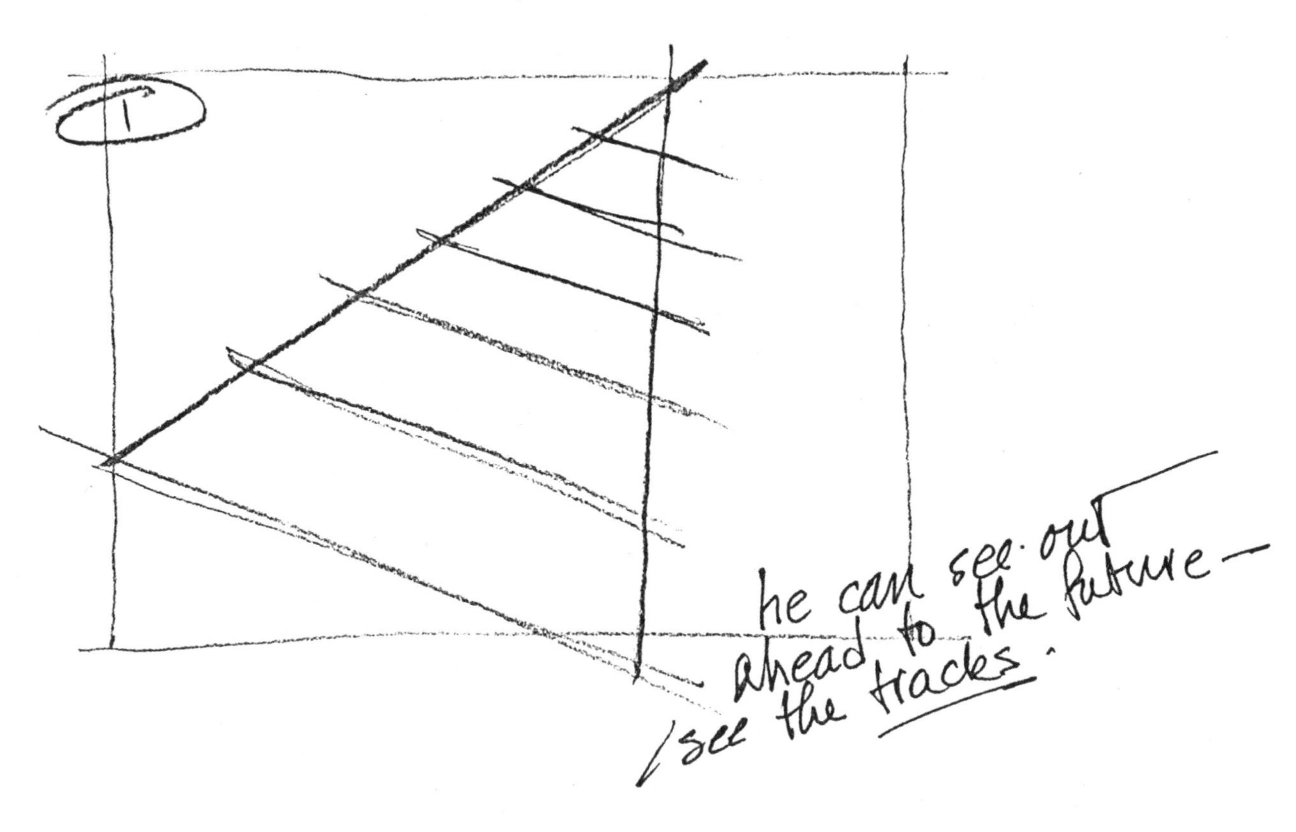

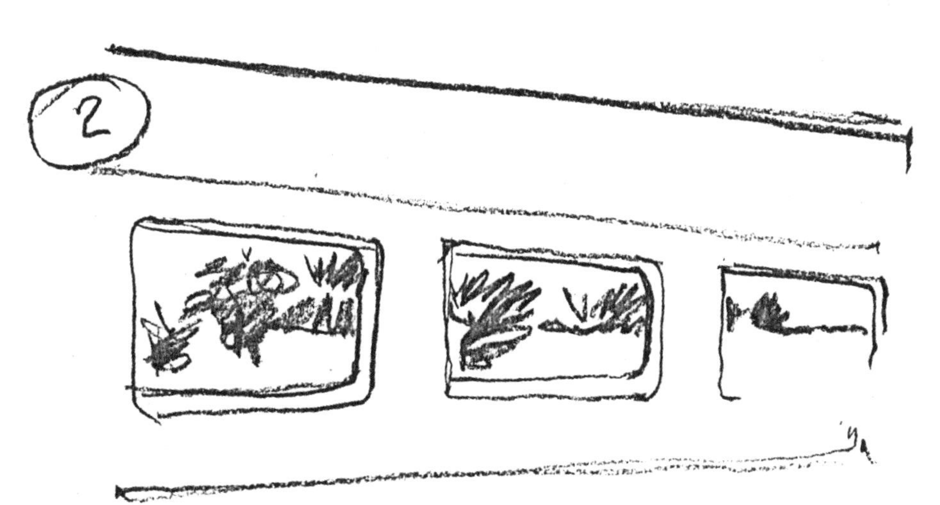

the others just see
the landscape passing-by
- 2D as a movie.
he sees where they meet—
but, they keep going on
+ never do . . .

NOTES
(TO) TRAIN
ON
HISTORY

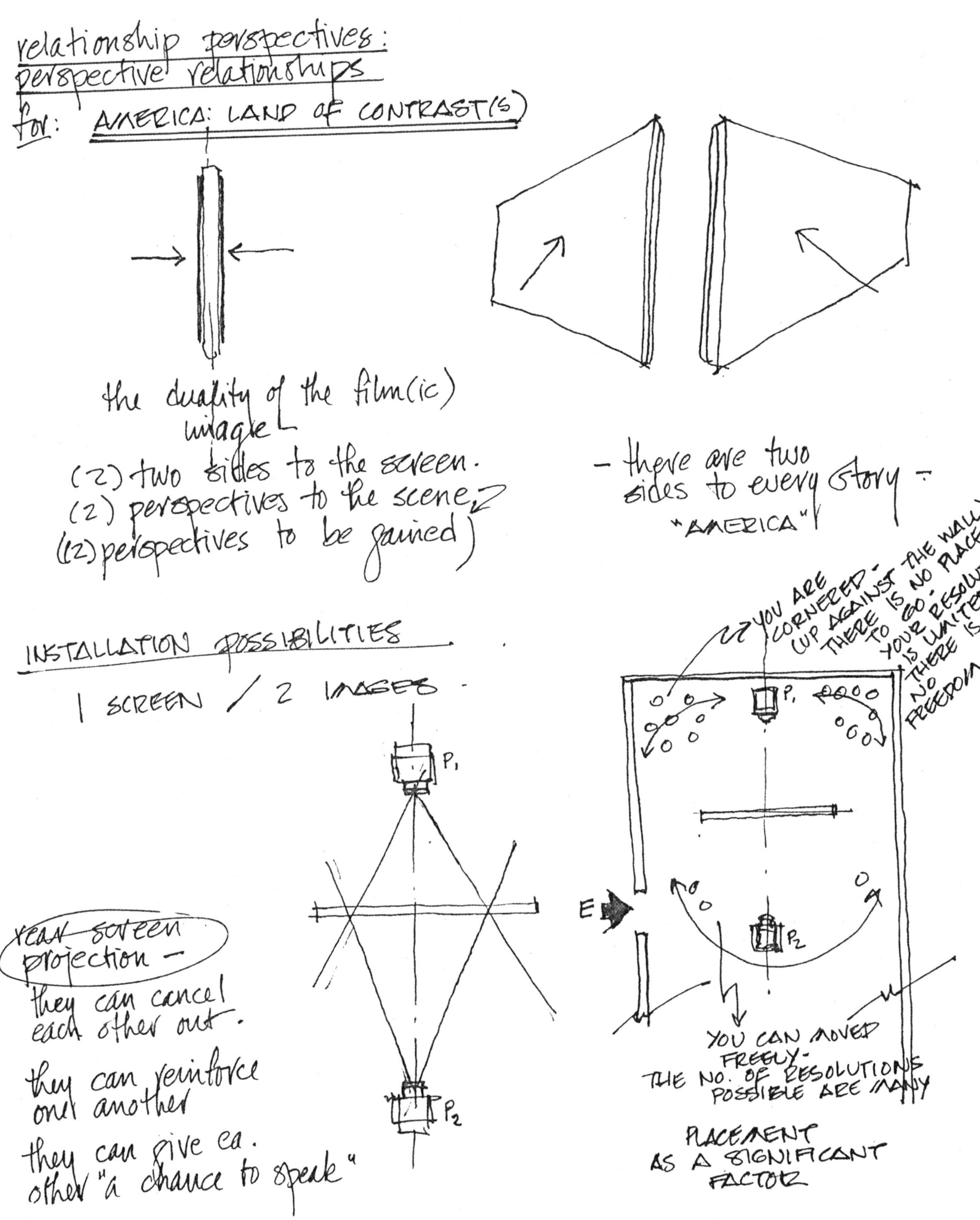
relationship perspectives:
perspective relationships
for: AMERICA: LAND OF CONTRAST(S)
the duality of the film(ic) image
(2) two sides to the screen.
(2) perspectives to the scene
((2) perspectives to be gained)
- there are two sides to every story -
"AMERICA"
INSTALLATION POSSIBILITIES
1 SCREEN / 2 IMAGES -
P1
P2
rear screen projection -
they can cancel each other out.
they can reinforce one another
they can give ea. other "a chance to speak"
YOU ARE CORNERED - (UP AGAINST THE WALL) THERE IS NO PLACE TO GO - YOUR RESOLUTION IS LIMITED THERE IS NO FREEDOM
E
YOU CAN MOVE FREELY - THE NO. OF RESOLUTIONS POSSIBLE ARE MANY
PLACEMENT AS A SIGNIFICANT FACTOR

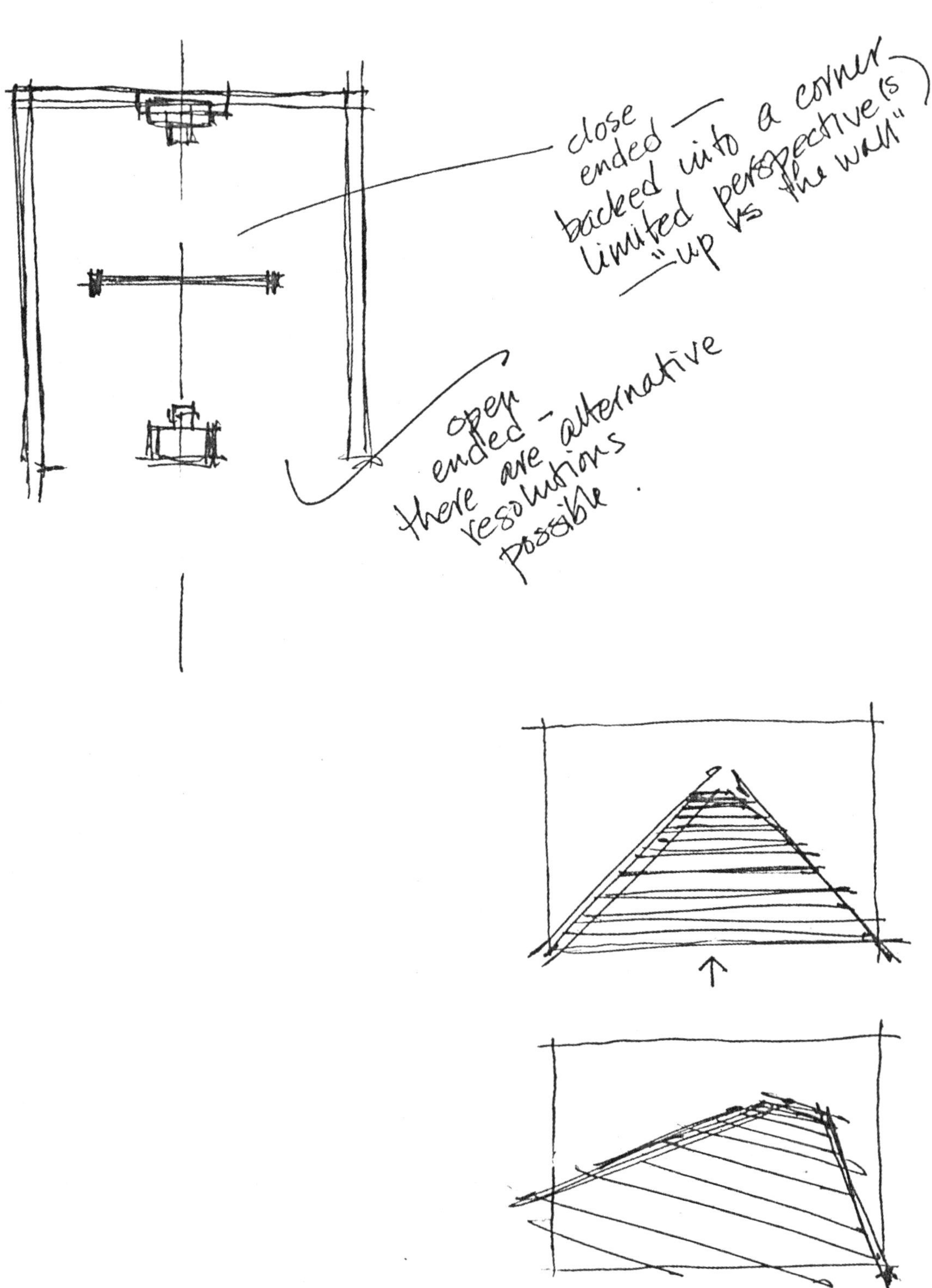
close ended
backed into a corner
limited perspective(s)
"up vs the wall"
open ended -
there are alternative resolutions possible.

age quality and the immediacy, you can be convinced you're seeing the reality of the moment.

SW: What are you working on now?

DB: A film and a video that go together. In film the audience is a voyeur in the darkness. In video the audience is in a light room and can relate to each other. The two parts are going to deal with day/night imagery. The video is going to be called *A Day of Awakening* and deal with things that have been revealed, for example, the public's feeling that things in our current politcal situation must be brought to light. The film will be *A Shot in the Dark* and deal with the fact that so much is still hidden. It will be about what we protect ourselves from facing directly.

SW: You've also been interested in transferring one medium to another?

DB: I want to see what film can do for video and video for film. When I put images that flicker on the video screen, you realize they're filmic and react to them according to the vocabulary you have built up for dealing with film. It makes it clear to the viewers that they are being manipulated. Too many artists deal with one medium or the other. When you cross boundaries, each medium's manipulative tendencies are more clearly defined, and new insights develop.

LESSON PLANS TO KEEP THE REVOLUTION ALIVE
NEW INFORMATION NEEDS NEW STRUCTURE

A WORK IN PROGRESS

" there is a simple and effective way
for public officials to regain public
trust - be trustworthy ."

Jimmy Carter
A Leader, for a change

election campaign 1976

NEW INFORMATION NEEDS NEW STRUCTURE -

lesson plans to keep the revolution alive
introduce revolutionary film structure
structure ie:
the Chinese would have to employ to reach the "masses"
who do not know (or are familiar with) "cutting" - as
in Western films / time - space distortion

/ ∴ reintroduce the "lessons" as to children -
who do not know the way to advancement -
in a new society ...

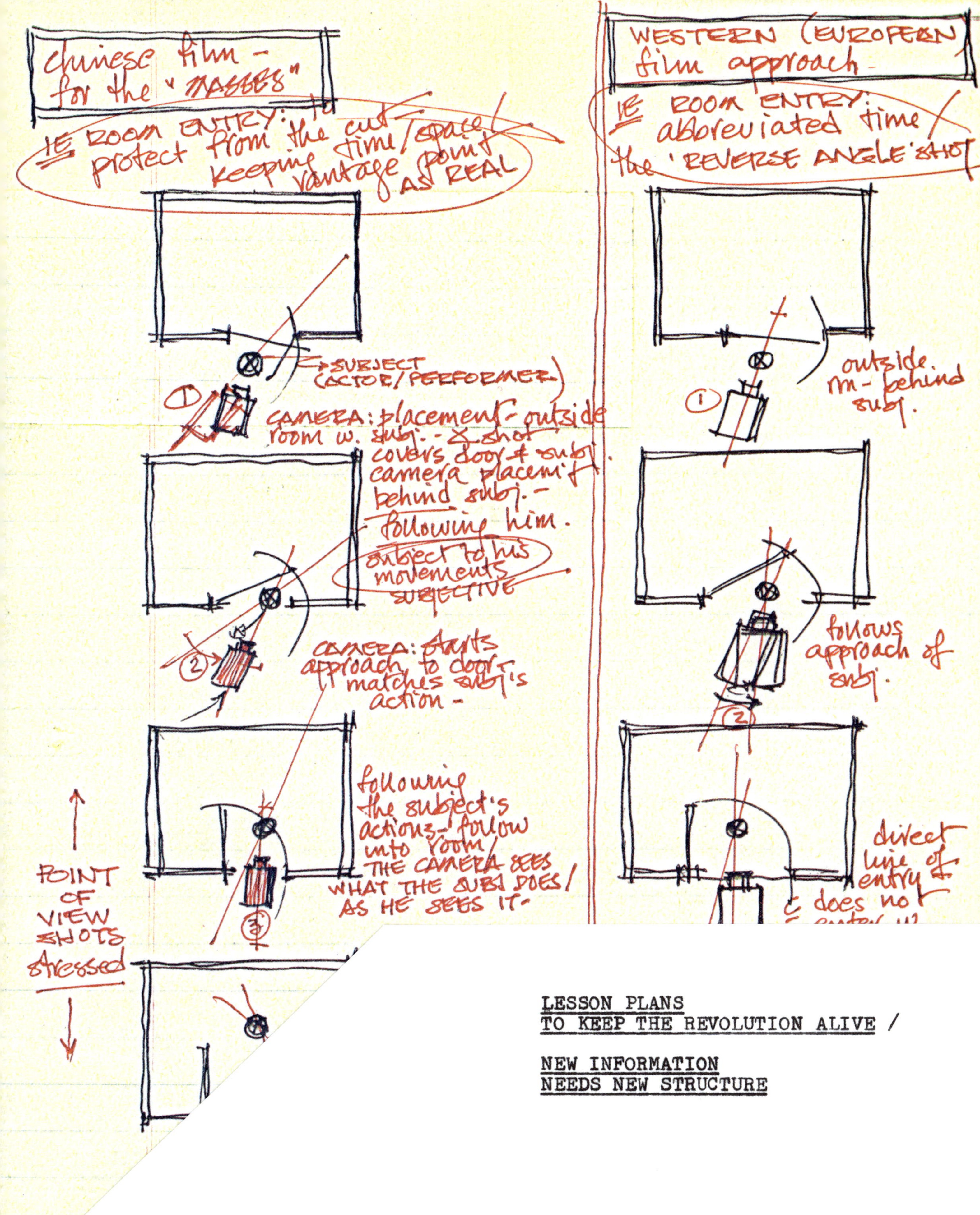

LESSON PLANS
TO KEEP THE REVOLUTION ALIVE /

NEW INFORMATION
NEEDS NEW STRUCTURE

NEW INFORMATION NEEDS NEW STRUCTURE

LESSON PLAN: FILM FOR THE ENTRY INTO A CONTAINED SPACE
FILM FOR THE MASSES - THOSE UNEDUCATED IN FILMIC TIME AND SPACE AS USED IN WESTERN DEVELOPMENT

the camera starts on the subject outside the space

the introduction is first to the subject - the contained area (doorway to room) is kept in the background

the subject starts the movement - the camera follows

the camera (eye) is subjugated - it becomes the third party's point of view shot

the subject goes to open the door / view from behind

the door is pushed opened / we see it as an over the shoulder shot - trying to closely associate with the original subject's viewpoint

the subject passes through / we wait a moment to allow for his/her entry / then we approach and pass through in the same manner

we see in room as the original subject sees it - our position is always related to his the information is presented to subject and third party POV always in the same manner

the subject turns to view his surroundings (the closed container)

the camera's eye parallels his movement - sees what he sees as he sees it

the subject turns to face the original entry way this shot is to establish the degree of containerization and location of original point of entry (a kind of establishing shot in reverse)

only then can we face the entryway to establish our own position as well / we see it from the point of view of the original subject (though this time he is out of frame). We have taken over his position. We have become one with the subject - his view is our own - through close association.

there has been no cut. The action must be continuous. We become a whole with the subject. At the end of the sequence, the subject's viewpoint, the camera eye's view and the POV SHOT are ONE.

NEW INFORMATION NEEDS NEW STRUCTURE

LESSON PLAN: FILM FOR THE ENTRY INTO A CONTAINED SPACE
FILM FOR THOSE PREVIOUSLY EDUCATED IN FILMIC
TIME AND SPACE AS USED IN WESTERN DEVELOPMENT

THE CAMERA starts on the subject outside the space

THE INTRODUCTION is first to the subject - the contained area (doorway to the room) is kept in the background.

THE SUBJECT starts the movement - the camera can follow (subjective) or remain stationary - becoming an OBJECTIVE OBSERVER / we may already start forming a detachment from the original subject...

THE SUBJECT goes to open the door - we remain behind (we can protect ourselves through distance - both physically and in the relationship)

THE SUBJECT passes through the doorway - we view him/her "framed" (frame within frame) . This affords us further protection if desirable.

CUT / POINT OF VIEW SHOT .... we take over the POV shot of the subject immediately. We see the interior (the containerized space) from his POV (instead of an over the shoulder slow intro). This has been made possible in this time element due to alienation instead of association from the very beginning.

THE SUBJECT enters the space - we have taken over his POV and it remains this way. From the interior there is one on axis shot aimed at description - straight ahead feeling of entry completed - the "space" itself comes into being.

CUT / REVERSE ANGLE SHOT ... DISASSOCIATION FROM SUBJECT . The shot is taken on axis - 180° from the first shot. THE CAMERA reclaims its own point of view. We see the original subject facing the camera directly (we are opposite to him / opposed him). We have even disassociated from the original camera POV that was somewhat "sympathetic" to the subject - to a now totally alienated (potentiality of hostile) 3rd POV.

THERE has been at least two direct CUTS. THE ACTION is discontinuous. At the end of the sequence, the subject's viewpoint, the camera's eye, and the 3rd POV (other) are all disassociated one from the other. In fact, in the last sequence the subject himself becomes SUBJUGATED TO THE "OTHER('S)" POV. WE HAVE ALIENATED THE SUBJECT / WE HAVE GAINED CONTROL OVER HIM / WE ARE A POTENTIAL THREAT IF WE CHOOSE TO FURTHER EXERCISE OUR POWER POTENTIAL.

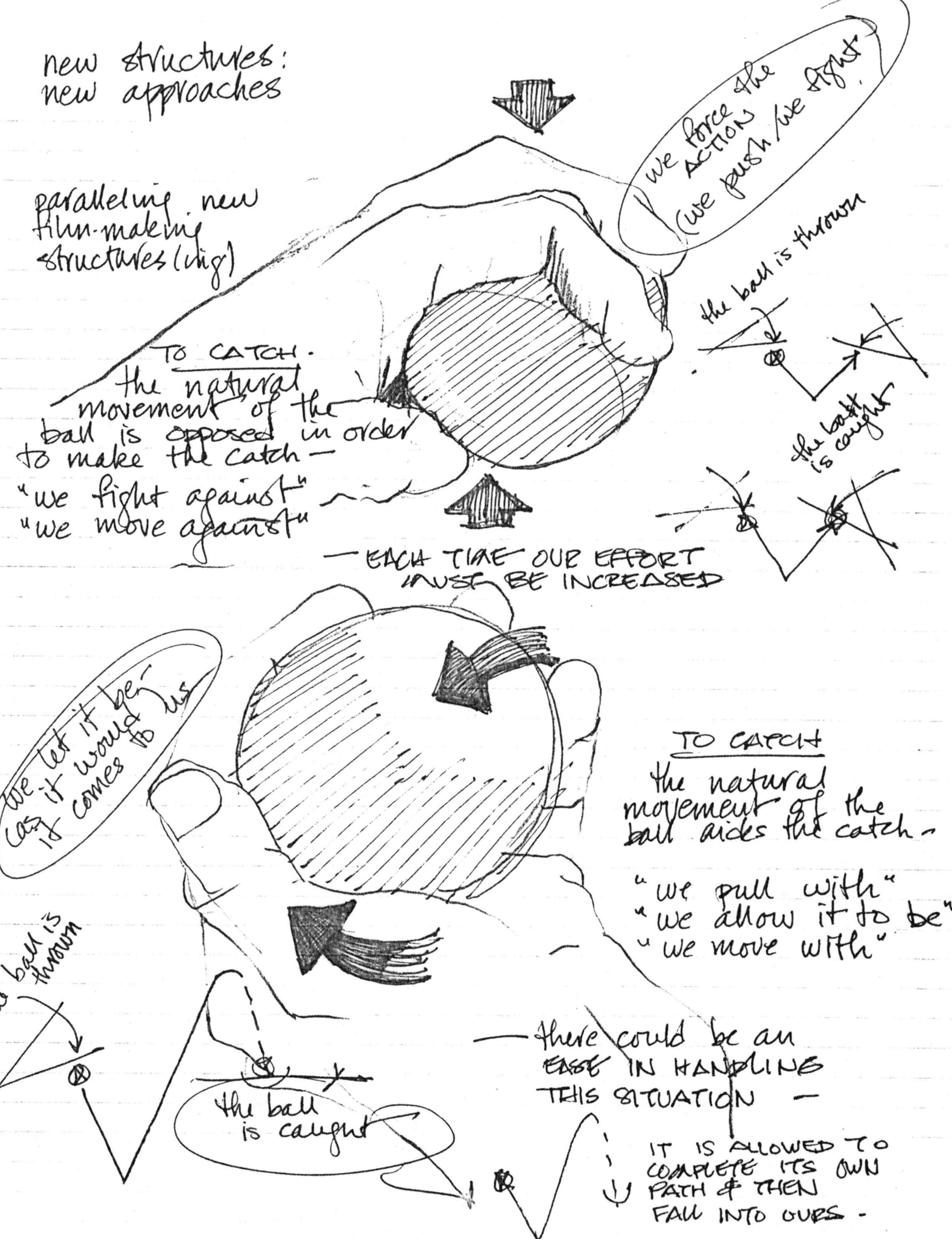

new structures:
new approaches
paralleling new
film-making
structures (dig)
we force the
ACTION
(we push / we fight)
TO CATCH -
the natural
movement of the
ball is opposed in order
to make the catch -
"we fight against"
"we move against"
the ball is thrown
the ball is caught
- EACH TIME OUR EFFORT
MUST BE INCREASED
we let it be
easy it would
it comes to us
TO CATCH
the natural
movement of the
ball aides the catch -
"we pull with"
"we allow it to be"
"we move with"
the ball is thrown
- there could be an
EASE IN HANDLING
THIS SITUATION -
the ball
is caught
IT IS ALLOWED TO
COMPLETE ITS OWN
PATH & THEN
FALL INTO OURS -

ie

as in
TO CATCH

①

②

controlling
WORKING vs
(working against)
putting stops on.

controlling
WORKING WITH
employing an
understanding of the
"natural" way it will go
(+using up on it →).

As different physical structuring would begin
to determine different psychological structuring

As one opposes (the natural order(ing))
The other works with / and unifies

As this occurs in the physical act,
its premises are extended towards psychological
action(s) / determinants / theories to be formulated
ideologies to be achieved

The media becomes the determinant
The structure inherent in
The camera formulates the view (POV) / determines
the course of action / takes the direction (towards)
It can be made to isolate / alienate
It can be made to consolidate / unify

The POV shot becomes sympathetic towards (takes over)
We are ONE (and the same)
The POV shot becomes alienating - opposed to (subject)
The camera choices to remain its own / as "Other"
There is (always) a force opposing us
We become DISUNITED (we must choose / we must fight
against that which can choose to remain undisclosed)
Our strength is fragmented

TO CATCH

EMPLOY(ING) an understanding of the NATURAL LAWS OF (the "natural way(s)" IT WILL GO ± USING UP ON IT —
(an Americanization of —)

as in
IE: TO KICK ↑

RE:
football kick
'STRAIGHT ON'
(as in/to attack · directly)
as in directly approaching the problem(s)

RE:
soccer kick
'FROM THE SIDE'
(as in/side attack -
side-step(ing))
as an issue

TO CATCH

EMPLOY(ING)
THE NATURAL STATE OF...

as in LAWS

natural laws of
(states of being)
(ie: HOMEOSTASIS)

natural state of

LAWS OF THE STATE
(as in "governments"
political bod(ies))

as in
IE TO THROW

underhand
(as relating) to
SOFT BALL - as
relating to
children play
softball - children are
introduced to hardball
through soft-ball)
under-hand - AS IN
UNDERHANDED
(as in approach to)

overhand
(as relating) to
HARD BALL - as
relating to an
'adult' game -
(the 'adult'
reality is 'hard')
as in -
IT IS ABOVE
+ OVER -
(as in excess of)

TO CATCH

IE AS in
TO TOSS - from the FOUL LINE
into

AS IN
WHAT DETERMINES "FAIR"
AS IN
"FREE-THROW LINE"
AS IN
A BOUNDARY LIMITING.

as in

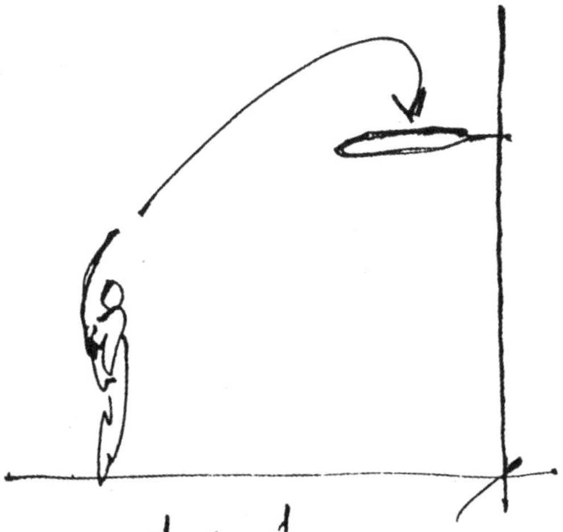

overhand
toss into -
as in TO SINK.

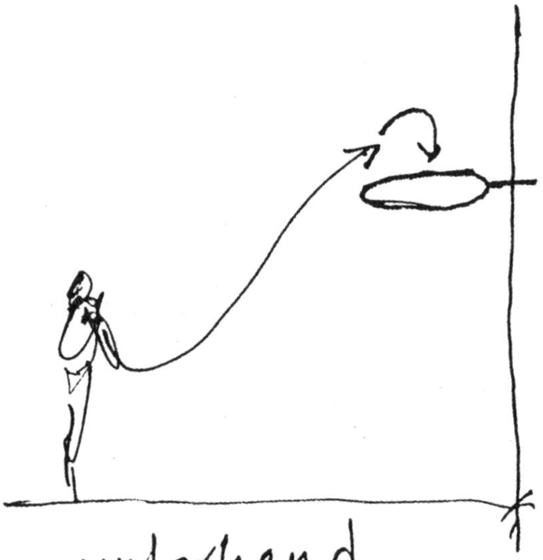

underhand
toss into -
as in UP + OVER

TO CATCH

IE as in

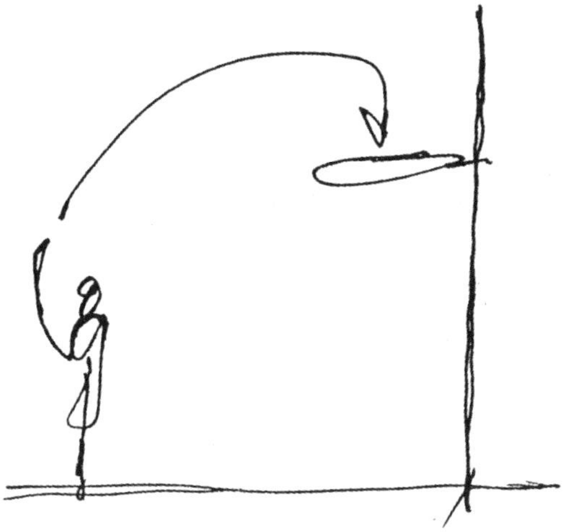

overhand looped

as in

TO GAIN HEIGHT

→ greater chance to score

greater chance to rebound

(AS IN OFF OF)

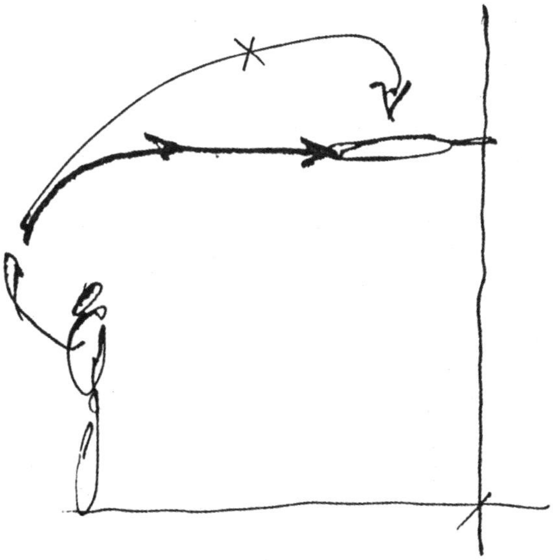

VS DIRECTLY ON

→ less chance to score

→ rebound possibilities limited.

DIRECTLY ON THE RIM (OF)

as in TO rebound out (OFF OF)

TO CATCH

IE as in

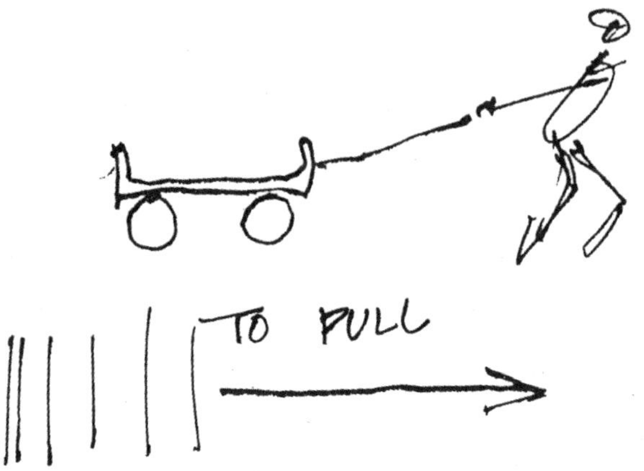

TO PULL

as in

TO PULL
AWAY FROM

as in

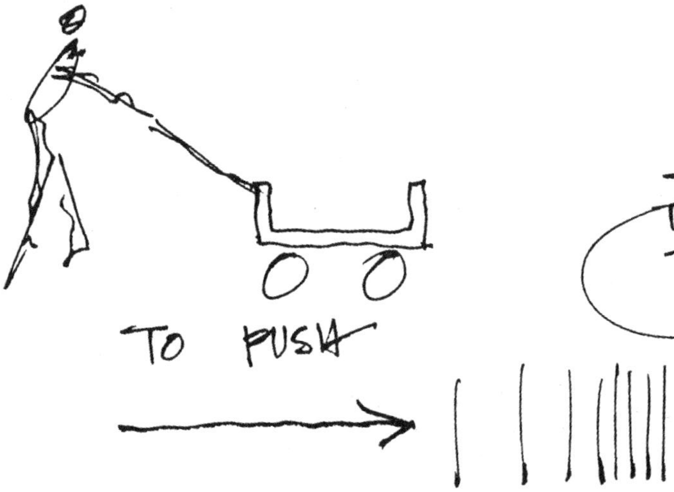

as in

TO PUSH
TOWARDS

TO PUSH

grasp
(AS IN TO GRASP
@ AN IDEA +
when it becomes a
necessity)

grasp
clutch
twist
brace
pull

as in

A GOAL
AN IDEOLOGY

TO CATCH

IE as in

grasp
clutch
twist
brace
pull

as in

grasp (at)
clutch (at)
twist (at / on or off)
brace (against / or up against)
pull (at / or to / or away from)

AS IN SQUAT VS BEND
(IE over as in TO LIFT)

push

pull

to push

IE: WITH

AGAINST

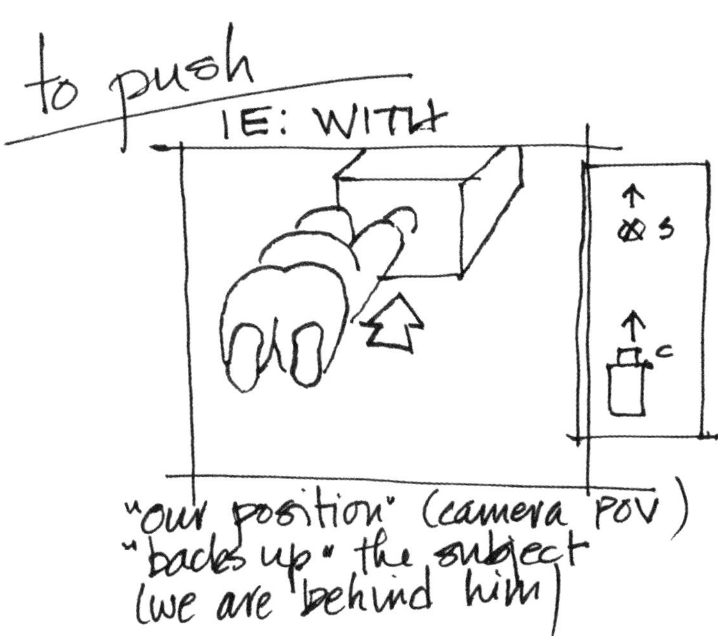

"our position" (camera POV) "backs up" the subject (we are behind him)

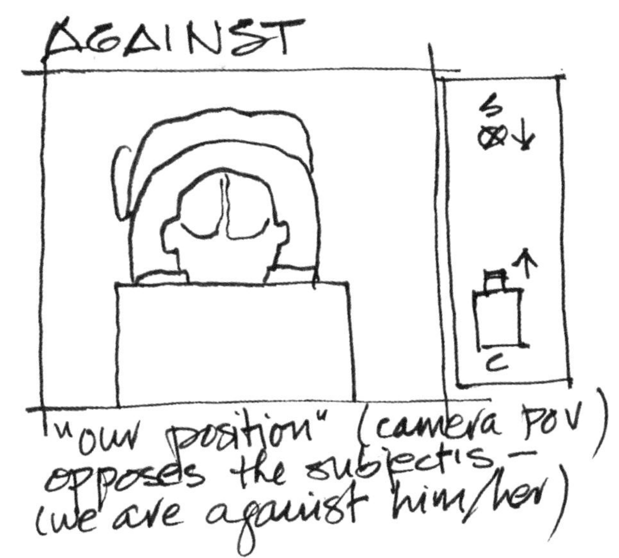

"our position" (camera POV) opposes the subject's — (we are against him/her)

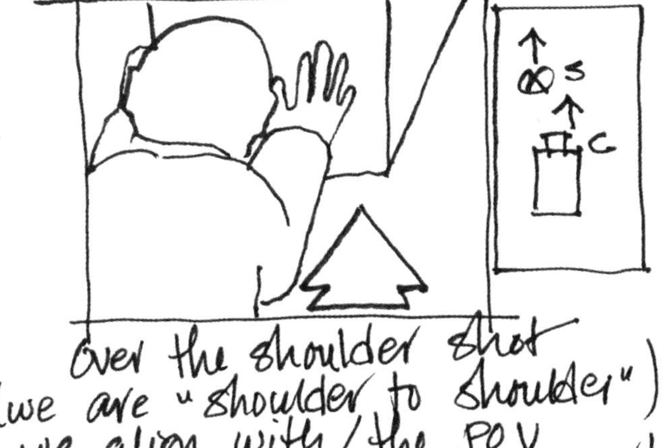

Over the shoulder shot (we are "shoulder to shoulder") we align with / the POV shot aides empathy towards

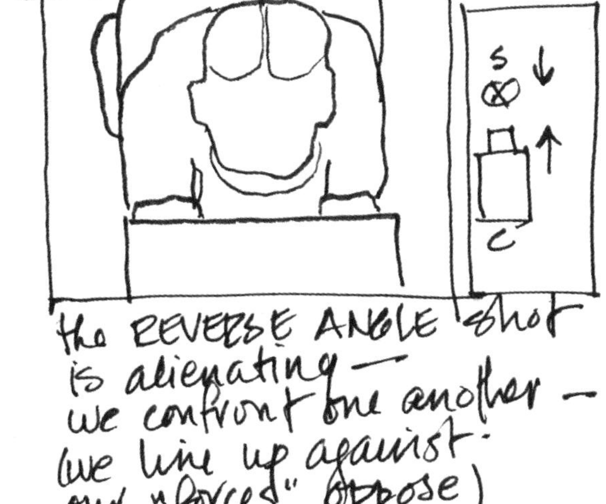

the REVERSE ANGLE shot is alienating — we confront one another — (we line up against our "forces" oppose)

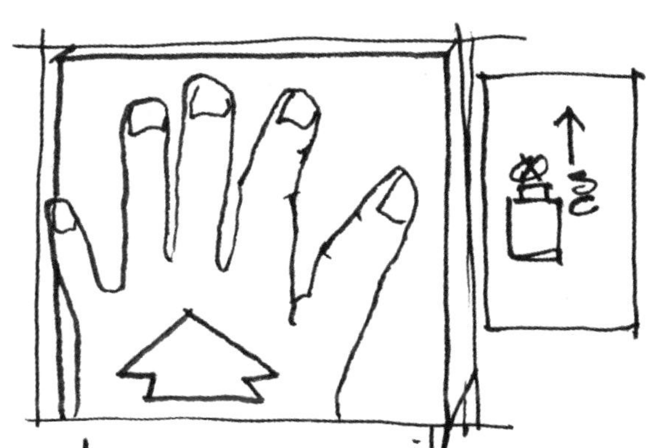

we become one with the camera's POV + the subject's POV are ONE AND THE SAME UNITED (with)

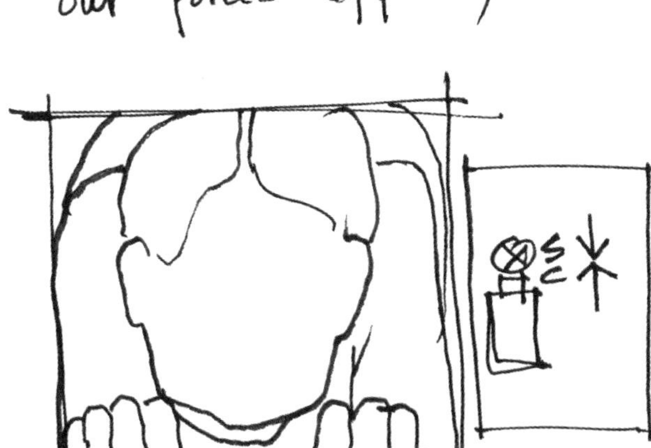

we become disunited — the camera's POV and the subject's are 'IN OPPOSITION (TO)' CU SHOT = FULLY OPPOSED.

__RE__: __CONCERNS (THAT TAKE ON / DEAL WITH)__
__INTER·PROCESS(ES)__
__INTER•PLAY(S)__

__IE__: __WORK(ING) NOTES__

CONCERNS:
SLIDE / VIDEO / FILM (ie)

① SLIDE

movement frozen

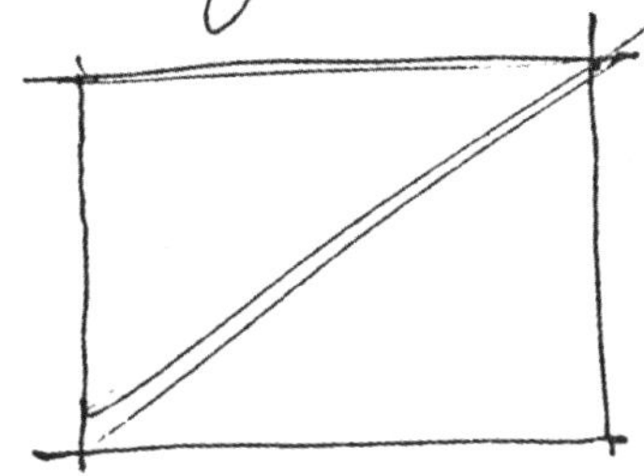

ie conditions as they still are —

we are still "in the government yard in Trenchtown"

(movement frozen: moment frozen — @ a point in time) (@ that moment in time)

② VIDEO

live movement in time

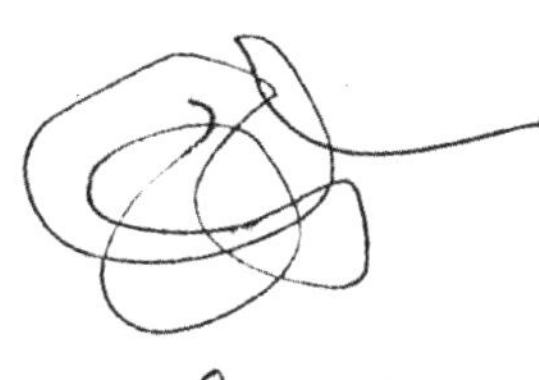

ie a dancing couple

continuous —

PUSHING SOMEONE INTO THE DANCE

the conditions we make inside as avoidances.

(movement in time: moments existing only in relation to the passing of time).

③ FILM

the frozen moment passing continuously —

THE PRESENT

— as it relates to a history of itself

— as continuous (eternal)

— as extended

— as contracted

"history makes the revolution"

VIDEO/FILM INTER•PLAY(S)

RE: (mass) media manipulation(s)

> video piece / film intervention

shoot video of catch

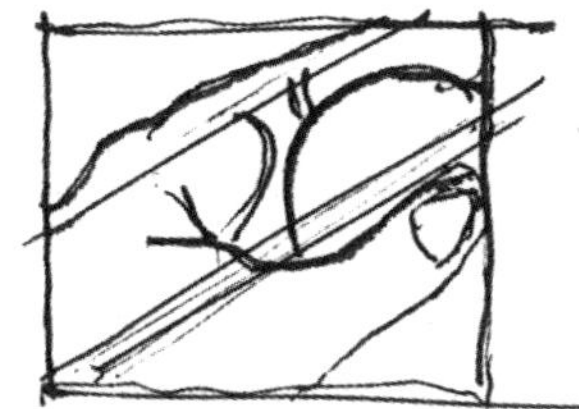

shoot super 8 off monitor (scan lines will show in film frames)

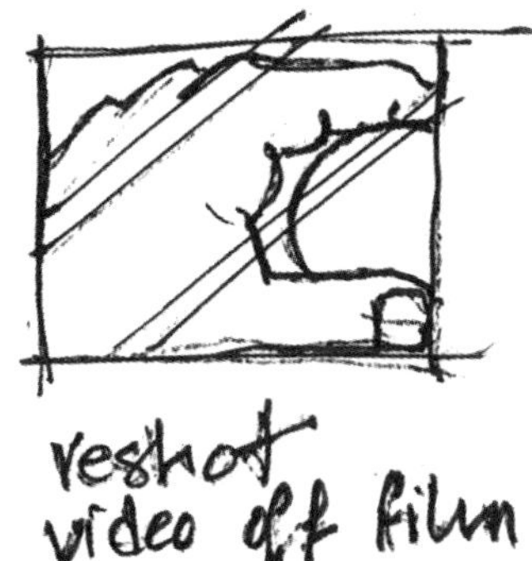

reshot video off film

>> or could be a graphic ie.

drawing of the filming effect (mirror reversed)

to

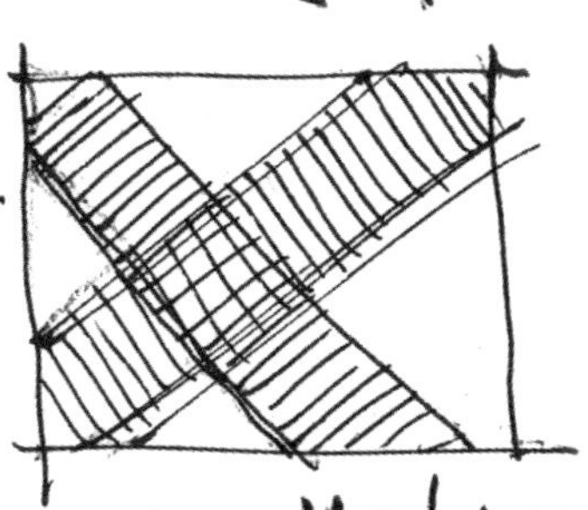

cancellation (becomes the statement)

>>> or shoot video of a film (or of film) originally.

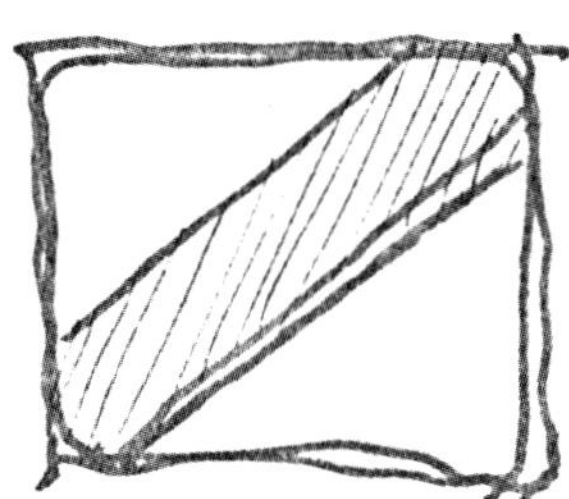 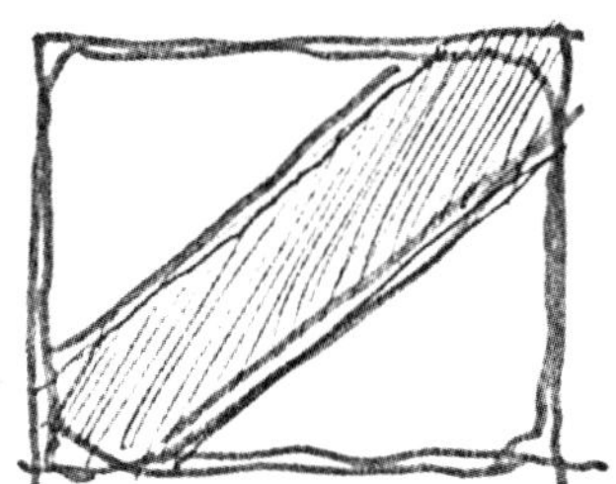

to stress the medium alone here -
to make one awares of manipulation -
(broadcast TV - film reference here) -
in broadcast TV / the quality of - film
becomes reduced to the quality of the TV
receiver - in this sense, the TV receiver
becomes the manipulator.

changing this - opposing it
interjecting the film as the catalyst -
it now reacts with the video - the
manipulation becomes visual (receives physical
form) / hence the filming will determine *
the quality of the video . . . .

(opposite to video (receiver) determining
quality of film)

hence - one is the same
yet, one is different

2 are the same
yet, 2 (both) are different

CONCERNS THAT (TAKE ON / DEAL WITH) FILM - VIDEO FORMAT(S)

SIMULTANEOUS PROJECTIONS
PROJECTIONS THAT REINFORCE / THAT OPPOSE / ONE ANOTHER

(1) A SUPPORTIVE SYSTEM

IE: WE ALL FEEL GUILT
WE ARE ALL THE BETTER
FOR IT

THERE IS A GUILTY
PARTY IN THE MASS

WE ALL FEEL HIS GUILT
FOR HIM

- THERE IS RELIEF

(2) A SUPPORTIVE SYSTEM

IE: NONE OF US FEEL
GUILT ...

WE ARE ALL THE
BETTER FOR IT

THERE IS A GUILTY
PARTY IN THE MASS

NONE OF US WILL
ALLOW THE OTHER
TO FEEL GUILTY

WE ABSORB HIS
GUILT -
THROUGH DISPERSION

- WE DISSOLVE

- WE ABSOLVE IT.

/ THE 'ART OF POLITICS'
THE 'CORPORATE UNITY - IDENTITY')

NOTE: (COMPARE TO 'SCAPEGOAT METHODS' IE: UNSUPPORTIVE SYSTEMS / OR SYSTEMS THAT WILL ONLY SUPPORT THEMSELVES - HE WILL FEEL ALL OUR GUILT FOR US (HE WILL TAKE ALL OUR GUILT) / WE WILL BE ALL THE BETTER FOR IT - RELIGIOUS IDENTITY (DEITY) VS CORPORATE (STATE) IMAGE) .

ROLE·PLAYING.

who are you to fit me into these roles?
who can I be when you fit me into these roles?
who should I be when you fit me into these roles?

who am I when you fit me into these roles?

Reversals.

becomes ↓
time is questioned
↑ (becomes relevant)

i. "who am I when you fit me into these roles?

the subject trying to reach an 'identity'.

here is the act what "the doer" is doing to the subj.

a preposition leading to the object roles.

ii. ① WHO AM I WHEN YOU FIT ME INTO THESE ROLES?

Reversal.

ii. who are you when you fit me into these roles?.

there has now been a shift – a questioning of the very identity (realing turning into the very essence) of the doer.

really is mystification in the sense of who are you why are you doing this to me?

here we can now lay a "supposed" guilt / questioning of one's self (an internal problem becomes externalized) leads to questioning the intent of "the other" –.

who am I ⟶ who are you?

ROLE· PLAYING

why are you doing this to me?
entails
guilt (a "supposed" act is occurring
by the other')

(the giving of) power (to the other—)
this is implied / though the power is probably
or most definitely with the questioner

why are you putting me into these roles? → questions intent REASON
who are you to put me into these roles? → questions (the identity) POWER

(see reason vs power in Castaneda's
↳ will Tales of Power
tonal vs nagual).

29-6-76

FILM•ING

FILM-ING

① lens distortion-
let the lens 'see' through a magnify'g lens -
bend the ∡ of the magn. lens to picture plane -
image distorts beautifully - wipes out

could bring back relation
again to 'beach boy lyrics'
+ 'film making process'
ie. WIPE OUT

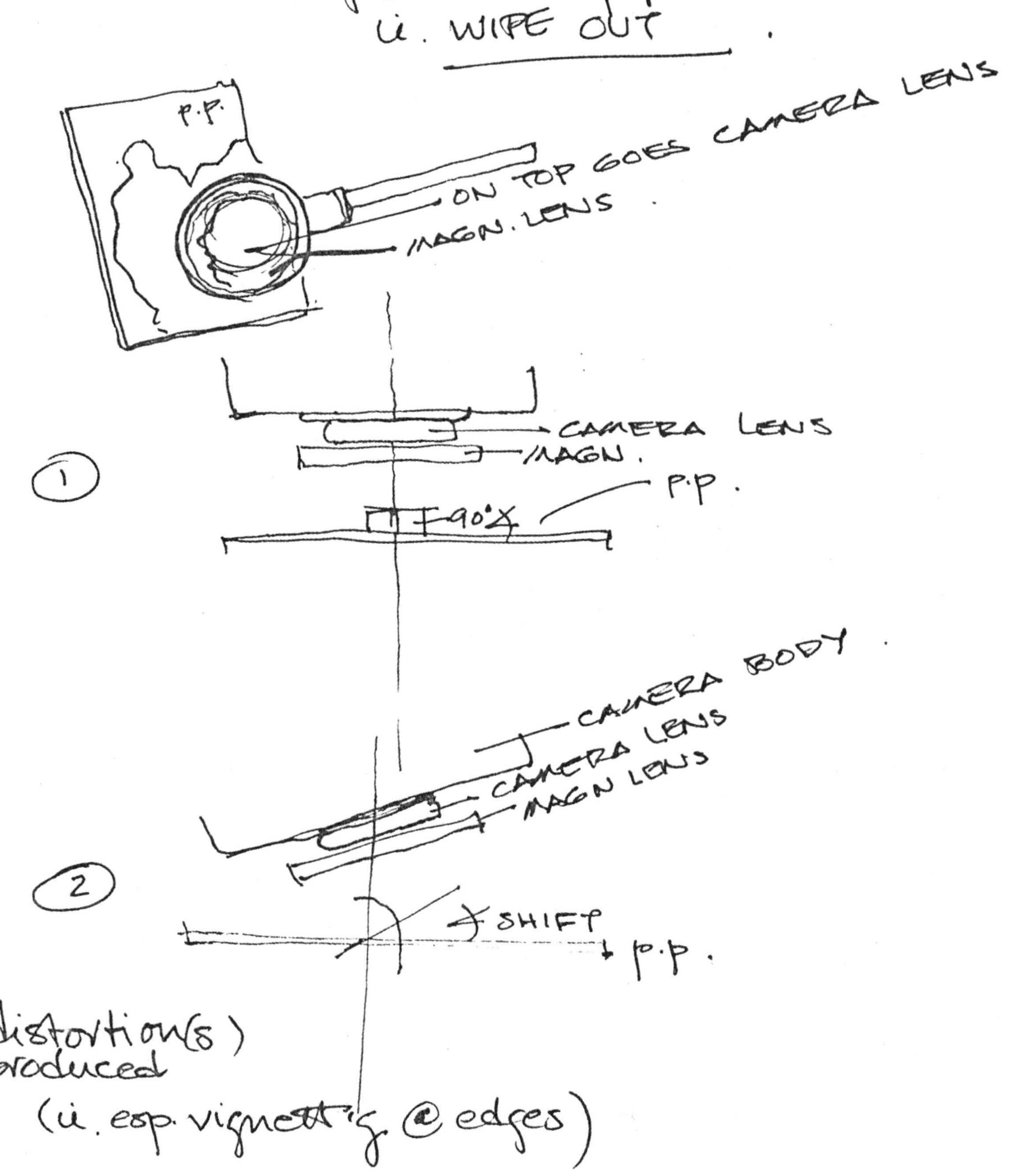

distortion(s)
produced
(ie. esp. vignett'g @ edges)

FILM 6

(2) slow down processes . . .
extended present

or
a slower / rhythmic timing that extents the present while changing it –

i.e. a focal pt. of action comes up – the 'extension' becomes slower still or speeds up to allow that action to occur in 'real time' –

>>→ "greater control over present conditions"

method of approach

shoot through the viewer –
you can control speed
seems fine to let blank'g ÷ frames to occur
also inequality of light on screen – ok –
re-emphasiz'g at medium that captures these actions through a continuous – equal runn'g
framing technique – can break this down as jonas broke down the 525 line scan (fought it) in VERTICAL ROLL.

FILM(IC) CONCERNS. "PROJECTION" (OF)

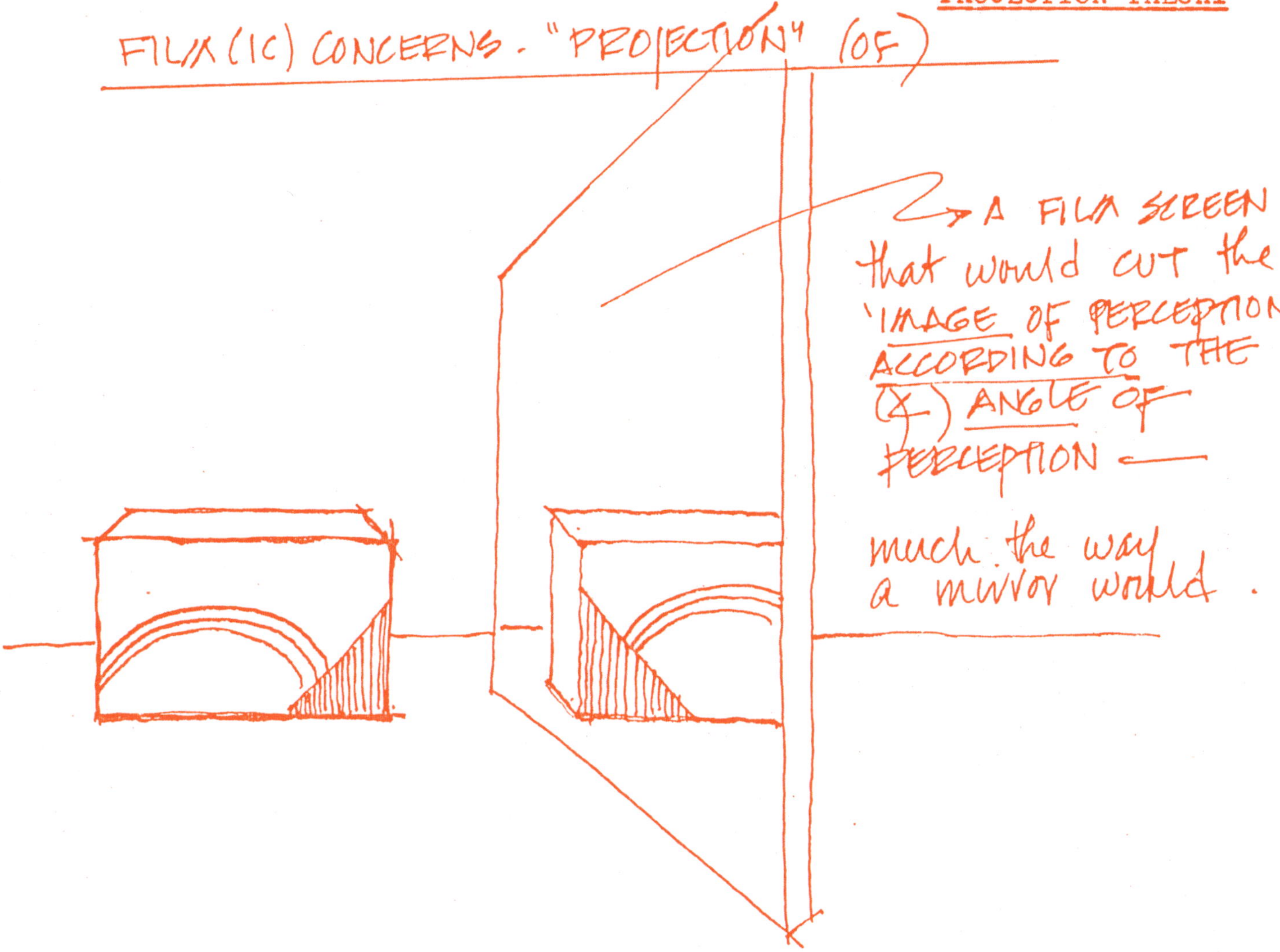

→ A FILM SCREEN that would cut the 'IMAGE OF PERCEPTION' ACCORDING TO THE (∡) ANGLE OF PERCEPTION ←

much the way a mirror would.

FROM (A)

TO (B)

the "object" AS WHOLE (a 2-D fully rendered perspective.)

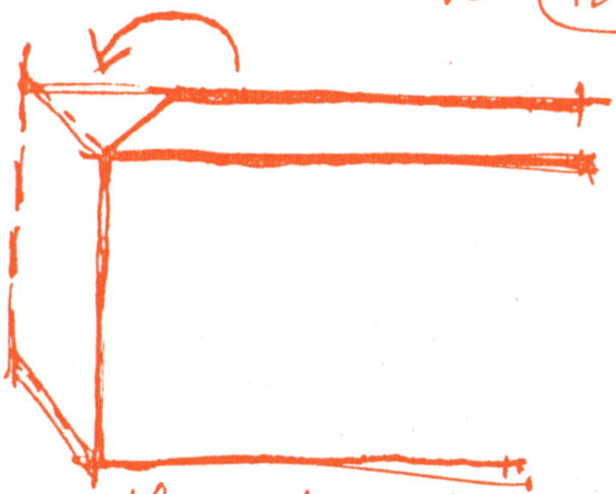

the "object" as MIRRORED - "CUT" (mirrored perspective - → reversal (of) / viewing & changed → cut - LESS THAN WHOLE RENDITION (OF)" (however, additional info may result).

THE CHARACTER IS BEING FORMULATED:
as if in a play
THE CHARACTER IS BEING ALLUDED TO:
as if in itself

CHARACTER - AS A CONSTITUENT / as the constituents of the person

CHARACTER - AS IN A PLAY / as a fictitious role
that is to be played out

ALLUDE - TO PLAY WITH: to make indirect reference

when the character alluded to becomes oneself
when I remains the "I" of the present which is both
the recipient and doer of the action /
when they both become one and can only be one in their reality ...

long shot - every movement of the body must be clearly visible

long shot - shows us as much of the subject as possible, but is long only in relation to the other shots associated with it.
ie: sequence about objects on table - shot covering entire table = long shot. / but if sequence = entire room, tabletop = close-up.

long shot - purpose: aquaint the audience iwth the overall appearance of the whole subject with the relationship of each of its parts. Orientation or establishing shot.

close-up - one of the best compensations for small screen
essential in creating intimacy
get viewer to see what is transpiring
dramatic effect due ~~to~~ as much to what is not shown as to what is./ draw attention to a particular detail - emphasized
limit audience to a small area of the screen
shown exclusively
director choses emphasis of details - change in detail = change in meaning

"tight close-up" /includes an even more limited area than a close-up
more than fills the screen
(TCU)

"extreme close-up" the camera approaches even closer to the subject
only a portion of ie: the face (ECU)

"combo" close-up with long shot
one close to the camera / another is seen beyond in the distance
adds depth to the scene
figures are of a different height and size (they become relative)

<u>in relation to the subject:</u>

the reverse-angle shot
the over-the-shoulder shot (OS)

the reaction shot

<u>in relation to the space:</u>

the establishing shot
the re-establishing shot

THE SUPER 8 LOOP
THREE (3) IMAGE PROJECTION(S)

ie "THREE SHOTS @ IT "

what intrigues me about 3 screens
3 visions.

draws ∥'s to relationships.

① long shot
SHOT
(establishing shot) → establishing - ① the background of the environment, the time / space that allows development (of plot)

② mid-shot → the development ② to current stages

③ close-up → breaking through ③ (the intrigue)

⇓

> moving in on something to uncover it

> going into the surface - or seeing surface from a distance + going in on it / attempting to break (break-through) it.

> going beneath the surface

(uncovering
digging out
getting @ the root of)

THE SUPER 8 LOOP
THREE (3) IMAGE PROJECTION(S)

assumption ①

long shot (establishing)
a relationship can only (develops) start
@ the correct time in the correct space.

relate to filmic time/space.
the elongated present
shortened present
video. real time
etc etc

mid-shot
it can only develop if there is
an attempt to get closer -
to move in on the other person.
to understand while still allowing
the other rm to breathe (his own space)

close-up.
we can only understand this
development by further moving in -
by allowing the space to become
at times too tight.

normally few people are allowed
to enter this tighter space

perhaps we have this as goal -
to move in systematically
"as tight as possible" until
one withdraws. until the 'couple'
choses to bind themselve closer
and systematically close out the
intruder -

we can further draw one out
through "intimation". etc. -
finishing without being provided
with info. from without + providing
within - would this produce a
"counter-move" (attack?).

THE SUPER 8 LOOP
THREE (3) IMAGE PROJECTION(S)

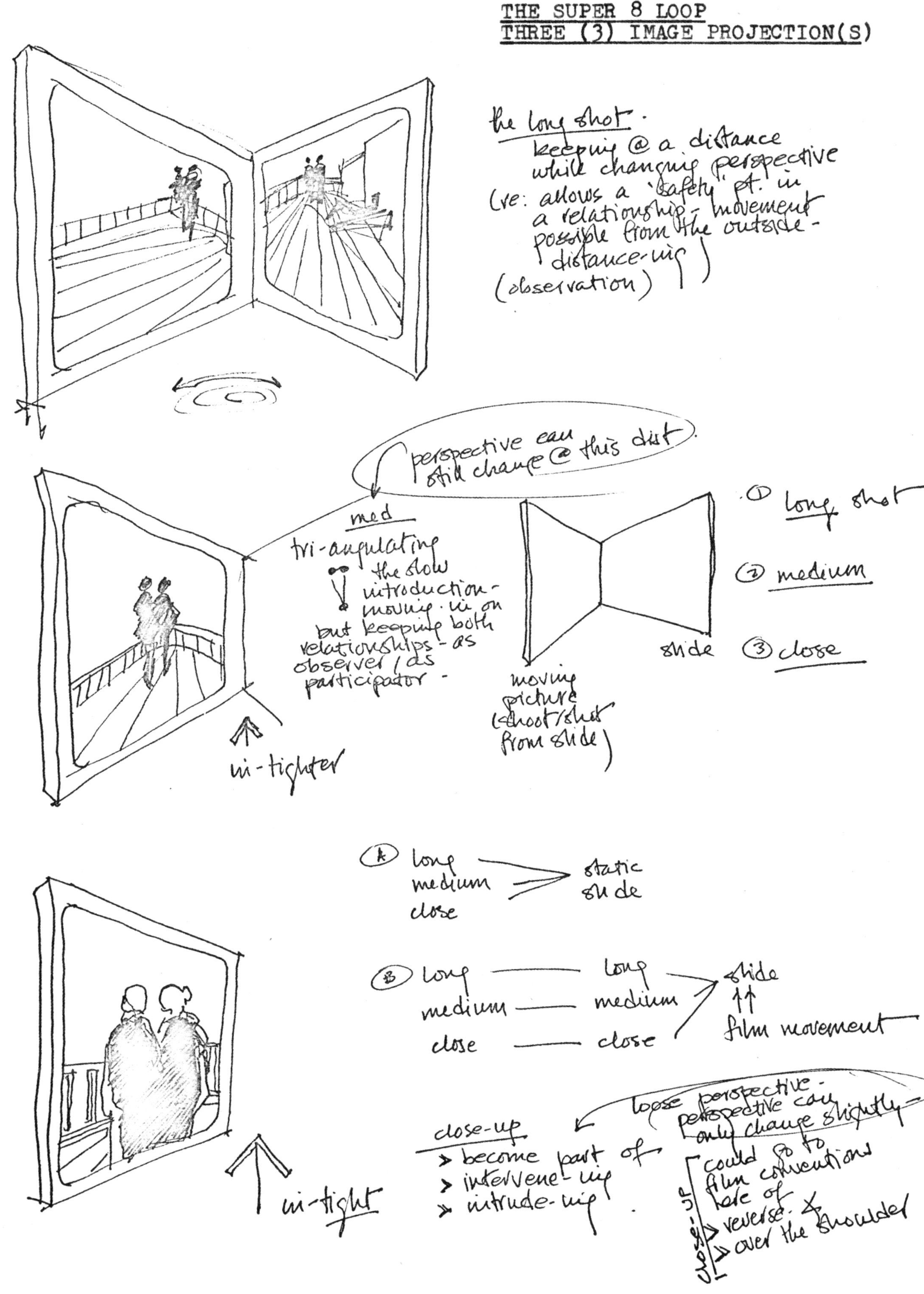

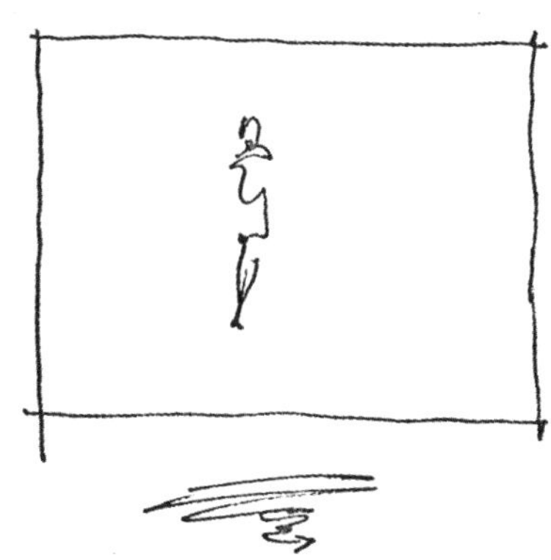

I move you. excite you—
(every movement of the body
must remain clearly visible)

to give me relevance.

you stand out / I make
you stand out through your
movements - I move you

to make me stand out
(for noticing you)

I acquaint you with each +
everything in your surroundings

so you may introduce
me into them

you are established

only to establish me

you are established

only in relevance to me

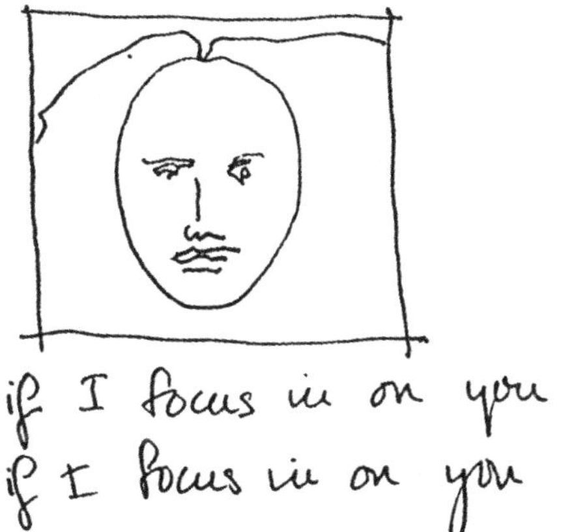

if I focus in on you
if I focus in on you

it is to give me relevance
it is because I choose what
I wish to see

the intimacy

depends on what I wish to
get intimate with

THE SUPER 8 LOOP
THREE (3) IMAGE PROJECTION(S)

ie
if I get intimate with you:

the intimacy

depends on what I wish to get intimate with
(what I wish to see)

extension

to culture:
mass audience — can 'they' relate to what I wish to get intimate with?
can it be introduced in a way that they will allow what hasn't come before —
does this take place / can it — due to convention (staying with it / breaking it)
techniques - staying with them — an old film convention enables a new view to get by — unnoticed?
(Altman - buffalo bill - failed to masses - they were disappointed old convention didn't bring entire, old package - unexpected 'newness' was rejected / esp. by backer - which is typical).
specific groups:
a "counter-culture"
(rejection of this country's conventions for those of another's — ie - Maoism / Marxism - to "transplace in space and / or time".)

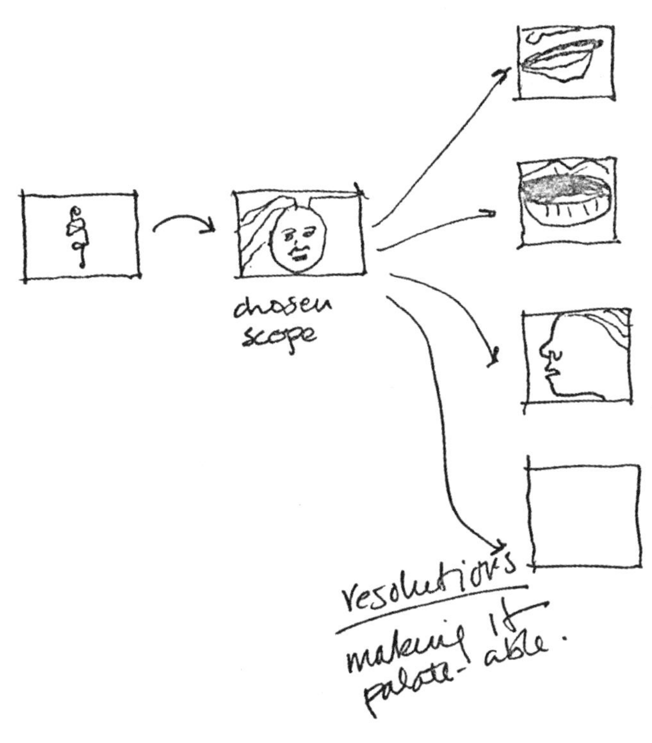

tension ÷ what I want / how I want it and sacrificing form — to show what I have gotten to others (another) so they will accept it on my terms.

mass media — what has been gotten — must be related the information / the slant it takes — is made digestable to control the message —
"the way something is affected can be sacrificed to make sure the effect will be there."

THE SUPER 8 LOOP
THREE (3) IMAGE PROJECTION(S)

STAGES OF INTIMACY

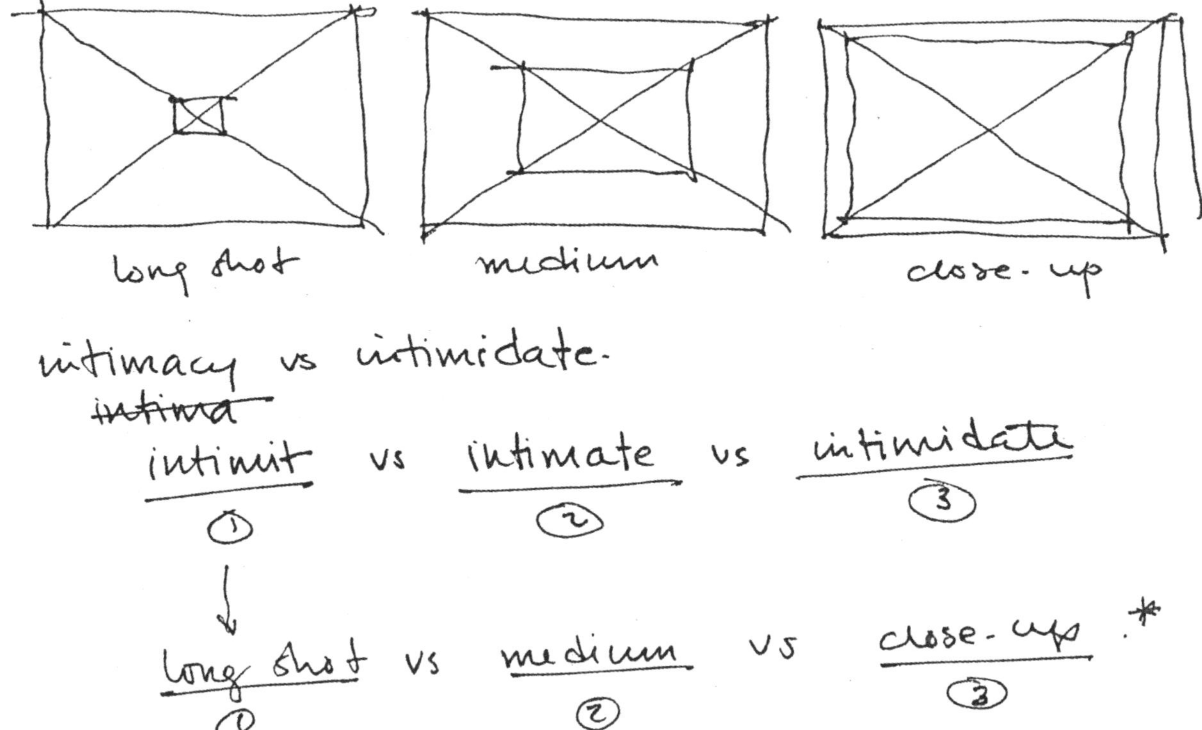

* not necessarily that the order follows
i.e. does intimit relate to long shot – even in a play on the converse of intimit naturally = close-up. ?

probably best to shoot 1 situation. talk-interview to asking questions – with 3 cameras – ca. placed very structured. distance varied. viewpt. the same. – i.e. on tripod. could give. locate all. just give order to roll – someone wouldn't even have to know how to shoot, focus: etc.

THE SUPER 8 LOOP
THREE (3) IMAGE PROJECTION(S)

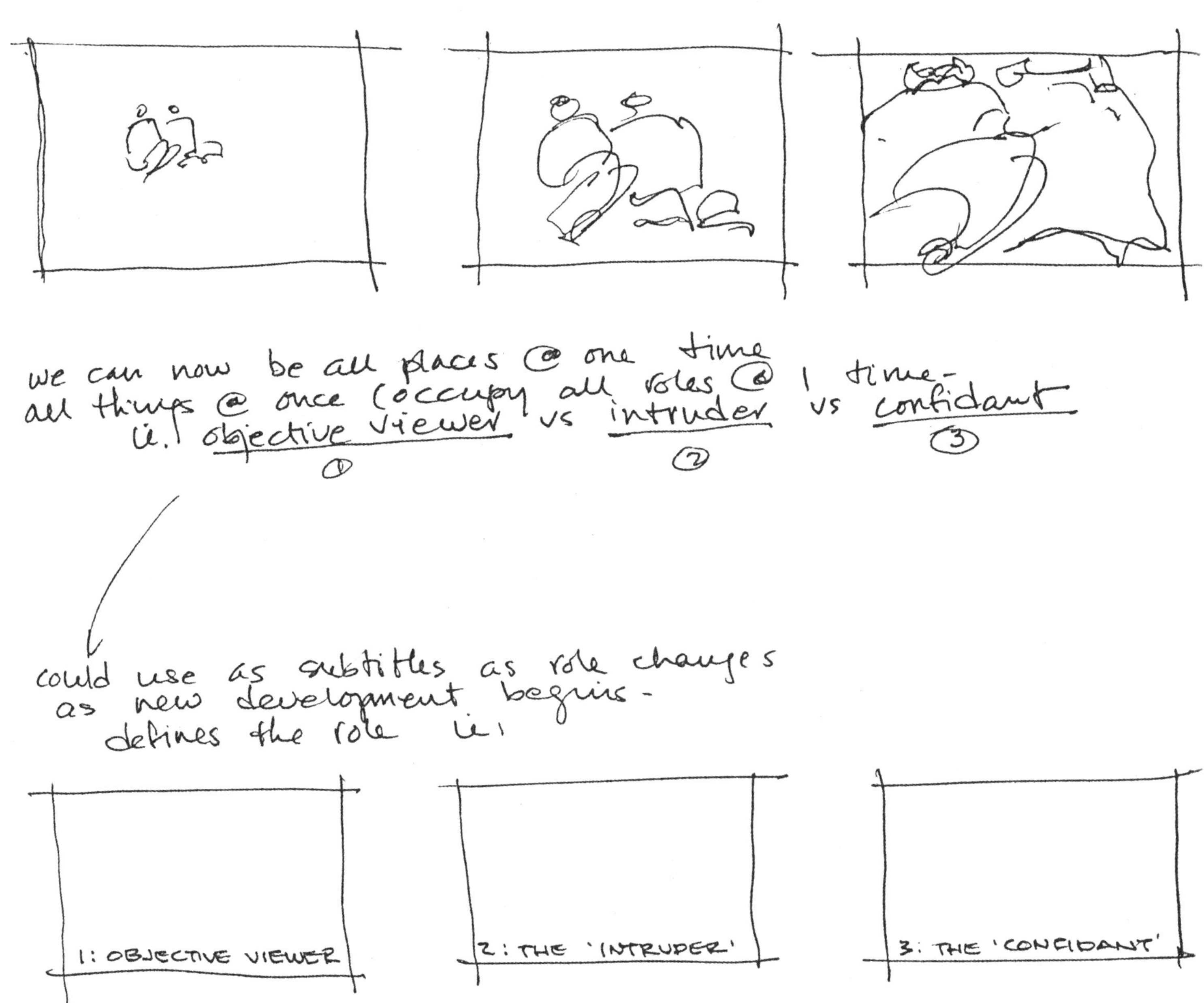

THE SUPER 8 LOOP
THREE (3) IMAGE PROJECTION(S)

CONCERNS THAT (TAKE ON / DEAL WITH) THREE (3) FILM(IC) PROJECTIONS

(1) (THE) DIRECTIVE	(2) (THE) ACT	(3) (THE) FOLLOW-UP
(gesture)	(note: 1 + 2 + 3 =	THE STORY LINE THE NARRATIVE)
SPEAK OUT !!	ENUNCIATE	EMASCULATE
	ARTICULATE	EMANCIPATE
CAUTION !!	DELINEATE ALLEVIATE DISSIPATE	DISSEMINATE ANTIQUATE DELINEATE
	SUFFOCATE ATTEND (TO)	ATTAIN
WARNING !!	WAVER (V. - TO WAVER)	WAVER (N. WAVER) A WAVER A WAGER AS A BET TO WAVER A WAGER
REGULATE !!	SITUATE	SUFFOCATE
DELINEATE !!	PROCEED	PROCURE
	COMMISERATE	CONSUME

FILM FORMAT (S)

NEW DIRECTIVES FOR WINNING

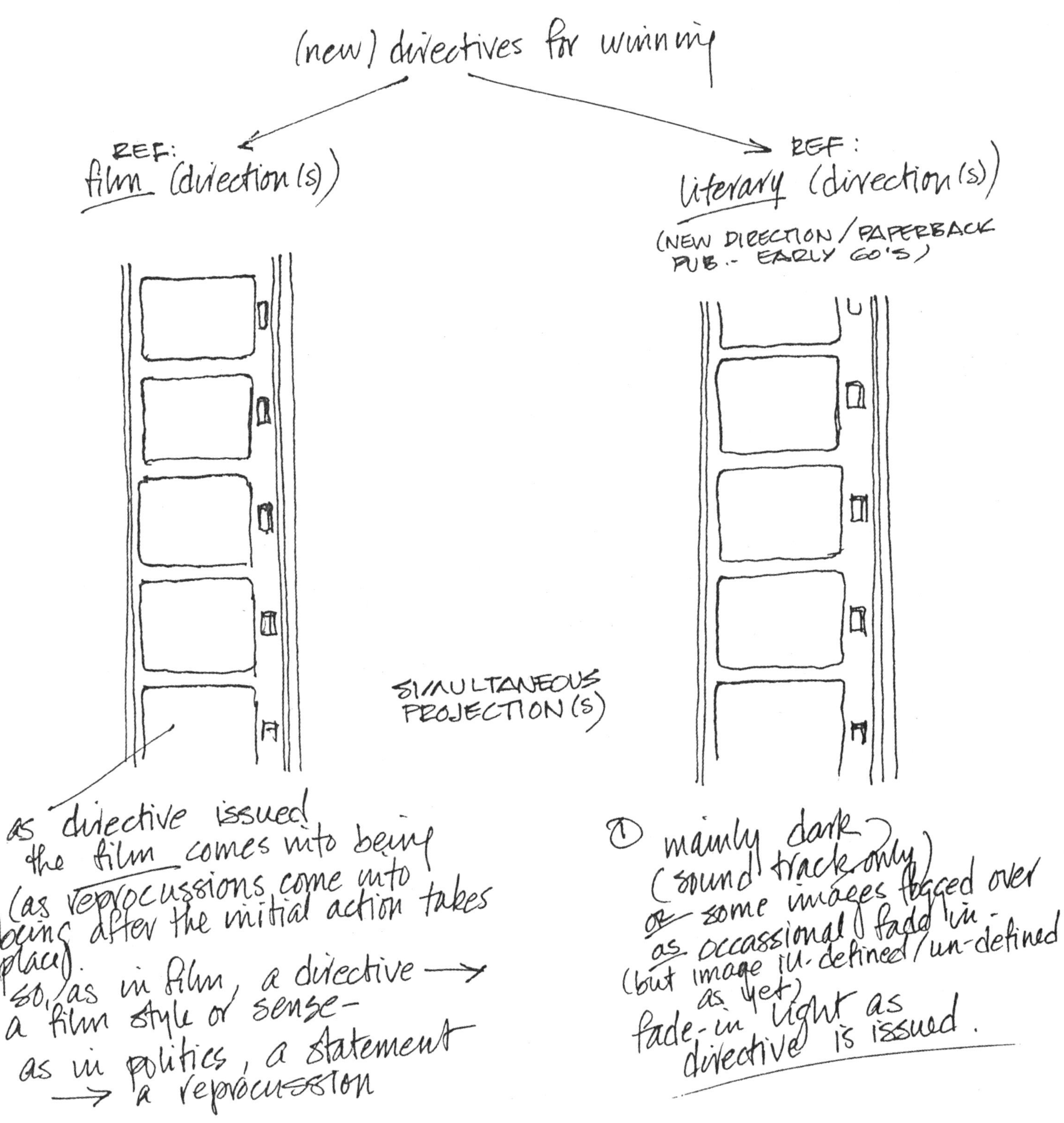

sound
the directive
said:

(politicized)
appeal to the
public ie.
rendered from Mao

super 8
proceeds
to direct —

to place
movement
onto a static
object
ie. z.i. on
ambiguous slide (space)

the space is contained
within

the space is static
until the directive
prompts movement

what directment —
could movement of
such the problem
here — a new source of a
lies — a needed or a
energy is of command
new form to start a
(directive)
flow (a movement)

coming in on a
static space +
awakening it

(opposite is to take an
awakened space + make it
static — ie. catatonic
people on bowery — play off
this — hold the flow back —
reverse — start / increase the
flow / or make sure it flows —

the
2 could
wk. off
(against
ea. other)

▷ equate flow + movement

of energy
thru directive

a psychological
energy band

ie as in
camera —
a mechanistic

pejorative
erudite
recondite

ambiguous spaces
referring to (relating to)
psychological (spaces) frames of mind / **FILM FORMAT**

~~[illegible]~~
analysis
of what is
needed to fill
the frame

ideological
(political)
notion of what
is needed to
fill the state of being -

related physical to psychological
states of being

places to be @ - ideologically (psychologically)
- physiologically -

ambivalent space ⇅
ambivalent states (of mind)

what is needed to get going
to fill the void again.

ambiguous - lacking clarity of meaning
1. susceptible of multiple interpretat'n
2. doubtful or uncertain.

ambiguous. indicates the presence of 2 or more possible meanings, usually because of faulty expression.

ambivalent. exhibiting ambivalence (the ~~existing~~ existence of mutually conflicting feelings or thoughts, such as love & hate together, about some person, object, or idea.

ambulant - moving or walking about
shifting from place to place.

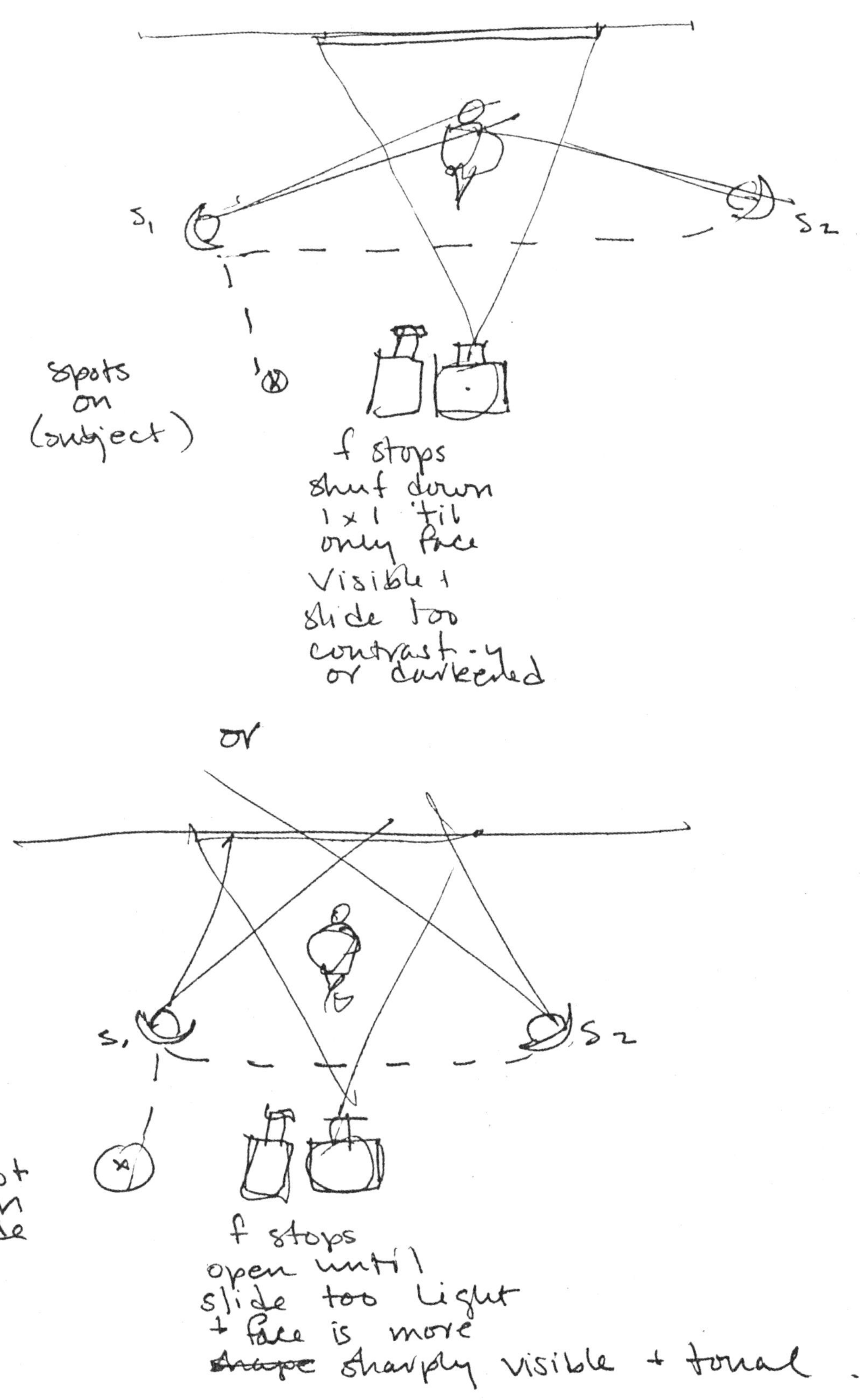
S1
S2
spots
on
(subject)
f stops
shut down
1 x 1 til
only face
visible +
slide too
contrast-y
or darkened
or
S1
S2
spot
on
slide
f stops
open until
slide too light
+ face is more
~~shape~~ sharply visible + tonal.

NOTE(S): SLIDE/FILM FORMAT

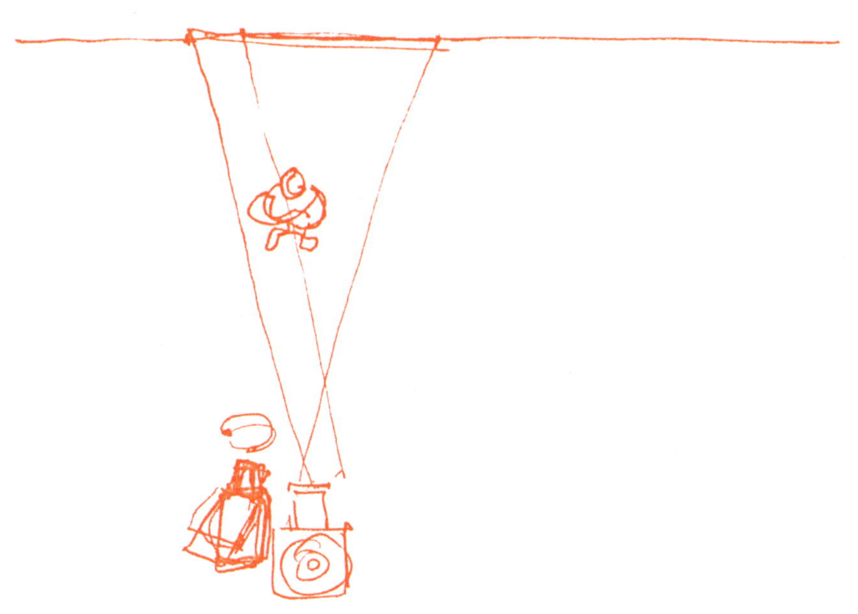

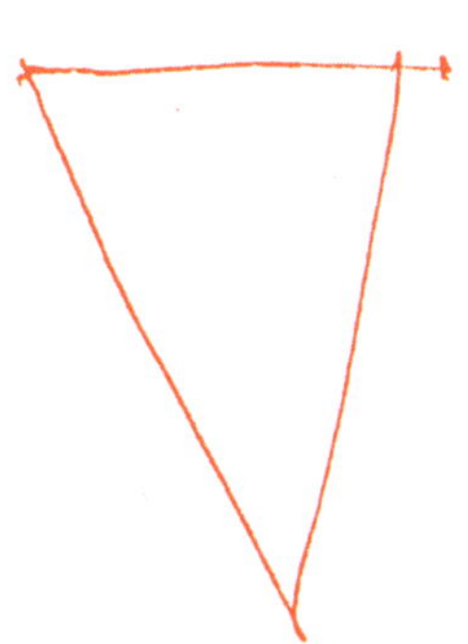

proj on blank.

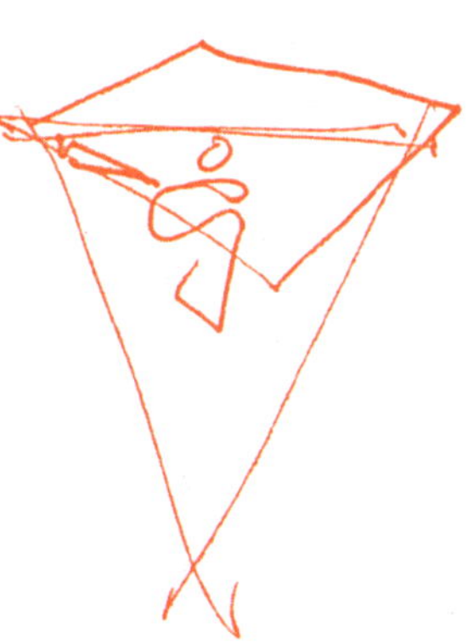

figure in defining the space. (or looking for it) (or remembering it) (could come on very light – spots on slide that are eventually turned out)

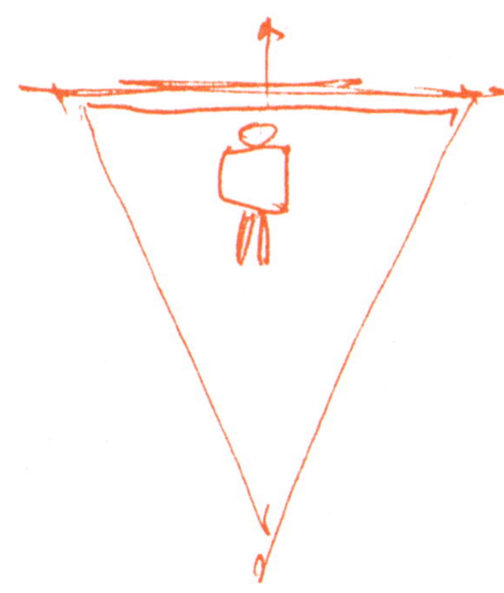

space appears facing screen

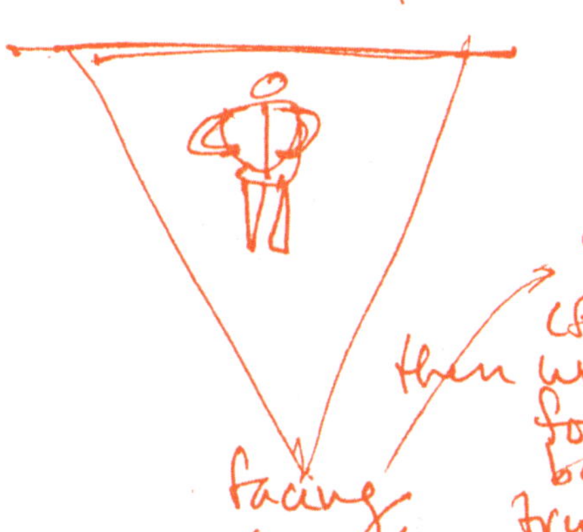

facing camera. start circular rotation (focus-in/out) then walk (in) forward back – trying to catch it.

ISBN: 978-1-7344897-7-4

Managing Editor: James Hoff
Managing Designer: Rick Myers
Copy Editor: Allison Dubinsky

Primary Information
155 Freeman Street, Ground Floor
Brooklyn, NY 11222
www.primaryinformation.org

Printed by KOPA, Vilnius, Lithuania

Primary Information would like to thank Alex Kitnick, Tyler Maxin, Alec Petty, and Harley Spiller at Franklin Furnace Archives, Inc.

This publication is made possible through the generous support of the Graham Foundation for Advanced Studies in the Fine Arts.

Primary Information is a 501(c)(3) non-profit organization that receives generous support through grants from the Michael Asher Foundation, the Greenwich Collection Ltd, the John W. and Clara C. Higgins Foundation, the National Endowment for the Arts, the New York City Department of Cultural Affairs in partnership with the City Council, the New York State Council on the Arts with the support of Governor Andrew Cuomo and the New York State Legislature, the Orbit Fund, the Stichting Egress Foundation, The Teiger Foundation, VIA Art Fund, The Jacques Louis Vidal Charitable Fund, The Andy Warhol Foundation for the Visual Arts, the Wilhelm Family Foundation, and individuals worldwide. Primary Information is a W.A.G.E. certified organization.